ALSO BY MARY ANN MADDEN

Thank You for the Giant Sea Tortoise
Son of Giant Sea Tortoise

MAYBE HE'S DEAD

MAYBE HE'S DEAD

And Other Hilarious Results of *New York* Magazine Competitions

Edited by
Mary Ann Madden

Random House
New York

Published in the United States by Random House, Inc., New York,
and simultaneously in Canada by Random House of Canada
Limited, Toronto.

All competitions, some in slightly different form,
have originally appeared in *New York* magazine.

Grateful acknowledgment is made to the following for
permission to reprint previously published material:

New York magazine: The copyright to all the responses
to the Competitions is owned by News Group Publications,
Inc. Reprinted by permission of *New York* magazine.

Library of Congress Cataloging in Publication Data

Main entry under title:
Maybe he's dead.

1. Literary recreations. 2. New York.
I. Madden, Mary Ann. II. New York.
GV1493.M33 793.73 80-6021
ISBN 0-394-51190-5
ISBN 0-394-74918-9 pbk.

Manufactured in the United States of America

9 8 7 6 5 4 3 2

FIRST EDITION

For my friends Helen Dolby
and Stephen Sondheim.
And for my fiancé,
Watch This Space.

Acknowledgments

Having done a competition on prolix dedications and/or acknowledgments, it is with self-conscious but genuine gratitude that I express my thanks to Herb Sargent, John Berendt, Burt Shevelove, Tom Guinzburg, Richard Maltby, Jr., Nora Ephron, Peter Stone, Bob Brown and Martin Yerdon for their help and friendship. To Jimmy Elson, Virginia Feine, Michael Stamos, and Paul Desmond for theirs. Thanks to Rusty Unger for bringing me to Jean McNutt, Alice Fahs and Random House.

Preface

I wonder if anyone actually reads a preface. God knows writing one is not, how you say, art. Or perhaps it is an art, and I simply haven't the knack.

I think a preface should contain some information about the matter in the book. What was culled, what included, and why. Well, this book is a collection of *New York* Magazine competition results. With one or two exceptions, all appeared in the magazine between December 1973 and January 1978. The ones included seemed funnier than the ones excluded. "Special Mention" attributions and the like are again omitted for reasons of sanitation. Now. If you're still with me, perhaps you would enoy knowing how these competitions are devised. Thought up. I would enjoy knowing that, too. Often a friend (almost usually Herb Sargent) says something funny and it remains to work out a competition around that premise. When nothing whatever comes to mind, I reread a master list of past masterworks and steal from myself. This is known in the trade as lack of imagination. A technical term. Of no importance.

I work at home. I've only visited the magazine once—when I was hired by Clay Felker in 1968. I guess the old place has changed. Entries are delivered to me by messenger. After sorting through the postcards-only-please (I read everything at least twice, and yes, work alone) I make piles of "wonderful," "okay" and "repeats." This is known in the industry as time-consuming.

Eventually, and painfully, one isolates winners, lists duplicated entries and makes notes for a report. (When the first collection of competitions appeared, some benign critic allowed as how the reports should have been included. So now they are. In publishing circles, this is known as suggestibility.)

Next. Type up results. Hand all this to a messenger, and next day galleys are delivered. These I check with my contact at the magazine. We make cuts according to space allotment, fix changes and discuss world events. Over the years, I've shared bizarre intimacies with the women and man with whom I've worked. It's odd that if I walked into the office, none of them would know me. Odd, and comforting. This is known in psychiatric circles as Carmelite Syndrome.

One does this on two out of three weeks for a number of years, and then one collects oneself and the material and puts the latter into a book. Then one writes a preface. (See above.)

Before completing the preface to a collection of NYMCR, I should like to thank the aforementioned associates at *New York* Magazine: Laurie Jones, Sandy Morehouse, Fred Allen and Jan Cherubin. Thank you for wisdom, understanding, counsel, fortitude, knowledge, piety and fear of the Lord. Not necessarily in that order.

And my gratitude to competitors who have been with us all these years. They raised me from a pup, and I think of them as family. For serious indefatigability, my thanks to: Miles Klein, Larry Laiken, the Wilens, the Ellners, Jacqueline Fogel, Alan Levine, Alex Vaughn, Robert M. Hunt, Cynthia Harrison, Arthur Ash, the Quirini-Brennans, Sal Rosa, Jay McDonnell, Nancy Joline, the Crystals, Ruth Migdal, James Fechheimer, J. Bickart, Jack Paul, Fran Ross and Phil Levine. Many more. I should also like to thank Robert Redford. But it would be wrong.

And thank you for buying this book. And for reading the preface. If you did and you are.

Contents

Preface *xi*

What I Should Have Said/What I Said *3*
First Day at School *9*
Answer Game with Switch *16*
Fractured Definitions *21*
Near-Miss Play Plots *31*
Sequels *37*
One-Letter Omissions *44*
Musicals from Classics *52*
Critique of Poor Reason *59*
Answer Game *68*
Fractured Names *75*
Redistributed Names *98*
Ciné Qua Non *104*
World's Longest Books *115*
Kangaroo Joke *120*
Fractured Fables *130*
Mind Reading I *136*
Mind Reading II *142*
Unusual Classified *148*
Oppress Clippings *155*
Unconventional Greeting Cards *160*
Conversation Openers *165*
Conversation Stoppers *171*
Two for the Opening *183*
Added Attractions *190*
Famous Line, Flawed Tag *195*

Jacket Copy *200*
Random Lines from TV *206*
Near Misses *213*
Literary Limericks *219*
One-Sentence Book *223*
Punned Foreign Phrases *229*
Book Retorts *234*
TV Guide Listings *240*
Whimsical Etymology *250*
Punned Quatrains *254*
Who's Who in the Cast *260*
Famous Guide to New York *268*

MAYBE HE'S DEAD

What I Should Have Said/ What I Said

1. "I'm a writer.
2. "I do this thing in the back of this magazine—like a puzzle, only not really. It's—uh—sort of a contest. I work at home. It's kind of a game where people send in things—look, can I get you a drink? Oh, sorry, here's a napkin. I'm sure it doesn't stain . . ."

Above, 1. what you should have said, and 2. What you did say. Competitors were asked for one sample of same.

Report: 1. See, we've set this one before, so the repeats were plentiful, and really too numerous to list. **2.** The repeats: **1.** Yes. **2.** No. **1.** No. **2.** I do. **1.** Of course, on the other hand. . . . **2.** Care to step outside? **1.** I'm dabbling in ceramics at the moment. **2.** A housewife. **1.** Hello dere, ossifer, how fast was I goin'? **2.** Sorry. Here's my license. **1.** Yes mother, I'm living with him. **2.** I've smoked a pipe for months. **1.** I loved last night, Jane. **2.** I loved last night, Joan. **1.** I'll just clean up and get the other turkey. **2.** Oh, god, it slipped off the platter and I've ruined everything. **1.** Who cares? She never picks the really good ones, anyway. **2.** Enclosed, my entry to the competition.

---

1. "Look, there's a lot of traffic, and he's probably been stuck in a meeting all day and didn't get your message, or he'd have called. I'm sure there's nothing to worry about."
2. "Maybe he's dead."

Cynthia Harrison, Rockville, Md.

1. "Mass? Last Sunday."
2. "They say it in *English?*"

Ida Campbell, White Plains, N.Y.

1. "Broken left upper window."
2. "Eight ball, side pocket."

Alan Levine, Massapequa, N.Y.

1. "Blake, Proust and the *O.E.D.*"
2. "One of those Euell Gibbons books would make sense on a desert island. I'd like a collection of crosswords to keep me busy. And then, if I were shipwrecked today, I'd take *Aunt Erma's Cope Book* since I just barely started it."

James W. Penha, Jackson Hts., N.Y.

1. "We both have such good taste."
2. "When you took your coat off, I almost died . . . nothing like this has ever happened to me before—do you mind if I ask you how much you paid for yours?"

Joan Corr, N.Y.C.

1. "No, thanks, I'm trying to quit."
2. "Hey, wait! Don't shoot yet! The blindfold's too tight. Stop! Help!!!"

Tommy Wino, N.Y.C.

1. "A hat."
2. "When it's this cold I like something I can pull down over my ears. I mean, they just kill me when it's cold like this. When I put it on I didn't realize one side was . . ."

Lee Bailey, N.Y.C.

1. "Some tuna, some shrimp, a little yellowtail, and maybe some of that pink stuff."
2. "Two uchimatas and an uke goshi, kudasai."

Stephen Pearlman, Los Angeles, Calif.

1. "How do you do?"
2. "How do you do your Highness, Excellency? Worship. No, Grace. Uh . . ."

Andrew Mezzetti, Flushing Meadows, N.Y.

1. "Thank you."
2. "It's really a mousy brown, but I use Stardust Blonde #4 and henna for body."

Anne Scott, Solon, Ohio.

1. "If you'll forgive me for not answering that question, I'll forgive you for asking it."
2. "Forty-two."

N. Schaaf, N.Y.C.

1. "Salaam!"
2. "Shalom!"

Carol Falcetti, Whitestone, N.Y.

1. "You're having a baby! How wonderful!"
2. "Who's the father?"

Brenda Lindberg, Little Silver, N.J.

1. "We hereby declare that we are king for the rest of our natural life."
2. "I am not a crook."

Mimi Kahn, Oakland, Calif.

1. "Some look at the future and ask why. I look at the future and ask why not."
2. "Some look at the future and ask what. I look at the future and ask what not."

Robert M. Hunt, Cambridge, Mass.

1. "He's dead, Doctor."
2. "Is he dead, Doctor?"

Anne Fruchtbaum, R.N., Gaithersburg, Md.

1. "*The Journal of Critical Analysis.*"
2. "*TV Guide.*"

A. Shulman, Villanova, Pa.

1. "That's really none of your business."
2. "Because nobody ever asked me."

Ellyn Polansky, N.Y.C.

1. "Of course, I have Perrier in the fridge."
2. "Will Grand Union seltzer do?"

Marsha La Greca, N.Y.C.

1. "No, it's too expensive."
2. "Oh, I'm sorry. I misread the price tag. I'll—uh, of course I'll take it."

Bill Anthony, N. Hollywood, Calif.

1. "Honk."
2. "Hi. I'm Harpo Marx. Welcome to the costume party."

Louis B. Raffel, Skokie, Ill.

1. "How can I ever thank you for pulling my grandson from that icy river?"
2. "Where are his mittens?"

Paul A. Zurkuhlen, Alexandria, Va.

1. "The relationship between the discussion in your introduction and the assigned subject is unclear. Similarly, your reasoning . . ."
2. "Stay off the grass when you're writing a term paper."

Page Collier, Thibodaux, La.

1. "You have quite an attractive mother."
2. "Who is that incredibly large and vulgar-looking woman?"

Scott L. Haskell, Stockton, Calif.

1. "Judy Garland."
2. "Liza Minnelli."

David J. Mackler, N.Y.C.

1. "Can I bring you anything from the coffee room, Ms. Steinem?"
2. "I'll have my girl bring us coffee."

Joel F. Crystal, Scarsdale, N.Y.

1. "What's an amulet?"
2. "Isn't that what doormen wear on their shoulders? Oh, no—that's armlet . . . gee, this sounds like *It Pays To Be Ignorant*—that old radio show. Er, of course I never actually heard it myself, but my mother told me . . ."

Anna Lambiase, Brooklyn.

1. "I'm an atheist."
2. "The Unification Church? No, I haven't. What is it?"

Greg Collins, N.Y.C.

1. "I hate cats."
2. "No, they're such fascinating creatures—the way they just look at you—so mysterious. It's not true that they're not affectionate—No, it doesn't matter at all, it's an old suit . . ."

Roderick Cook, N.Y.C.

1. "Libra."
2. "*Smoking and Spitting Are Prohibited By La* . . . hey, come back I was only . . ."

Jacqueline Fogel, Jamaica, N.Y.

1. "Yes, we're the Doyles."
2. "Well, yes and no. I'm Chris Doyle and this *is* my wife Karen. But she kept her former married name, Bracey, because . . ."

Chris Doyle, Burke, Va.

1. "I can tell that's a pure-bred Lhasa apso."
2. "What a cute little pussy cat!"

Tom Morrow, N.Y.C.

1. "Too bad you're busy, because a friend just gave me a pair of front-row seats to Saturday's Stones concert."
2. "Oh, well, what about next Saturday night?"

Larry Abramsky, N.Y.C.

1. "Break a leg."
2. "Break your legs."

Jay McDonnell, N.Y.C.

1. "I'm single."
2. "Uh, I *was* married, but he, er, that is, I uh, it didn't . . . we, uh, I'm not married now—at the present time, that is."

Jacqueline Richman, Long Beach, N.Y.

1. "The house, the Mercedes and $500,000."
2. "Please don't leave me."

K. R. Steele, Vernon, N.Y.

1. "He was the only one killed, and the car, a Facel Vega, was totally destroyed. The legend surrounding his death has been largely romanticised; and he was not the driver."
2. "I always get Sartre and Camus confused."

Jack Krug, N.Y.C.

1. "Edna St. Vincent Millay."
2. "Edna St. Vincent Mulcahy."

Ken Coleman, Woodstock, Conn.

1. "If I do, I'll get carsick."
2. "Oh, sorry, driver. Of course I'll put it out. How long have you been allergic?"

James Elward, N.Y.C.

1. "Mind your own damned business."
2. "The house cost $190,000; my husband earns $65,000 a year; my daughter is adopted; and three or four times a week."

Leonard Osterman, Potomac, Md.

1. "The cavity preparation process on a mandibular first molar may involve some instrumentation placement difficulty. . . ."
2. "Oops!"

Paul Kokesch, Minneapolis, Minn.

First Day at School

"April Rane shuddered into the clinging Pucci and turned to appraise herself in the full-length mirror. "Perfect," she thought, "the body of a twenty-year-old." She held the large gold hoops to her ears. "Too much," she decided. No sense diverting attention from the sleek chestnut hair caressing her shoulders. Once more she twirled before the mirror—a flick of mascara—and smiled at her reflection. April tiptoed across the bedroom (Brick was still asleep), picked up her pencil box, and with a soft click the door closed upon summer. "P.S. 501 look out," she breathed, "here comes April Rane."

Above, an excerpt from "First Day at School" by little Judith Krantz. Competitors were asked to provide an extract from a composition on this topic in the style of any well-known writer, age ten.

Report: Par Lagerqvist, Dylan Thomas, H.P. Lovecraft, W. Shakespeare, J.D. Salinger—if you really want to hear about it. Tom Tryon, F. Kafka, N. Hawthorne, A. Conan Doyle, Julia Child, Kahlil Gibran, Aileen Mehle, Jean Genet, Isaac Singer, Damon Runyon, Dos Passos, F. Dostoyevsky: all represented. Also: the Wolves, Virginia, Tom and Tom. Robert and Michael Crichton, the Barretts, Rona and Elizabeth. Gael and Graham Greene. And so forth. You work and play well with others. Promoted to 6-A.

Jocelyn was waiting for the light to change when she heard her name being called. She turned. Asta Roberts came running up to her. Asta went to P.S. 41. "Jocelyn! How was school today?" Jocelyn hesitated. "Fine, but . . . well, St. Mary's is rather strange." "How do you mean?" queried Asta. "For one," Jocelyn replied. "I'm the only girl in my class. And then, there are all these statues of the Virgin all over, and they're . . . sort of scary. I know it sounds stupid, but they look just like real girls, only they're . . . statues." She shuddered.

—IRA LEVIN
Philip Jerry, N.Y.C.

No because the covers were warm and I stretched and the torrent of sunrise sometimes like fire no hit the flowers ranged in rows where I played in summer no and got up when I wanted and wore jeans and old shirts no and she held up a dress no and pulled off the covers no and she said it's time no and notebooks and pencils no and then she asked me would I get up no and I put my arms on the covers and drew them down to me no and my heart was going like mad and no I said no I won't No.

—JAMES JOYCE
Patricia Nelson, New Haven, Conn.

Young Biffy trousered his lunch quid and, with a cheery "Tinkerty-Tonk," toddled off. "Rummy day," he thought, "not quite the sporting thing, to be trundled off to school so dashedly soon after having floated the sizzling eggs and b. to their destination with only a spot of milk." Thoughts of being conspic. by his a. at rollcall throbbed in his youthful lemon. But Biffy bit the bullet and smiled bravely. It was to be the last time he was to smile that day.

His man had put him out with mismatched spats.

—P. G. WODEHOUSE
Harold J. Ellner, M.D., Richland, Wash.

Already the sun was hot, working the earth into red dust, searing the jacarandas while a thin, slip-like dress she had made only the night before out of her mother's discarded dishtowel, stood at the doorway, waiting. Now she would meet them all, the anxious, bony, well-read Jews who would be the revolutionaries and expect too much of her, the stolid, giggling girls who, in only sixteen years, would give themselves up to babies and slight security, and the thick-legged, big-chested boys who would die badly in new but ancient wars. "This will never be enough," she said to herself and to the heavy, worn-out African morning.

—DORIS LESSING
E. Klein, N.Y.C.

"It is no longer enough to skip into one's classroom, shout 'Here!' and expect our problems to vanish. We have done that in the recent past: when not enough crayons were available, we looked to our allies for help. This is not playschool; it is a new era. Some matters—spelling, to cite an obvious dilemma—are too complex to solve by a wave of the hand. Let us put away our coloring books and face the future—not with a pout but with hope that the chief executive, Miss Murphy, will lead us through the long days ahead . . ."

—JAMES RESTON
Gerald Nachman, N.Y.C.

The first day of school dawned appropriately bleak. I retrieved my Harrod's school bag noticing by the single hair still in place across the hasp that it hadn't been touched. Methodically, I inspected the contents: three medium Crown lead pencils, Strand pen nib and two points, Mayfair composition book, and a box of Crayolas in assorted colours. Shrugging into a Mark & Spencer pullover, I proceeded to the kitchen where my mum was preparing breakfast. "Just a bit of porridge," I said, "sprinkled with 10X confectioner's sugar, a splash of warm milk, and stirred seven times *counter*clockwise."

—IAN FLEMING
Norton Bramesco, N.Y.C.

You just have to love a spunky school like this one—a thousand miles from the Great White Way, Sticksville personified, but still strutting like the Big City. Teacher has airs too. "Treat me like a lady and you've got me where you want me," was her opening number. I gave her the apple. She devoured it with sharp little cries of pleasure. All the kids did mysterious, infinitely sad, rural double-takes and muttered gutsy cornfield witticisms. Spirit they've got, but couth may take a while.

—BRUCE JAY FRIEDMAN
Anthony Gray, Closter, N.J.

She was looming over me, the wall eye careening into Zooks McCaffrey on my left, the other pinning me to the desk. Her upper lip curled hideously, towards her nostril. "Holy poop, she's going to *bite* me!" I rammed three red ones and two green ones down my throat, holes and all. She was still there, but the eye glowed now . . . a furious cherry-Jello red. I followed with a four-inch stick of Tootsie Roll.

"The wrapper, you crazy fool. You ate the darned *wrapper,*" McCaffrey hissed in my ear. —HUNTER THOMPSON

Ian M. Irvine, Cambridge, Mass.

. . . I find nothing to recommend *School.* Unfortunately, it's the only thing running. —JOHN SIMON

Arthur B. Rubinstein, N.Y.C.

Desist, good mother, no more play the fool; / Beseech me not to quit my bed for school. / Consider, parent: wide-browed Plato finds / The Child knows first, the Teacher but reminds. / The Bard reveals—nor can you, Ma'am, dispute it— / How Wisdom oft in Solitude is rooted. / One further thought, that I to Chaucer owe: / "Ful wyse is hee that doth hemselven know." / Thus rests my case; at rest I'll too remain, / And know myself beneath my counterpane.

—ALEXANDER POPE

Trudy Drucker, Newark, N.J.

. . . Squinting in the early light which polished the crumpled garbage cans rolling at the curb, he watched the pumpkin coach grind to a halt and as he climbed the first high step he remembered with a sudden strange feeling the whiteness inside the teacher's thigh when she perched atop his desk. —JOHN UPDIKE

Louis Devon, Turnersville, N.J.

Penmanship. That's what's selling at Hollywood Grammar. But not everyone's buying . . . Seated in a room where sunmotes crawled off the syrupy, ocher walls like flies stuck in a jar of U-bet, little Candice Bergen, whose father plays with puppets, so she'd have you believe, stalks across the toy-strewn floor like a palomino filly who's suddenly lost her stride. "School, I've decided, is a trap for little rich girls. What I want now is simply a good camera." —REX REED

James Fritzhand, N.Y.C.

CHAPTER XXXVIII—Revolt at Snack Time—Detention of Malefactors by the Headmaster—Manners and Customs of the Class—Fall of the Playground to Vandals—Last Hours—General Observation Upon the Period—Outline of Book Four. A loud and licentious mur-

mur was echoed throughout the class at the appearance of juice and cookies, and as the mild indolence of Miss Smith, magistra, neglected to extinguish the first symptoms of discontent, the want of honour and respect was supplied by the fearful discipline emanating from the High Office of the Headmaster, Britannia fertilis provincia tyrannorum . . .

—EDWARD GIBBON
Jack Ryan, N.Y.C.

This glorious day of crisp yellow and blue suddenly red bricked around Blessingworth's small life. Mustiness in the nostrils. Shouldering through the older ladies of the sixth grade, rife with possibilities, foregoing a possible perfunctory tweak of a cheek. Noel Blessingworth, scholar, displaying detachment as I slide into this arse-polished seat. To glimpse Miss Pennyquick's hallowed ground as she places it desktop and crosses the legs. Picking up the golden rule. With which she lacerates a geography book. Angry chip of sound. For punctuation. To begin the first period. O, school days. / But my nights / Are still / Free.

—J. P. DONLEAVY
Ford Hovis, N.Y.C.

My uncle gave me the box. He warned me not to open it until October. When I shook the box the pencils rattled and the box groaned. Today, Herr Klabendich called the class to order. I shook the box and he took it away from me. He was so angry his high stiff collar shook. Then he opened it. The groan became so loud I hid my head. When it became quiet, only the collar lay where Herr Klabendich once stood. School begins in Glumpelsdorf on September 5.

—E. T. A. HOFFMAN
James M. Green, M.D., Livingston, N.J.

We have learned from reliable sources that Teacher Eleanor Carlisle worked out a deal with Principal Ronald Geevers to eat hot lunches in the cafeteria for nothing, over what may have been many months. Close associates of Carlisle have told us her flagrant misuse of taxpayers' dollars was linked to a cover-up for Geevers, who, you may recall, came under attack only a year ago for suspected Crayola pilfering and report-card doctoring. When we questioned Carlisle on the alleged meal freeloading, she flatly denied taking part, and then dumped a load of homework on us.

—JACK ANDERSON
Toby Smith, N.Y.C.

Drive on, O Bus of State / Proceed, O driver, strong and great. / Hank Longfellow, and all his peers, / With lessons planned for future years / Are riding, breathless, in this crate.

—HENRY W. LONGFELLOW
Benjamin Ivry, Fresh Meadows, N.Y.

Daddy, I know why you sent me to school. / They wait in rows: / Desks, chairs, minds— / Nailed tight to the floor / Like clothes upside down on a line.
Smell of felt and chalk dust. / Insistent bell— / Daddy, I must, I must / Find the room, pass the door, lose my face, / Go to school, to school, to school.

—SYLVIA PLATH
J. Bickart, N.Y.C.

The schoolroom is just as I described it to Mama and Daddy this morning at the breakfast table. Little Peggy Sommers sits next to me. Poor thing. She's going to break her shoulder bone while ice skating this winter. That's nothing compared to what's going to happen to the boy two seats in back of me. I like school this coming year even though I'm going to get a "C" in arithmetic.

—JEANE DIXON (As told to RUTH MONTGOMERY, age eleven)
Lydia Wilen, N.Y.C.

It's the sort of day for fishing, if you know what I mean, / It's the sort of day for walking, or conversing with the queen. / It's the sort of day for skipping, or swimming in the pool, / 'Cos it's definitely not the sort of day for school! // "Yes," said Christopher Robin, "it's the sort of day that's sunny," / "And of course," said Pooh, "it's the sort of day for hunny." / I sort of think I'll skip it, tho' I may be thought a fool, / 'Cos it's definitely not the sort of day for school!

—A. A. MILNE
Andrea Harris, New Haven, Conn.

Carol had learned to keep her balance while dressing, in spite of the incessant swaying of the building. Dabbing her fork into the rouge-pot, she carelessly smeared four-tined auguries on each cheek. Then after tying her mother's hands together with pantyhose, she leaped through the nearest window, not forgetting to tap the radiator for the super as she passed. Today was a school day.

—DONALD BARTHELME
M. M. Bogle, Syracuse, N.Y.

Who amongst them could imagine that, unlike this first day at The Chadsforthrun, there would be but one child left out of ten by next semester?

—AGATHA CHRISTIE
R. Gelfond, Phila., Pa.

Jack woke up. It felt good to wake up. He stood and dressed in flannel shirt and flannel trousers. They felt good. Jack walked downstairs. The stairs felt good against his feet. In the kitchen he warmed his hands over the stove. Jack liked the warmth. It was good to feel warm. His father sat at the table drinking milk. "First day of school, eh, son?" You weak bastard, thought Jack. "There's no time for breakfast," said Jack. "I'll just slip this slab of beef in my pocket and take the wineskin of Pernod for lunch."

Jack left. It felt good to leave.

—ERNEST HEMINGWAY
Laurence Rosen, Chicago, Ill.

Today, the firste day of schule year 1652–53, I did walke to schule. Passing under an apple tree at MacDonwald's farm, I was hitte bye a rotten apple, soyling mye shirte. I did complayne to Schulemaster, and he did questionne Old MacDonwald and his kerns. Alle said that theye did throw nothinge. Being wroth, I wished them taken up for the Assizes. Schulemaster said it was follie to hale them to court on a matter of no gravity.

—ISAAC NEWTOWNE
Louis Kleinman, Louisville, Ky.

I was late for my scheduled appearance. The summons had been quite specific: nine o'clock. I'd lingered in the street, and was late. I handed my credentials to the Examining Magistrate and she—SHE! but I'd known all along, hadn't I?—the Examining Magistrate indicated the defendant's booth. My jurors, done up to resemble me, sat stiffly, silently, in individual stalls, hands folded, eyeing me sternly. I glanced about the courtroom. The walls, othertimes hopeful, otherwhere gay, were hung in black, with the single, damning chalk relief, "What I Did This Summer."

—FRANZ KAFKA
John Hofer, Southborough, Mass.

"My First Day at School and Suicide Note" (to be forwarded to my teacher, Mrs. Fleck, so she wouldn't think I didn't do my homework).

—GAIL PARENT
Ronnie Warren Ashcroft, N.Y.C.

Answer Game with Switch

ANSWER: "Skip To My Loo."
QUESTION: What was the postscript on the invitation to Lord Braithwaite's "Come as a Silly Billy" party?

Above, the Answer Game with a switch. Competitors were asked to provide an aphorism altered by a one-letter substitution and a clarifying riddle.

Report: "Friends, Romans et al, lend me your eats." "I've Got You Under My Skis." "Take My Life, Please" (by Patrick Henny). "Mary Had a Little Limb." "Jeannie with the Light-Brown Heir" and *Gone With the Wand.* As to which, a covey of homosexual riddles appeared. (See finale.) Herewith the winters of our discontest:

A. "Who was that mashed stranger, anyway?"
Q. What did they say as the Lone Potato rode out of town?

Martin Israel, Bklyn. Hts., N.Y.

A. Hell hath no furs like a woman scorned.
Q. Where in hell can you get a good fur?

Richard J. Hafey, Morningdale, Mass.

A. A rolving stone gathers no moss.
Q. What is a rolving stone?

Katherine Mount, Teaneck, N.J.

A. Don't book a gift horse in the mouth.
Q. Where should you not let your new pet perform?

Max Dixon, Westminster, Md.

A. Monkey pee, monkey do.
Q. What do you like least about being a zookeeper?

Jerry Wachtel, Columbia, Md.

A. Sugar and spice and everything mice.
Q. What is Rodent Thermidor made of?

Capo di Fugawi, Dahlgren, Va.

A. "I am the captain of my shul."
Q. How does an Israeli chaplain identify himself?

Ilene McGrath, Englewood, N.J.

A. In days of old when knights were bald.
Q. When were armor-plated toupées popular?

Hyman Levy, N.Y.C.

A. He loved not wisely but two well.
Q. What was the bigamist's defense?

Paul Weiss, Washington, D.C.

A. *All's Well that Ends Welk*
Q. What did the man say after he shot the accordion player?

William Cole, N.Y.C.

A. Minty Python
Q. What does Baskin-Robbins call its new snake-flavored ice cream?

James C. Perrine, Lawrenceville, N.J.

A. *Dolce for niente.*
Q. What's the title of the Neapolitan free candy program?

Mobil Rm. 303, N.Y.C.

A. *The Man in the Glass Boots*
Q. Which one did you say was Alice Cooper?

Joshua Daniels, Hewlitt, N.Y.

A. *Duce Soup*
Q. Name a film starring Mussolini and the Marx Brothers.
David Levine, Brooklyn.

A. "The Girl That I Marry Will Have to Be as Soft and as Oink as a Nursery"
Q. What did Brad say to make you stop dating him?
Tom Morrow, N.Y.C.

A. *Ten and Sympathy*
Q. What's the most you can expect from your brother-in-law?
Ms. Gene Winslow, Summit, N.J.

A. Mr. Snowden (3,560 feet).
Q. Mrs. Snowden is 3,545 feet tall. How tall is her husband?
Bernetta Nelson, N.Y.C.

A. *The Return of the Dative*
Q. What is the dream of every Latin lover?
Lelia Vincent, Providence, R.I.

A. *The Poisoner of Second Avenue.*
Q. Describe McDonald's.
C.P. Jones, N.Y.C.

A. *Watch on the Rhino.*
Q. What was the title of John Cameron Swayze's autobiography?
Gerard J. Cook, Westbury, N.Y.

A. Julius Cnesar.
Q. What Roman emperor's last words were "Achoo, Brute"?
Rick Jaconson, Stamford, Ct.

A. "Eine Kleine Nacht Musak"
Q. What do they play in the Vienna Hilton?
Robert Barrie, N.Y.C.

A. "Now is the winter of our discontent / Made glorious . . . by this son of Pork."
Q. Cite a quotation from *King Richard III* by Bacon.
Fred Berg, Boston, Mass.

A. Manuel of Arms.
Q. Who's in line to succeed José of Feet?

Charlie Laiken, N.Y.C.

A. Bubonic plaque.
Q. What was the leading destroyer of teeth during the Middle Ages?

Rich Sylvestri, Valley Stream, N.Y.

A. Catherine the Greet.
Q. Who was the Perle Mesta of Ole Russia?

George Fairbanks, Nutley, N.J.

A. "Somewhere in the night, a dog barfed."
Q. What line follows, "Oh, Jerry, don't let's ask for the moan, we have the stare"?

Charlotte Laiken, Bayside, N.Y.

A. Doc Quixote.
Q. Who was the fastest lance in the west?

James R. Dalin, Avenel, N.J.

A. Alternate side of the street barking
Q. Why did the puppy cross the road?

Henna Arond Zacks, Brooklyn.

A. The Roman umpire.
Q. What caused the decline and fall of Italian baseball?

Lecia Dellamano, Southold, N.Y.

A. One fool in the grave.
Q. Who was Yorick?

W. H. Richardson, Peace Dale, R.I.

A. Tranks for the Memory.
Q. What's the name of that drug that helps you forget?

May Maher, Montclair, N.J.

A. Ritual Tire Dance.
Q. What is the initiation at a Goodyear convention?

Joel Crystal, Scarsdale, N.Y.

A. Bruce Force.
Q. What's another name for Gay Power?

Richard Fried, Brooklyn.

A. *The Gay of the Locust.*
Q. What do you call a closet grasshopper?

Richard J. Hafey, Morningdale, Mass.

A. "A thing of beauty is a boy forever."
Q. What motto appears on Dorian Gray's family crest?

Robert Ross, N.Y.C.

A. Two Gays from Harrison.
Q. Who supplies the best discount drag?

James Fechheimer, Glen Head, N.Y.

A. Down to the Sea in Skips.
Q. How did everybody leave Lord Braithwaite's "Come as a Silly Billy" party?

Similarly from: Many

Fractured Definitions

polyglot, 1. substance found on the plumage of an ill-kempt parrot. 2. *obs.* the raucous call of an aunt. (*See* tomsawyer)
tabloid, 1. any species of brindled cat having the ability to swim underwater. 2. a newspaper for consumers of diet beverages.

Above, further extracts from our "Fractured Dictionary." Competitors were invited to invent appropriate definitions for words beginning with the letters "P" and "T."

Report: A lively group, *q.v.* You'll note, with good humor, one hopes, the scheduled reappearance of ethnic jokes: Polish, Jewish, Italian, Oriental. And drunk jokes. The repeat "Ps": **paterfamilias:** sound of little feet. **propaganda:** formal goose. **penchant:** convict's hymn. **pigtail:** *cf The New Centurions.* **privilege:** shelf for plumbing facility. **pungent:** Bennett Cerf. **platoon:** ornate cuspidor. **psoriasis:** an optometrist's nurse. Or the capital of Poland. Whichever comes first. Do you know what they call an ill wind? **Pariah.** Which see. The repeat "Ts": **teetotaler:** golf scorekeeper. **tintinnabulary:** Hollywood dog catcher. **tango:** breakfast drink for ballroom dancers. **tapioca:** nostalgic Latin American soft shoe. **trifle:** small gun. Altogether a satisfying group. Which see.

---

precedent, 1. First person ever to occupy White House. **2.** First toothpaste ever marketed. **3.** First person in White House using first toothpaste. **4.** First newspaper release regarding first person in White House using first toothpaste.

Jack Paul, Bklyn.

pandemonium, bear-owned and -operated apartment building in Miami Beach.

Susan Wolfson, Little Falls, N.J.
Henry Hirschberg, Bayside, N.Y.

Poland Water, H_3O

Dan Greenburg, N.Y.C.

purvey, sound made by overwrought Jewish cat.

Peter Meltzer, N.Y.C.
Miles Klein, E. Brunswick, N.J.

pronto, the Lone Ranger's faithful Italian companion.

Dr. S. Kelz, Rye, N.Y.

phlegmatic, *Israeli.* a pennant that unfurls without human assistance.

Lee Greene, Briarcliff Manor, N.Y.

purloin, school for pussycats, Brooklyn.

Anne M. Bartine, N.Y.C.

plume, the ball point belonging to the sister of one's father or mother.

Eileen Tranford, Dorchester, Mass.

podium, 1. intense hatred of ravens and ushers. 2. a feeling of weariness induced by attending a Vincent Price film festival.

Ruth Brewster, Hillside, N.J.

plutocrat, an important executive at Walt Disney Studios.

Ann Schwartzman, Essex, Md.

placebo, an ornamental outdoor structure that has no effect on the landscape.

Bernetta Nelson, N.Y.C.

pasturella, Elsie the Cow's youngest daughter.

Jay McDonnell, N.Y.C.

powwow, the bark of a boxer.

Mary Conte, N. Miami, Fla.

pulverize, *Naut.* to promote to the rank of ensign (the sailor was p . . . d during the battle).

Harris Ruben, Berkeley Hts., N.J.

purple, throaty sound of contentment uddered by cattle.

Rosenthal Family Rm., Roslyn Hts., N.Y.

Pooh Bah, short review of works of A. A. Milne.

William Cole, N.Y.C.

pungent, a feminist puppet show. (*see* **Judy**)

Msgr. A. V. McLees, St. Albans, N.Y.

pocket, at Radio City Music Hall, a dancer with acne.

Stanley Wettan, Bklyn.

picador, the climax of "The Lady or the Tiger."

Jack Ryan, N.Y.C.

pylon, a Greek orgy.

Jack Neal, N.Y.C.

pneumonoultramicroscopicsilicovolcanoconiosis, 1. supercalifragilisticexpialidocious. 2. the word generally conceded to be erased from tape by Rose Mary Woods during telephone call.

Rose Kahn, New Orleans, La.

prairie, *Colloq.* a religious homosexual.

Peter Howard, N.Y.C.

pimiento, *Reader's Digest* edition of playwright's memoirs.

Frank McAteer, Maplewood, N.J.

penultimate, member of an Ivy League college precision dance team.

Norton Bramesco, N.Y.C.

Palermo, Sicilian transsexual sitcom loosely based on role created in America by Marie Wilson. (*see also* **Palmyra**).

Philip Edinger, Cloverdale, Calif.

polyester, a Jewish princess.

Patricia Cary, Trenton, N.J.

prism, 1. a jail with windows. 2. *Obs.* (*see* **Sam Quentin**).

1. Mrs. Robert I. Polunsky, San Angelo, Tex.;
2. Jonathan Abrams, Bklyn.

penknife, 19-cent Bic.
passé, a citizen's group on harses riding after a rabber.

Baylor Bd. of Old Trustee, Chatt., Tenn.

periscope, the mouthwash of fairies.

Harold Brewster, Hillside, N.J.

pacifist, a cannibal's request.

Michael Bromley, E. Hampton, N.Y.

plasma, a very posh hotel in Transylvania.

Joshua Daniels, Hewlett, N.Y.

Polish Corridor, a wooden plank set on four bricks.

Phyllis Kelly, Locust Valley, N.Y.

Pollyanna, 1. a synthetic fiber simulating certain tropical vines. 2. an elaborate fabric made from this fiber (*see* **Gladrags**)

Roger Wykes, Ann Arbor, Mich.

prop, the sound made when Oriental food is spilled.

George Fairbanks, Nutley, N.J.

pastry, the wardrobe room at Minsky's.

Bunny Daniels, Hewlett, N.Y.

publican, a member of the political party that instigated the Whiskey Rebellion.

Joel Frome Crystal, Bklyn.

psychic, an ol' drinkin' buddy.

Steve Diamond, N.Y.C.

precocious, the reason Sammy Davis Jr. ate pork chops as a boy.
Andrea J. Goldberg, N.Y.C.

Panzer Division, a gay brigade, Germany, W.W. II.
Steven Weinberger, Beechurst, N.Y.

pter-o-dac-tyl, *Poet.* on the wings of Higgledy-Piggledy.
Harlow T. Mapes Soc., Chatt., Tenn.

pampas, disposable diapers used extensively by mama llamas.
Carol Drew, Palisades Pk., N.J.

phlegm, 1. native of Flanders. 2. *Dial.* moth's destiny.
Albert G. Miller, N.Y.C.

parrot, a talking orange vegetable.
Martin Schlesinger, Bklyn.

parallelogram, a message sent by wire from one math teacher to another.
Mrs. Joel F. Crystal, Bklyn.

panhandler, 1. one who accosts the Greek god of pastures. 2. *Colloq.* John Simon's copy boy.
Frank Shanbacker, N.Y.C.

postnasal, a difficult equestrian maneuver in which two horses are required to pass each other's right flank while moving backwards.
Peter Slade, N.Y.C.

pickerel, prize-winning doggerel.
John Hofer, Southborough, Mass.

pistachio, hair or bristles on the face of a pig. adj. Music slightly faster than palmetto but slower than pellagra; as, *pistachio ma non troppo.*
Marie Longyear, N.Y.C.

perquisite, *Chiefly Brit.* The wife or widow of a perque (*see* **marquisette**).
John S. Spano, N.Y.C.

participle, one who spends limited time as the follower of a guru.
Irwin Vogel, Bklyn.

preposition, an offer made to or by a prestitute.
Mel Taub, N.Y.C.

parsimony, 1. marriage between two grammarians. 2. divorce settlement paid by clergymen.
1. John J. Coniglio, Bklyn.
2. Linda J. Kern, Midland, Mich.

pedagogue, house of foot worship.
Barney Shiffman, Bayside, N.Y.

polaroid, a very cold heavenly body.
R. Schulman, Merrick, N.Y.

pesky, *Colloq.* means of gaining access to apartment by custodian.
Joseph Falk, E. Elmhurst, N.Y.

poinsettia, a red dog with a long tail.
Herb Lessell, Bklyn.

prayer wheel, Billy Graham.
Sal Rosa, N.Y.C.

Pensacola, beverage served in club car.
Stanley Stone, Oceanside, N.Y.

prizewinning, 1. this entry. 2. *Obs.* my last entry.
M. Anesh, Teaneck, N.J.

Tong, 1. formerly a secret society of Chinese icemen in the United States noted for their violent street fights. 2. A breakfast drink made from wet sandals.
George Fairbanks, Nutley, N.J.

tetrahedron, 1. Film festival showing at least three movies featuring the star of Hitchcock's *The Birds.* 2. A cheer for the same star originated during a Vietnamese holiday.
Jack Riley, Los Angeles, Calif.

tokenism, cult centered around author of epic tale *Lord of the Subways.*

Giff Crosby, Bloomfield, N.J.

tactics, Polish breath mints.

Judith Klein, E. Brunswick, N.J.

turtleneck, the practice, now obsolete, of petting a turtle above the waist and outside the shell.

Dan Greenburg, N.Y.C.

thanatopsis, 1. Famous radio game show featuring cash prizes to contestants with best death stories. 2. *(colloq.)* Expression of an incest taboo (i.e., I'd rather be right thanatopsis).

1. Walter I. Epstein, Cedarhurst, N.Y.
2. Joyce Harrington, Parkersburg, Va.

Tuscaloosa, Ivory League dental college.

Albert G. Miller, N.Y.C.

tammany, overabundance of Sandra Dee movies.

Kate Dwyer, Orange, N.J.

toadstool, a frog that's turned state's evidence.

Gabrielle Benigno, Glen Oaks, N.Y.

therapy, poncholike garment for a gay caballero.

Frances Kaauamo, N.Y.C.

talisman, a male talisperson *(see below).*

Anne Milton, San Francisco, Calif.

Tashkent, mild-mannered, bespectacled reporter for Tass known to the world as **supertovarich.**

Jacobi Radiology, Bronx Mun. Hosp., N.Y.

taxidermy, a dance hall elephant.

Lydia Wilen, N.Y.C.

teacup, bra size of woman listed in the *Guinness Book of World Records.*

Oscar Weigle, Whitestone, N.Y.

tamper, A disposable paper hat.

Mark Wolfson, Spring Valley, N.Y.

tachometer, device for measuring audience response at Bette Midler concerts.

J. Bickart, N.Y.C.

tachycardia, 1. Rejection slips from Hallmark. 2. A bridge club for senior citizens who always wear white socks.

1. Norton Bramesco, N.Y.C.
2. Sy & Carmen Fisher, Newton, Mass.

trout, banish or expel, as in grid of.

John Hofer, Southborough, Mass.

tempest, 1. Person who keeps calling you up and telling you how hot or cold it is outside. 2. List made annually by film critics.

1. Oliver Katz, N.Y.C.
2. Mark Kabat, N.Y.C.

Tomboy, the Waltons' pet cat.

Richard Fried, Bklyn.

troupe, wig worn by members of acting group.

Tom Robinson, Bayonne, N.J.

transcendentalism, the basic tenet of an obscure Protestant sect believing that tooth decay is divine retribution for spiritual transgressions. Doctrine fell into disrepute following introduction of stannous fluoride.

Joe E. Forrester, N.Y.C.

truncheon, afternoon meal, especially one at which club sandwiches are served.

Mel Taub, N.Y.C.
Also: Connie Garretson, E. Orange, N.J.

Tangelo, chief of the Miami Beach Mafia.

Erna Lovett, Hillside, N.J.

twitch, mechanism for changing track on the Atchison, Topeka and Santa Fey.

Warren Randall, Levittown, N.Y.

terris, pacem in, too many people at a Vatican garden party.

S. Rosmarin, Scarsdale, N.Y.

toga, the mental discipline concentrating on the crossing of pedal digits.

Alan Levine, Copiague, N.Y.

tombstone, building material utilized by prisoners of well-known N.Y.C. penitentiary. (See also JAILHOUSE ROCK.)

Gerald J. Levy, N.Y.C.

tilt, to plow with a lance.

Anne Feldhaus, Cincinnati, Ohio

transylvania, new AC-DC lightbulb.

C. Spenker, N.Y.C.

telephone pole, employee of P. T. & T.

Anna Brennan, E. Greenwich, R.I.

tadpole, 1. A skewer for inexpensive steaks. 2. Any small, round native of Warsaw.

Gerald Nachman, N.Y.C.

toad, poem on a Grecian Tern.

Conant Moulton, N.Y.C.

tangible, a blimp camouflaged for reconnaissance in sandstorms.

Mobil Rm. 304, N.Y.C.

tickle, proposed U.S. 2 1/2-cent piece.

W. M. Campbell, N.Y.C.

tallyho, a Vietnamese census-taker.

David M. Taub, Claverack, N.Y.

Tyrannosaurus, dictionary of fascism.

Patrick Killpatrick, Alexandria, Va.

tarnished, a German youth who is not a sailor.

Cynthia Dantzic, Bklyn.

trivet, sound of no consequence made by a frog.

Lynn Gross, N.Y.C.

terra cotta, derisive term in ancient Rome applied to pins securing chariot wheels. (*See* unsafe at any gallop.)

Anna Koppersmith, N.Y.C.

Tsetse, twin rulers of the Mao dynasty.

W.H. Rossmassler Jr., Flourtown, Pa.

trollop, a streetcar men desire.

Elliott Sperber, W. Hartford, Conn.

trumpet, 1. A rostitute. 2. A treetwalker.

C. N. Troller, Willow Grove, Pa.

Near-Miss Play Plots

Mr. and Mrs. Dinner of New England and their entire family slip, fall, and break their legs on the doorstep of famous lecturer-writer, Sheridan Mann. They move in, and . . .

Above, the final plan of a stage Near-Miss. Competitors were asked for the brief plot outline of a Near-Miss play.

Report: A word on plays. Almost all the near-miss plots hatched in a satisfyingly silly way. Repeats either were, or easily might have been, entitled as follows: AUNT VANYA. *Mishap To a Salesperson. Teeter-Totter. Violinist on the Roof. Vitalis! The Three Siblings. Romeo and Mercutio. Who's Afraid of a College President's Daughter?* (or, *Here's Our Son Now, Home From School*). *Oedipus Regina* (or, *Here's Our Son Now, Home From School*) and *Hamlet* (or, *Here's Our Son Now, Home From School*). Plus sundry deus ex machinery. And *you* wanted to know where all the new young talent is coming from?

Gilbert and Sullivan wade satirically through the straits of Quaker dogma in this comic opera spun round the two spinster aunts of William Penn and a merry band of New World pirates they come to lead . . .

John Hofer, Southborough, Mass.

1787—A musical adaptation of the events leading to the ratification of the U.S. Constitution, featuring the Bill of Rights . . .

M. Borowka, Mineola, N.Y.

A sensitive lad at a boys' school is accused by his peers of being a possibly gay person. The sympathetic and winsome wife of the headmaster takes pity on the lad, invites him over for tea, and decides the only way to bolster his shaky masculine ego is to jump him. Unbuttoning her blouse, she whispers: "When you speak of this, and you *will,* please—don't lisp" . . .

Dan Greenburg, N.Y.C.

Prince Hoglet to Playactors in Billy Shockspur's *Hoglet,* Act III, Scene II: "Talk the talk, I pray you, any way you like, use your own discretion. . . . Sawing the air wildly with your hand certainly ought to help. . . . Show emotion, make plenty of faces. . . . Improvise your own actions and words. . . . Clown it up. . . ." . . .

Jack Paul, Bklyn.

Phoebe (*Phèdre* de Racine, adapté par Melina Mercouri et Abe Burrows): Phoebe décide à pointer le finger à her stepfils, Hippy, pour making une passe à her (un grand fib). Elle goes blabant à her hubbi, Théodore, père of le "perpétrateur." Teddy dit, "Grouvi! Le garçon obvieusement has le bon taste. Hitchez les chevaux et haverons une grande wingding!" Et tout le monde chariote à la seashore pour un moonlight pique-nique . . .

Fran Ross, N.Y.C.

A devious guy tells his buddy, the King of the Moors, that his wife is fooling around. The king is madder than hell and gets a Haitian divorce.

Maurice Katz, N.Y.C.

Six authors come out onstage and horse around looking for a character to write a vehicle for. Failing to find same, they take a cab to Elaine's and spend the rest of the evening playing backgammon . . .

Oliver Katz, East Hampton, N.Y.

The Stopover. When Clara Zachanassian returns to the place of her birth, the train she is on accidentally kills her former beau and now mayor-elect. Swept up with guilt, she offers to give the town one billion marks as compensation for its loss . . .

Stephen Gelb, Allston, Mass.

Forty-year-old woman refuses to marry twenty-year-old boy. He tells her that she is childish, stupid, and age doesn't matter. So she elopes with a childish, stupid sixteen-year-old . . .

Sam Bassin, Bklyn.

The Elder sisters, kindly spinsters, make a delicious wine with the help of their nephew and their brother, who thinks he's General Grant. Word of their local success reaches Ernest and Julio Gallo, and . . .

David E. Cassidy, Salem Center, N.Y.

Sluice—One person plays all roles. Triptych screen provides cover for lightning changes. Plot involves lesbian who, disguised as husband, inveigles their lover, disguised as dentist, into heisting bank fronting for gasoline ring, inducing guard to stab lover with rubber knife. In second act, lover disguised as maid returns to frighten lesbian disguised as butler. Lover then unmasks to reveal bank president, and lesbian unmasks to reveal police officer who makes arrest . . .

Michael Schreiber, Bklyn.

Ensemble. All Robert's married friends have gathered to throw him a surprise party, but are instead surprised themselves when Robert shows up with a new bride . . .

Jack Sharkey, Elk Grove Village, Ill.

Three elderly women, who have gone into the occult thing pretty heavily, tell a Scottish lord that if he and his wife play their cards right, they can rise in the local social order. Macbeth forgets to tell his wife, and . . .

Barbara G. Sambol, Winchester, Va.

Eliza Lerner-Shaw, elegant Mayfair debutante, is seen rushing from Covent Garden in a drenching rain. "Flowers for the lady," cries a seedy, fiftyish Cockney street vendor with a blackened tooth and virtually unbearable charm. Rising to the moment, Eliza observes, "Give that man a bath and a diphthong or two, and in six weeks I'll pass myself off as his niece and ward." As the sniggering of her companions subsides, music starts up under . . .

Edward Kleban, N.Y.C.

A professor of phonics decides to make a lady of a poor Cockney flower girl. He begins an intensive campaign to improve her speech. At last, he thinks he has succeeded and takes her to a fancy ball to show her off. The strain of all the diction lessons, however, has made the girl so hoarse that no one can understand a word she says . . .

George Fairbanks, Nutley, N.J.

Male Chauvinist Pygmalion persuades the haughty only daughter of the Earl of Slowdon to attend the Queen's garden party, dressed in rags, hawking her wares in the atrocious Cockney accent he has been teaching her for months. Pyg falls madly in love with her, but she treats him with the hauteur of an earl's only daughter. In desperation . . .

Judith R Goldsmith, Woodmere, N.Y.

Haplet. A Danish prince returns from college to discover his recently widowed mother has married his uncle. He is happy. He'd never liked his father anyway . . .

James Elward, N.Y.C.

Claudius, brother to the King of Denmark, pours poison into the king's ear while he is asleep in his orchard. After being laid up a few days with a bad earache, the king decides to . . .

Thom Molyneaux, N.Y.C.

M. Bilder, Scandinavian architect, struggles hopelessly to encourage his chief assistant. . . . The assistant is talentless . . .

Sterling E. Lanier, Sarasota, Fla.

An unscrupulous but utterly charming young man succeeds in business without really trying—to be honest, that is. His methods of climbing the ladder of success are unethical but hilarious. Unfortunately, the Senate Committee on Business Practices investigates him and he is eventually indicted by a federal grand jury. His boss's nephew, in the meantime, becomes chairman of the board . . .

Teresa Gerbers, Glenmont, N.Y.

Pardoned by the governor after spending twenty years in jail, Lucky Louie decides to get the judge who sent him away. He discovers, to his chagrin, that the judge is now the governor who pardoned him. He seeks the aid of a well-known psychiatrist . . .

Alissa Abrams, Bklyn.

Dolly, after spending most of her working life in a match factory making matches for everyone else, finally makes one for herself. As she takes a break and lights up a cigarette, her boss proposes and all the factory workers assemble to sing, "Hello, Matchmaker . . ."

Edmund Conti, Summit, N.J.

A bullfighter brings his wife home to meet his father (a retired college professor) and his two brothers (a priest and a social worker). After an hour or so he realizes that they have nothing at all in common so he and his wife get up and leave . . .

Eileen Tranford, Dorchester, Mass.

A bunch of guys who play together in an orchestra get together for a little birthday party/jam session. Slapstick hilarity ensues when it is discovered that one member of the group is locked in a closet. The others try to coax him out . . .

Susan N. Klein, Pittsburgh, Pa.

The marriage of Paula and Gregory Anton is threatened. He can't abide her continual lowering of wattage in the household. Her tap dancing in the attic at unseemly hours is bugging him. If she hides just one more thing from him . . .

Gene Oberg, Richmond, Va.

Two young men, Americans, on a trip to Scotland, stumble upon a golf course which appears only once every 100 years . . .

Bryan Spencer, N.Y.C.

An aging king decides to retire and divide his possessions among his three daughters. They refuse his offer, saying that they already have far more than they need. The two older daughters then realize that their father needs someone to share his golden years with. They arrange for him to meet the Duchess of Gloucester, hoping that marriage will result . . .

J. Bickart, N.Y.C.

Agamemnon (revival). *Cassandra.* "Now I will tell you plainly and from no cryptic speech. You shall look on Agamemnon dead. *Cassandra & Chorus* (music). "Que será, será. Whatever will be, will be . . ."

Larry Laiken, Bayside, N.Y.

Flo Ziegfeld sends invitations to every showgirl he's ever employed to come to his theater before it's ripped down for one last evening of nostalgia. Nobody shows up because the invitations get lost in the mail, so Ziegfeld hops a cab to Elaine's and plays backgammon all night . . .

D. Kotteb, N.Y.C.

Sequels

Barbra Streisand in FUNNY CORPSE
HOW TO BE YOUR OWN NEW BEST FRIEND, by Newman/Berkowitz
Jean-Charles Taccefia's SECOND COUSIN, COUSINE

Above, the forthcoming. Competitors were asked for the compelling title for an inevitable sequel to a well-known film, play, etc.

Report: Son of Repeats: Stephen Sondheim's SEND IN THE LION TAMERS. Michael Bennett's A FEATURED PLAYER. BOB & TED & CAROL & ALICE & BENJI. WHERE WERE YOU WHEN THE LIGHTS WENT OUT AGAIN? WHAT KEPT YOU, GODOT? And THE GREATEST STORY EVER TOLD, PART II.

THE NEW IMPROVED TESTAMENT

Michael J. Barkan, Levittown, N.Y.;
Brenda Spisto, Marlboro, N.J.

LAST YEAR AT MARIENBAD—POSITIVELY

Dorothy Green, Yonkers, N.Y.

A BRIDGE J-UUUUS-T RIGHT, by Cornelius Ryan

Nan Fornal, Dennis Port, Mass.

THE RETURN OF THE SCREW

Henry Morgan, Truro, Mass.
Ellen Burr, New Paltz, N.Y.

Lisa Alther's NEXT OF KINFLICKS

Gene Goott, Silver Spring, Md.

IN THE REALM OF THE SENSES GOES TO MONTE CARLO

Belenis Schnappapopolis, Southfield, Mich.

August Strindberg's MISS TRICIA

Lewis Ware, Montgomery, Ala.

Frank Sinatra sings HAVE IT YOUR WAY

Linda Rizzo, N.Y.C.

T. S. Eliot's PLOP, PLOP, FIZZ, FIZZ, OH WHAT A RELIEF IT IS

Raymond S. Kauders, Pittsburgh, Pa.

SEQUUS

M. Barden Prisant, Roslyn, N.Y.;
D. R. May, Syracuse, N.Y.

MORE KING OF KINGS

Byron Fink, Philadelphia, Pa.

LOVE, YOUR MAGIC SPELL IS EVERYWHERE, PARTOUT

similarly: Grace Katz, Rutland, Vt.;
Bob Kocheck, Perth Amboy, N.J.

LIFE AFTER DEATH IN VENICE

Ethel McConaghy, Boston, Mass.

Saul Bellow's HUMBOLDT'S THANK-YOU CARD

Greg Collins, Bellerose, N.Y.

RIVER OF NO RETURN REVISITED

Helen Zimmerman, Freehold, N.J.

FAT WILLIE WONKA AND THE CHOCOLATE FACTORY

Anita Greenberg, Flushing, N.Y.

THUNDERHEAD, SON OF EQUUS

Beverly Nancy Salter, Southfield, Mich.

THE BAD NEWS BEARS IN HIBERNATION

Jean T. Cook, Bethesda, Md.;
Ann Smith, N.Y.C.

BERNADETTE SINGS AGAIN

Charlotte F. Curtis, N.Y.C.

THE SUN ALSO RISES, AGAIN

Walter Hathaway, Columbia, S.C.

THE BRIDE OF FRANKENSTEIN'S PERIOD IS LATE

Judith Klein, East Brunswick, N.J.

WINNIE THE POOH TOOH

Carolyn Hymson, Cincinnati, Ohio

Woody Allen in THE FRONT'S BACK

Ellen Proscia, Orangeberg, N.Y.

Engelbert Humperdinck's RE-RELEASE ME

H. H. Hammer, N.Y.C.

SUPERSTAR SPANGLED BANNER

Dr. Myron Leiman, Mineola, N.Y.

MARY FOLEY, MARY FOLEY

Ilene McGrath, Leonia, N.J.

Jean-Paul Sartre's RETURN TO NO EXIT

Steven G. Kellman, San Antonio, Tex.

PORCA, THE KILLER PIG

David Richards, Allentown, Pa.;
Daniel Cohen, N.Y.C.

LORCA, THE KILLER POET

Jan Leighton, N.Y.C.

LES MOPEDS DE BELSIZES

Julian Bradford II, East Providence, R.I.

ABA DABA ALIMONY

Carleton Carpenter, Warwick, N.Y.

I HEARD THE OWL CALL MY NAME—I MUST HAVE BEEN MISTAKEN

Miles Klein, East Brunswick, N.J.

THE KING AND II

Diana Harding, Yonkers, N.Y.

ANOTHER BOOK, by Desi Arnaz

Frank Di Palma, N.Y.C.

THE EFFECT OF DELTA RAYS . . .

A. Kaufman, Scarsdale, N.Y.

THE OTHER SIDE OF MIDNIGHT

Michael Seymour, N.Y.C.

HARRY AND WALTER LEAVE NEW YORK

Mrs. Anna Lambiase, Brooklyn

Dee Brown's NOW BURY THE REST OF ME

Caryl Lee Rubin, N.Y.C.

THE WIZARD OF OZ AND HARRIET

Linda Neukrug, Brooklyn

DON JUAN, TWO

Ruth Surrey, Kew Gardens, N.Y.

WHY NOT THE BEST—COMPLETE WITH ANSWER BOOK

Judith A. David, Cambridge, Mass.

Dostoevski's THE REPOSSESSED

Dora Ullian, Newton, Mass.

HOW THE WEST WAS WON, TWO

Edward Ferron, N.Y.C.

SON OF NAUGHTY MARIETTA

Michael Deskey, Wauwatosa, Wis.
A. C. Beattie, Washington, D.C.

I LOVE YOU, SON OF JUNIE MOON

Heidi Jackson, Amherst, Mass.

A 35-MM SLIDE OF THE ARTIST AS A YOUNG MAN

Paul Walker, Cambridge, Mass.

THE INTERNAL REVENUE CODA

Robert S. Holzman, Danbury, Conn.

ONE MORE TIME AND AGAIN

Lydia Wilen, N.Y.C.

THE TAKING OF THE 14TH STREET LOCAL (ALL TIMES)

Jeff Monasch, Brooklyn

Tom Laughlin is WILLIAM JOHN

Eugene Brunner, Buckeye Lake, Ohio

ALL THE PRESIDENT'S MEN ON PAROLE

Gene Brown, Hollywood, Calif.

SON OF THE SUN ALSO RISES

Tadas Osmolskis, Richmond Hill, N.Y.

KING KONG

R. Sander, N.Y.C.

CARRIE GOES HAWAIIAN

Madelyn Kaplan,
Croton-on-Hudson, N.Y.

Holden and Dunaway in RERUN

David Yarnell, Los Angeles, Calif.

LIFE AFTER LIFE AFTER LIFE

D. Schoenberg, New Brunswick, N.J.

CAT ON A SOLAR PANELED ROOF

Allan B. Smith, N.Y.C.

APOCALYPSE NOW, PART II: THE CLEAN-UP

Janet Herbert, N.Y.C.

I WAS—I'M DEAD, by Neil Diamond

Ann Wilson, Chapel Hill, S.C.

1984 REVISITED

Holly Sean Kennedy, Yardley, Pa.

SUPERDUPERCALIFRAGILISTICEXPIALIDOCIOUS

Mimi Cohen, Orange, N.J.

ABSOLUTELY YOUR LAST CHANCE DIET

Alice Poch, East Brunswick, N.J.

Broadway's rock musical, THE NATURAL LOOK

Bruce Karp, N.Y.C.

WHY WE WERE THE WAY WE WERE

Eileen Barken, Brooklyn

THE RUSSIANS HAVE ARRIVED, THE RUSSIANS HAVE ARRIVED

Alan Levine, Copiague, N.Y.

John Updike's RABBIT RERUN

Mark Sardella, Wakefield, Mass.

Billy Wilder's ONE, TWO, THREE, TWO

Dan Cane, Greenbrae, Calif.

SAME TIME, NEXT YEAR AT MARIENBAD

E. Rubinstein, N.Y.C.

THE CHARGE OF THE LIGHT BRIGADE RIDES AGAIN

Jan Marie Sarro, Hewlett, N.Y.

YOUR ARMS LONG ENOUGH TO BOX WITH GOD

Joan Honymar, N.Y.C.

43 • Sequels

JONATHAN LIVINGSTON SEQUEL

Paul Ambos, Linden, N.J.

JUDE THE INVISIBLE

Robert M. Hunt, Cambridge, Mass.

One-Letter Omissions

STAND UP AND CHER—New Television Comedy Hour
SONY AND CHER—Expensive Japanese/French TV Set
JOHN CANCELLOR—Eminent Television Journalist Who May —Or May Not—Do the Evening News.

Above, Omissions Impossible. Competitors were asked to define a name or catch phrase altered by a one-letter omission.

Report: Here Come the Jude. Most of the repeats may be appreciated without accompanying definitions: BAREFOOT IN THE ARK. MOO FOR THE MISBEGOTTEN. LICE IN WONDERLAND. THREE CONS IN THE FOUNTAIN. OEDIPUS RX. THE OYS OF YIDDISH. MUCH AD ABOUT NOTHING. THEY SHOOT HORSE, DON'T THEY? ZERO MOTEL. SAMMY DAIS. JOYCE BOTHERS. MICKEY MUSE. ZORBA THE GEEK. And NORMAN MALER. Obviously you can't please everbody. As Judge Cater said.

VENI VIDI VII—Father of Veni VIII

John Hofer, Southborough, Mass.

THE KING AND —Royal Family's Reference to Wallis Simpson, 1936

Karl Levett, N.Y.C.

JOSEF VON STERNBEG—Adamant Panhandler

Robert Struzik, Amherst, N.Y.

TEAK & BREW—New Restaurant Chain Serving All the Wood You Can Eat

Gerald J. Levy, N.Y.C.

WALT OF THE TOREADORS—Star of the Mexico City Basketball Team

J. Bickart, N.Y.C.

SAMMY DAVS JR.—Handcapped Entertainer

Jack Rose, N.Y.C.

THE LADY IS A TRAM—A Streetcar Named Desire

Roy Rubin, Margate, Fla.

DAID HARUM—Late Dixie Concubines

David G. McAneny, Rumson, N.J.

BEER BARREL POLK—Unflattering Presidential Biography

Toni Marco, Bklyn.

OMEN'S WEAR DAILY—Astrological Guide for the Sartorially Superstitious

Fred Berg, Boston, Mass.

GEORGE M. CHAN—Immortal Star of the Chinese Musical Theater

Margot Howard, N.Y.C.

THE LONE RAGER—The Last Angry Man

P. Quinn, Boston, Mass.

MATTHEW, MARK, UKE, AND JOHN—Bible Belt Folk Singers

Mrs. Robert Polunsky, San Angelo, Texas

MORNING BECOMES ELECTRA—Daytime TV Serial Sponsored by Con Ed

Andrew E. Beresky, N.Y.C.

UP THE DON STAIRCASE—Novel About a Young Oxford Professor

Jeff Pope, Hopkins, Minn.

FIBBER MCGEE AND MOLL—Nostalgia Crime Show

Arnold Bennett Glenn, Eastchester, N.Y.

HENRI SOUL—Creator of *Les Chitterlings en Gelée*
Mark & Myra Perel, Baltimore, Md.

GAIL HEEHY—Hilarious Writer
Jessica Z. Nichols, Burnsville, N.C.

SOCKS AND BONDS—Putting Your Money Where Your Foot Is
Virginia Herzfeld, Linden, N.J.

QUEEN ANNE'S ACE—Hole Card in a Royal Flush
Gilbert M. Krebs, Rocky River, Ohio

GRAD SLAM—52 Interviews and No Job Offers
Alan Wall, Dellwood, Mo.

STAR TEK—Interplanetary Toothbrush
Michael Schreiber, Bklyn.

THE VOLGA BATMAN—Russian Comic Strip
Joan Lester, N.Y.C.

ABBA BAN—Father of Israeli Antiperspirant Industry
J. Berkowitz, De Kalb, Ill.

TUPPERWAR—Gunpowder Preparation Sold Only at Home Parties
B. Culligan, Westfield, N.J.

THE PRICE OF WALES—Has Gone Up Since Charlie Took Over
Marguerite Marra, Bklyn.

MOO GOO GAI PA—And Ma's a Real Sweetheart, Too
Pat Carroll, Asbury Pk., N.J.

THE ENGLISH CHANEL—Mary Quant
Jay McDonnell, N.Y.C.

THE BOYS OF SUMER—Championship Ball Club of Mesopotamia
Stephen B. Yohalem, M.D., N.Y.C.

THE FALL OF THE HOSE OF USHER—Sequel to *Getting Gertie's Garter*
Phyllis Taub, Bklyn.

GREGORIAN CHAT—Mutter in the Cathedral

Burton Seife, M.D., Bronx

GARB—Swedish Dressmaker with Passion for Privacy

E. Rubinstein, N.Y.C.

BABE RUT—Consequence of Zero Population Growth

Bruce Karp, Flushing, N.Y.

THE WIZARD OF Z—Amateur Magician Who Hung Around Set of Costa-Gavras Movie

David Axlerod, N.Y.C.

THE ACADEMY WARDS—Neuropsychiatric Wing, Cedars of Lebanon Hospital

Jerome Coopersmith, Rockville, Ctr., N.Y.

HENRY IV, PAT I—White House Tennis Score

Joel F. Crystal, Bklyn.

THE GREAT WHITE HOP—Harvey

Dorrie Ameen, Lisa Golbitz, N.Y.C.

SY AND THE FAMILY STONE—Hebrew Monument Sales

Edward Silver, Bronx

"FRANKLY, MY EAR, I DON'T GIVE A DAMN"—Last words of Rhett Van Gogh

John J. Coniglio, Bklyn.

THE HINDENBUG—Blimp by Volkswagen

Todd D. Ellner, Richland, Wash.

THE WALTON—John-Boy Arrives Home to Discover That Entire Family Has Deserted Him

J. E. Scharper, Hartford, Conn.

POLLO SPACE PROGRAM—Spanish rocket project to land a chicken on the moon.

Mavis A. Kauders, N.Y.C.

JOSEPH CHILDKRAUT—German kiddie actor of stage and screen.
Judith M. Kass, N.Y.C.

GIDE MICHELIN—Book listing French philosophers worth a detour.
The Welcomers, Lake Ronkonkoma, N.Y.

MACH HARE—Extraordinarily fast rabbit, defeated in fabled race by the Mach Turtle.
Bill Detty, Austin, Texas

OLDMAN SACHS—Door-to-door stock peddler.
Robbie Kempner, Hastings-on-Hudson, N.Y.

GEORGE GIZZARD—Actor noted for appearances in many turkeys.
Don Gibbs, Omaha, Neb.

EASTER AIRLINES—The Wings of Rabbit.
Judy Robins, Folcroft, Pa.

SEN SWENSEN—Swedish breath freshener.
Roger Grodsky, Madison, Wis.

SIR CHARLES CAPLIN—Furrier to Queen Elizabeth.
Mrs. Jack Kramer, Holliswood, N.Y.

G. B. SAW—1. Well-known literary hack, author from whose work *My Fair Lad* was adapted. 2. Historical retrospective of England.
Alfred Shoenberg, N.Y.C.

CARMELITA POE—Author of *The Pot and the Pendulum.*
John Coniglio, Bklyn.

POT LAUREATE—Honor bestowed upon Whitman for *Leaves of Grass.*
Rich Silvestri, Valley Stream, N.Y.

REX TOUT—Highly praised author of *The O.T.B. Mystery.*
Bobbi Martin, Portland, Ore.

JOHANN SEBASTIAN BAH—Contentious critic (Baroque) and composer of the B-Minor Mess.

T. D. C. Kuch, Vienna, Va.;
B. A. Huff, N.Y.C.;
Dorothy Stein, Miami, Fla.;
Jerry Dantzic, N.Y.C.

NAIVE SON—Jocasta's second husband.

Jane Dickerman, N.Y.C.

KINGMAN REWSTER—President of Barnyard College.

Edward Nickelson, N.Y.C.

WARREN BATTY—Sequel to *Watership Down* about deranged rabbits.

Jack Rose, N.Y.C.

WARREN BETTY—Featured dessert at the Playboy Club.

D. D. Heines, Albany, N.Y.

SALVADOR ALI—Leader of the surrealist school of prizefighting.

Bradford Willett, Stevens Pt., Wis.;
Carol O'Dell, Estes Park, Colo.

ARK VICTORY—Creatures, 2—God, 0.

Linda Quirini, Greenville, R.I.

DOROTHY PARER—Well-known wit who could cut anyone down to size.

James M. Green, M.D., Livingston, N.J.

AL A MATER—College cafeteria cooking just like mother used to make.

Adriane Greene, Sayville, N.Y.

POPEY—Catholic sailor man with large forearms.

Lelia Vincent, Providence, R.I.

"POP" PAUL—Much-beloved proprietor of malt shoppe in Vatican City.

Joshua Daniels, Hewlett, N.Y.

POPE PAL VI—The archbuddy of Rome and a real swell guy.

David Friedman, Chicago, Ill.
Mel Taub, N.Y.C.

NIKOLAI GOGO—Transvestite dancer in a Moscow discotheque.

Albert G. Miller, N.Y.C.

VALERY GISCARD D'ESTAIN—The most exclusive dry cleaner in Paris.

Ron Harvie, Montreal, Canada

CLARENCE ARROW—Marlon Brando's lawyer.

David Falk, N.Y.C.

"H - A - Single R - I - G - A - N spells HARIGAN"—One of George M. Cohan's least popular songs.

Solomon Bernard, Hillsdale, N.J.

YOU LOOK LIKE $,000,000—An unspeakable insult, usually a miscalculation.

Jack Labow, N.Y.C.

ML BROOKS—The 2,013-Year-Old Man's tailor (since 1050).

Richard J. Hafey, Morningdale, Mass.

CLIV BARNES—154 of Rome's severest critics.

E. R. Wallerstein, Raytown, Mo.

TOM IX—Early Pope of the Western World.

Walter L. Olesen, Westport, Conn.

LIV LLMAN—The jersey number and nickname of the man who fumbled half his receptions for the Tiber Tigers.

Jack Ryan, N.Y.C.

MAX FACTO—Ex-postman, brother of Ipso.

Miriam Blaufuss, Oakland, Calif.
Jill Sola-Rosenbaum, Chicago, Ill.

HUM CRONYN—Song stylist with a poor memory for lyrics.

Judith Maron, Englewood, N.J.

SUBWAY TOKE—What you smoke while waiting for the IND at 4 A.M.

M. Leslie Kayne, Baltimore, Md.

THE WIZARD OF O—Erotic adventures of a farm girl and her dog. (Olympia Press)

Madeline Falk, N.Y.C.

FRANK BUM—Beloved, besotted author of children's classic.

Milton Kass, N.Y.C.

SAM SADE—Private detective with a taste for violence.

Richard A. Rosen, M.D., Mt. Vernon, N.Y.

CHATEAUNEUF-DU-PAP—Vintage baby food.

Paul Grosvenor, Seattle, Wash.

POP GOES THE EASEL—Remaindered biography of Andy Warhol.

J. Bickart, N.Y.C.

GODFATHER, PAR II—Golf course where they really know the meaning of sudden-death playoffs.

Bernard Lovett, Hillside, N.J.

ERLE STANLEY GARNER—Pianist best known for "Play Mystery for Me."

Michael Alan Kay, Norfolk, Va.

Musicals from Classics

FETCH! (A Musical Nursery Rhyme)

A Drop in the Bucket (Entire Company)
Love Is All Uphill (Jack, Jill)
Falling for You (Jack)
You Look Like a King (Jill, Nurses, Doctors)
Falling for You (Reprise—Jill)
Blue Cross Blues (Ensemble)

Above, items brought forward from an unsuccessful backers' audition. Competitors were asked to invent titles for five songs suggesting the dubious quality of a musical based on a well-known work.

Report: Reading (or auditioning) these results was a little like reading (or auditioning) *Classic Comics.* Except I don't think *Classic Comics* closed out of town. A sweet disorder of repetition from Godiva to *The Godfather,* from Goethe to GWTW, from Darwin to David Reuben, M.D. Head-spinning musical numbers for *The Exorcist.* And God alone knows what inspired the musical *Oedipus:* "Outa Sight." Similarly represented: Tennessee Williams, the Bible, Chekhov, Mr. Nixon's *Six Crises,* Portnoy and Hamlet. The latter is still on the charts with such pop faves as "Prune Danish" and "Don't Stab Me in the Arras." Despite these toe-tappers, we ankled at intermission.

THE BROTHERS KARAMAZOV COME TO HARLEM

At the Candy Store—Where I Fell in Love With Feodor Pavlovich Karamazov, Leader of the Pack (Grushenka)
They Call Me Mister Alexei Fyodorovich Karamazov, the Mystic of Seventh Avenue (Alyosha)
Keep on Truckin', Ivan Fyodorovich Karamazov, Tortured Intellectual of the Ghetto (Vanya)
Knock Three Times, Katerina Ivanovna, and I, Dmitri Fyodorovich Karamazov, Will Meet You in the Hallway (Mitya)
Bad, Bad Smedyakov Brown, the Baddest Man in the Whole Damn Town (Chorus)

Jack Ryan, N.Y.C.

THE BOYS FROM ATHENS (Plato's Dialogues)

If You Were the Only Boy in the World and I Were the Only Man, Does Not the Public Good Require That We Get to Know Each Other Better? (Plato)
Is an Apple for the Teacher Proper Whose Pupil Is the Apple of His Eye? (Plato and Socrates)
We Have Often Talked on These Streets Before for Where Else but Athens Is There? (Entire Company)
Our Eyes Have Seen the Glory and Is That Not of Greece? (Socrates, Glaucon, Polemarchos, Thrasymachos, Adeimantos, and Cephalos)
I Drink to Thee Only With Mine Hemlock for Would Not to Flee the State Be Wrong? (Socrates)

Michael Schreiber, Bklyn.

BLUBBER (A musical tragedy)

*But Please Don't Call Me Izzy (Ishmael)
I'm Ahab the Whaler Man (Ahab)
I'm Gonna Squash That Man Right Down With My Tail (Whale)
Harp, Harp, Harp, the Boys Are Pooning (Crew)
*Drop Me a Line, I'm at the End of My Rope (Ahab)

Martin H. Belsky, Philadelphia, Pa.
**George Fairbanks, Nutley, N.J.*

LEAVE IT TO JOAN (A reverential musical)

Dom-Re-My (Joan and Children)
*There Are Voices In the Bottom of My Bouillabaisse (Joan)

*The Day of the Dauphin (Joan)
I Am Dauphin, You Are Maid (Joan and Claude Dauphin)
Is It Warm in Here or Is It Me? (Joan)

John S. Spano, N.Y.C.
**Chas. Kilcrease, N.Y.C.*

THE PRIDE AND THE PASSION (Browning)

I Wish My Paint Could Capture Her Joy and Rapture (Fra Pandolf)
My Heart Is Glad and Easily Impressed (Last Duchess)
Here Are Some Cherries for You (Officious Fool)
A Nine-Hundred-Years-Old Name Does Not Stoop (Duke)
The Count's Fair Daughter's Self (Duke)

T. E. Louis, Dobbs Ferry, N.Y.

FORUM FOLLIES

Spring Will Be a Little Strange This Year (Soothsayer)
With Friends Like This (Caesar)
Red-orange Julius (Senators)
Mire on the Pyre (Marc Antony)
All's Not Well That Starts Not Swell (Romans, Friends)

Allen Balla, New Hyde Park, N.Y.

WAITING FOR THE MAN

Nothing Happens, Nobody Comes, Nobody Goes, It's Awful (Estragon & Vladimir)
Nothing Happens (Pozzo & Lucky)
Nobody Comes (Estragon)
Nobody Goes (Vladimir)
It's Awful (Estragon & Vladimir)

Larry Woods, Middletown, Conn.

TWO HEADS ARE BETTER THAN ONE

I Have Mixed Emotions (Dr. Jekyll)
Who Was That Fellow I Saw You As Last Night? (Chorus)
I Had to Give Up House Calls (Dr. Jekyll)

Teresa Gerbers, Glenmont, N.Y.

ADAPT! ADAPT! *(Origin of Species)*

When We Were a Couple of Squids
If Ever I Survive You (It's Because I'm Fittest)
I've Got a Feelin' I'm Amphibian
Stand on Your Own Two Feet

John H. Dorenkamp, Worcester, Mass.

MIRACLE!

__________(Helen Keller)
__________(Helen Keller)
__________(Helen Keller)
______(Reprise: Helen Keller)
What? (Annie Sullivan)

Janis March, N.Y.C.

CATCH A FALLING TSAR

Walking Shoulder-to-Shoulder With My Dollink by the Volga (Nicholas and Alexandra)
Refutin' My Rasputin (Alexandra)
Ivan Was Terrible, Peter Was Great, But What Will They Think of Me? (Nicholas)
Finale: We're Knocking Off the Family Romanoff (Bolshevik Firing Squad); Not Quite (Anastasia)

John J. Coniglio, Bklyn.

MEET MILLIE! (From *Of Human Bondage*)

You Make Me Sick (Mildred and the Barmaids)
Lucky in Lab, Lost Out on Love (Philip)
Meet Millie! (Admitting Desk Personnel, Doctors)

Robert McHaffey, N.Y.C.

LEMUEL!

We're Just Small Town Girls (Empress & Ladies)
Be a Good Egg (The Lilliputians)
B-r-o-b-d-i-n-g-n-a-g Spells Brobdingnag (His Majesty's Scholars)
Yahoo! (The Yahoos)
Always Say Neigh (Gulliver, Houyhnhnms)

Bruce Clements, Willamantic, Conn.

SHIPWRECKED!

All Alone (R. Crusoe)
Big Foot (R. Crusoe)
T.G.I.F. (Crusoe, Goats, Birds, Mollusks)
*Thank God It's Crusoe (Friday)
*Tyb Umgah Kertyl? Do You Speak Kertyl? (Friday)
*All Alone (Reprise: R. Crusoe)

C. S. (Larry) Hanson, N.Y.C.
**Grace Katz, Rutland, Vt.;*

ALICIA GOES TO RIO (Hitchcock's *Notorious*)

Counterespionage Conga (Alicia, Devlin, Entire Company)
Sebastian's No Saint (Alicia)
You're the "U" in My Uranium (Devlin)
Next Time, Sanka (Alicia, Sebastian)
The Rescue Rhumba (Devlin, Alicia, Sebastian, Entire Company)

Eugene A. Padow, Pineville, Pa.

PREPPIE! *(Love Story)*

What Can I Say After I've Said She's Dead? (Oliver Barrett IV)
You Came Forth, Oliver Barrett (Jenny)

E. Showalter, Princeton, N.J.

FOG! (After Carl Sandburg)

Here I Come (Fog)
There's something on My Feet (Little Cat)
Sit a While and Look Me Over (Harbor, City)
We'll Never Say a Word (Haunches)
Time to Be Movin' On (Entire Company)

Skip Livingston, Baltimore, Md.

UNCLEAN *(A Journal of the Plague Year)*

Don't Come Too Close, You Don't Look At All Well (The Young Lovers)
Everybody's Leaving Town (Entire Company)
Ding-Dong, the Church Bells Bong (The Street Urchins)
1665 Was a Very Bad Year (Survivors)

Dori Anderson, La Jolla, Calif.

ME AND DOC

You Made Me What I Am (Frankenstein's Monster)
He's Not Frankenstein, I Am (Dr. Frankenstein)
I'm Not Frankenstein, He Is (Monster)
Just the Three of Us (Mrs. Frankenstein)
*Hey, There! Got a Light? (Townspeople)

Elsie Angell, Greenville, R.I.
**James Weaver, Pittsburgh, Pa.*

SHOW WHITE

The Reflection of Your Grace (Mirror)
If It's Thursday, You Must Be Grumpy (Show White)
God Didn't Make Poison Red Apples (Show White)
If It's Friday, You Must Be Sleepy (Reprise: Dwarfs)
A Nice Girl Like You in a Palace Like This (Company)

Edd. Morrison, Bklyn.

BLOOD! (A Bram new musical)

The One Bier to Have (Count Dracula)
Can This Be the Vampire State Building? (Harker)
In a Serious Vein (Count and Renfield)
I Staked a Claim on Her Heart . . . and I Claimed a Stake in His (Count and Van Helsing)
*We Always Get Stuck With the Drinks (The Entire Company)

Norton Bramesco, N.Y.C.
**Louis B. Raffel, Phoenix, Ariz.*
sp. ment.: V. J. Conroy, Astoria, N.Y.

HEIR (A musical tragedy)

Six Little Words, But What a Big Question (Hamlet)
*Big R, Little O, Double T-E-N (Marcellus, Guards)
**I Saw Mommy Kissing Claudius (Hamlet)
Don't Call Me Auntie, Call Me Mother (Gertrude)
Duet: It's Curtains for Me (Polonius); In One Ear and Out the Other (Claudius)

Alice M. Yohalem, N.Y.C.
**John Wrubel, Providence, R.I.*
***Leslie Wheeler, Lakewood, N.J.*

HAPPY RETURNS! (A musical form 1040)

*Income Other Than Wages, Dividends and Interest (CREEP Staff)
Withholding You (Mr. and Ms.)
You Depend on Me (Baby Jane)
We've Grown Accustomed to Your Case (I.R.S. Agents)
Everything We Are We Owe to You (Mr., Ms., and Baby Jane)

Fred Berg, Boston, Mass.
**Nancy M. Sobolevitch, Phila., Pa.*

VIVE LE CORE! (A musical "Genesis")

Anyone for Volleyball? (Adam, Eve, Hairless Animals)
This Is a No-No Tree (God)
Duet: A Little Nosh Can't Hurt (Eve); Fig Leaves for Two (Adam)
*He's Not Heavy (Cain)
They Went Thataway (Snake)

Albert G. Miller, N.Y.C.
**Thomas E. Bundrick, So. Salem, N.Y.*

Critique of Poor Reason

". . . interesting study of a young prince. Yet if Hamlet looked with such disfavor upon the alliance of his mother and uncle, it would seem a poor idea indeed to put on a little play to entertain them . . ."

"In this slim volume, Alex Haley has taught us much about the principles of gardening . . . "

Above, notices to overlook. Competitors were asked for an extract from a review of any literary or dramatic work based on ignorance, naïveté, or misunderstanding.

Report: Our reviewers complained of: the Bible (too wordy), Camille's cough, *Sleuth*'s lack of range, fairy tales (too Grimm), *Ulysses* and/or the White House transcripts (unintelligible). Occasionally, titles of deliberate ambiguity were selected. This is not so much humor as pointing at the duck. But, soft. On to the repeats: Liv Ullman on diapers. Stendhal on accounting. Roget and his tame pet thesaurus. Leon Uris on his alma mater, Trinity. *The Hite Report* on basketball. *Lists,* a biography of the composer and his family. *Soul on Ice* about a black hockey team. And William Peter Blatty on physical fitness. Not a moment too soon.

. . . and even the coarsest inquisitive appetite can readily appreciate that this latest and, certainly, most aesthetically repugnant addition to the current "how to" genre of sadistic literature moves most palatably from title to trashbasket. I can only assume that its musically sobriqueted author, one "Harper" Lee, a man of . . .

John Hofer, Southborough, Mass.

. . . [Mr. Bernstein's] somewhat distorted view of the Mass [is] by a non-Catholic. Seeing it does not fulfill your Sunday obligation . . .

Elsie Angell, Greenville, R.I.

. . . play purports to show the difficulty of maintaining a friendship with a six-foot rabbit. Poor stage lighting makes it difficult to see the rabbit. . . .

Linda Quirini, Providence, R.I.
John Michalski, N.Y.C.

. . . given that people of their social standing could be presumed to be well acquainted with and well able to afford the benefits of cosmetic surgery, why, then, did the Bergeracs allow their son . . ."

M. B. Sherman, Bronx

. . . someone was obviously trying to lure audiences with a catchy, family-oriented title [*The Seventh Seal*]. I have admired Miss Bergman's beauty and talent, but perhaps she should stick to acting. . . .

Michael Laser, Glen Oaks, N.Y.

. . . in view of the importance of Wilder's debut as a Broadway playwright, it is this reviewer's opinion that the producers could have budgeted at least a few dollars for scenery . . .

Anne M. Milton, San Francisco, Calif.

. . . at the risk of giving away the ending, let me add that the Godot of the title never bothers to show up. He probably saw a preview. Take my advice and follow his example . . .

Thomas K. O'Connell, Ridgewood, N.Y.

. . . depressed and worried about the future? You shouldn't be, if we can judge by Mr. Huxley's new book . . .

Mark Greenberg, Bronx

. . . I think [Crowley] should consider writing in a romantic female lead . . .

Deborah Sneol, Phoenix, Ariz.

. . . perhaps if Albee had allowed their absent son to appear in the last scene, it would have clarified . . .

Marianne Lester, Washington, D.C.

". . . and while the author may have been attempting a spare, Hemingway-like style, the result is mechanical rather than taut. The main characters, Dick and Jane, fail to move the reader. Only Spot, their quadruped companion, can briefly stir our interest. Indeed, one is intrigued by the questions of why Spot is running, and from what . . ."

Richard A. Rosen, M.D., Mt. Vernon, N.Y.

. . . what Mallomars are to me, *madeleines* are to this Frenchman who can't forget the cookie of his childhood. Nor, for that matter, has he been able to forget anything else in this exercise in total recall. If anything was lost in translation, I'd be very much surprised . . .

David E. Diener, Irvington, N.Y.

. . . the playwright seems to have ignored one important fact: Oedipus could *not* have married Jocasta because she is his mother. Perhaps Sophocles, having written himself into a corner, despaired of rewriting his play and left it as it was, in the hope that audiences would fail to catch this detail . . .

Anita & Steve Winkler, Binghamton, N.Y.

. . . [*Tiny Alice*'s] Julian wants to see a model home, yet turns curiously indecisive when his wish is granted . . .

Anthony Gray, Closter, N.J.

. . . how come Marlon Brando never took off *his* underwear?

Michael Panser, N. Brunswick, N.J.

. . . Mr. Hemingway's protagonist, whose ignorance on these matters is appalling, knows little—or has chosen to ignore entirely—the use of proper sporting tackle and line in modern game fishing . . .

Arnold Rosenfeld, Dayton, Ohio

. . . Robert Anderson . . . tells the tale of the love-starved wife of a schoolmaster . . . I bet she delivers that line to all the boys . . .

Andrew Mezzetti, Flushing Meadows, N.Y.

. . . what was Joseph K's crime? who was behind the effort to harass him through the "legal process"? These are some of the questions that are raised and never resolved in this ambitious but confused first . . ."

Martin Schlesinger, Bklyn.

. . . but we might caution the actress playing Mrs. Malaprop to consult more carefully her script . . .

George Shackelford, Hanover, N.H.

. . . *That's Entertainment* indeed . . . apparently the work of several directors, some of whom chose to shoot in black and white while others insisted on color . . .

Randy Brooks, Dallas, Texas

. . . *Six Crises* is a refreshingly frank book. The author is perhaps the first politician ever to disclose all the facts—even the embarrassing ones—of his political life . . .

Moshe Steinberg, Silver Spring, Md.

. . . Dostoevsky . . . breaks one of the most elementary rules of detective fiction: he lets us in on whodunit from the very beginning . . .

Anne Himmelfarb, White Plains, N.Y.

(Waltz of the Toreadors) . . . I'd give it a 75; it has a good beat, and the kids can dance to it . . .

Annlois Freedman, Brookline, Mass.

. . . Ulysses proved a good point: it doesn't matter how long it takes for a man to get home if he has a good story to tell after he gets . . .

Bertha Fraser, N.Y.C.

. . . the author has an interesting albeit pretentious premise—that of an omniscient being going on a creative spree. The archaic language lends an air of authenticity. The over-use of "begats" weakens credibility . . . we look forward to the author's next work . . .

Miles Klein, E. Brunswick, N.J.

. . . attempts to write the same story four ways with very little change in plot . . .

Amy Himes, Ridgefield, Conn.

. . . the highly improbable likelihood of such a disparate group of persons coincidentally coming together at the same time in one place; on a bridge which—fortuitously for the frail plot—collapses suddenly, bringing instant death to just these particular persons. . . .

Marion K. MacInnes, Memphis, Tenn.

. . . anyone in a more lucid state would no doubt have delighted in a Raven who could muster a vocabulary over and above "caw, caw." Had the "ungainly fowl" alit on an equally placid vase . . .

Mel Taub, N.Y.C.

. . . on the fingers of one hand *Oedipus the King, Hamlet, Faust.* Now there is *Dude* . . .

Laurence Laiken, Bayside, N.Y.

. . . *New York* is certainly a welcome addition to the local literary scene. The magazine's only weak point appears to be the "Competition," a reader participation game which the editors have wisely relegated to the magazine's last few pages . . .

Esther Preis, New London, Conn.

Hedda Gabler: "Show-biz veteran Buddy Ibsen's biting biography of the former high priestess of Hollywood gossip . . ."

Murry Harris, N.Y.C.

Cuisine Minceur: "In this guide to homosexual restaurants . . ."

David C. Pollack, San Diego, Calif.

Ms. Found in a Bottle: "In this gruesome tale, Poe describes the bizarre discovery of the pickled remains of a diminutive feminist . . ."

Guy Joseph Jacobson, Brooklyn

The Man in the Gray Flannel Suit: "Although this biography of Stan Musial, by Sloan Wilson, is well documented and informative, it cannot compare with Henry Morton Robinson's *The Cardinal,* which first appeared . . ."

Mark Wolfson, Spring Valley, N.Y.

"A. A. Milne's surprisingly scatological defamation of the usually revered prime minister . . ."

Joe Gluck, South Orange, N.J.;
Debra Larsen, Park Forest, Ill.

A Place to Come To: "Robert Penn Warren's exposé of the behind-the-scenes activities in the recovery room of a general hospital . . ."

M. C. Campbell, Lookout Mountain, Tenn.

The Hamlet, by William Faulkner: "Despite the title this is not *the* Hamlet. Mr. Shakespeare's version is more definitive."

William Brennan, East Greenwich, R.I.

Maxims: "M. La Rochefoucauld's history of the celebrated Parisian restaurant is destined to become a classic. . . ."

Mary Damsky, Brooklyn

The Screwtape Letters: "The collected correspondence of Rose Mary Woods has just crossed my desk . . ."

Paul E. Smith, Pittsburgh, Pa.

Thaïs: "For this historical work about the natives of French Indo-China, M. Anatole France might better have chosen a more recognizable title, such as 'Les Siamoix'. . . ."

Msgr. A. V. McLees, St. Albans, N.Y.

"Known worldwide as a playwright, Strindberg was known to almost no one as a collector of firearms. But Miss Tuchman, with her customarily painstaking scholarship . . ."

Alex Vaughn, Old Lyme, Conn.

I' MOK—You're OK: "This touching account of an Eskimo boy coming of age . . ."

Ellen Tanner, Cortland, N.Y.

The Bermuda Triangle: "When Bob and Barbara Bermuda first met Candy Miller, it was clear they would soon . . ."

Unsigned, Columbus, Ohio

"Poor Joe Miller may have written a book that is the laughingstock of the publishing world, but . . ."

Michael Schreiber, Brooklyn

Curtain: "With this warm and witty biography of the delicious star of *NBC Saturday Night,* Agatha Christie joins Jules Feiffer, author of last year's *Ackroyd,* on this publishing bandwagon. . . ."

James W. Penha, Jackson Heights, N.Y.

The New Columbia Encyclopedia: "That such a comprehensive compilation of knowledge could be successfully undertaken by one of the so-called underdeveloped countries is proof . . ."

John Falxa, N.Y.C.

Coma: "A clasic acount adresed to the acurate ussage of gramar."

Helen Levine, New Rochelle, N.Y.

Looking Out for #1: "Dry, practical advice for parents dealing with children's bed-wetting problems."

Sal Rosa, N.Y.C.

The Man Who Loved Cat Dancing: "A sensitive biography about the life of Gunther Gebel-Williams."

Melanie London, N.Y.C.

The Three Musketeers: "Does childhood money and fame lead to a life of unhappiness and despair? Read Alexandre Dumas's revealing story about the separate lives of Annette, Darlene, and Cubby . . ."

T. L. Bracken, Lyme, N.J.

Sondheim & Company: ". . . in this delightful little book he shares some of his secrets with the reader and offers some of the recipes that always leave guests smiling . . ."

Shirley Freiberg, Boston, Mass.

The Alexandria Quartet: "In a somewhat lengthy history of the barbershop group, Mr. Durrell . . ."

L. Zuckerman, Philadelphia, Pa.
Tim Houk, Carrboro, N.C.

"Ms. Stewart's charming book tells the delightful story of a small girl and her cat, Touch Not . . ."

Gregg Biggs, Moore, Okla.

Numbers: "In this, the fourth book of the Old Testament, God teaches his people how to count."

Shirley Boardman, Wayne, N.J.

The Best of Kipling: ". . . a must for anyone who has ever kippled . . ."

H. Ellner, Richland, Wash.

The Oxford Book of Literary Anecdotes: ". . . one is not sure just what poisons are counteracted, but . . ."

E. S. Franchuk, Quebec, Canada

"When's the best time to take *your* vacation? Middlemarch, says George Eliot . . ."

Michael Godwin, Austin, Tex.

Understanding Media: "Mr. McLuhan offers a somewhat convoluted analysis of the tragic Greek figure and her . . ."

Nina Hasin, Falls Church, Va.

The Story of Sigurd the Volsung and the Fall of the Nibelungs: "If you liked *Jabberwocky,* you'll love this one (or at least understand it)."

Stanley Stone, Oceanside, N.Y.

"Sammy Davis Jr. has captured the determination of industrial giant H. J. Heinz . . ."

Ms. D. Taub, Hazleton, Pa.

Atlas Shrugged: ". . . a must for indifferent travelers, this thick set of maps, specially designed by the senior partner of the Rand McNally team . . ."

Dolores J. Southard, Quincy, Mass.

Something's There: "Dan Greenburg's sequel to Joseph Heller's 1974 novel is . . ."

Pat Dutton, Rahway, N.J.

"Ornithologist-cosmetologist Jerzy Kosinski presents easy-to-follow steps towards sprucing up your canary. Detailed chapters on beak gloss and . . ."

John Ruppe, Ann Arbor, Mich.

"Maeterlinck traces causes and possible cures of depression plaguing the avian species. . . ."

Eve Thurston, N.Y.C.

Steppenwolf: "Slow-moving dog story by Hermann Hesse . . ."

Frank Visakay, Bloomfield, N.J.

On the Beach: "Frankie Avalon and Annette Funi . . ."

Rachel Friedenberg, Hunt. Wds., Mich.

To Have and to Hold: "Habeo and teneo, those pesky Latin verbs, are translated, conjugated, and explored . . ."

Edward R. Wallerstein, Raytown, Mo.

Bury My Heart at Wounded Knee: "Dee Brown, candidly sharing intimate details of her amorous but unhappy rendezvous with Joe Namath . . ."

Dr. Nicholas C. Romano, Westfield, N.J.

"We never find out in this book how Ulysses gets to Dublin from the Mediterranean. Not as inspiring as the author's *Trees.*"

Lelia Vincent, Johnston, R.I.

Baby and Child Care: "Writing under his favorite pseudonym, Mr. Nimoy has . . ."

Donald Saidel, Lafayette Hill, Pa.

The New York Times Book of House Plants: "A revealing newspaper saga of how secretaries, chauffeurs, aides, et al. are paid to spy . . ."

Warren Alexander, Brooklyn

Lays of Ancient Rome: "Sexual behavior described by the eminent Victorian, T. Babington Macaulay . . ."

Ruth von Phul, N.Y.C.
similarly: Marcel Henderson, Rye, N.Y.

Sometimes a Great Notion: "Being a well-chronicled telling of the life and career of the late F. W. Woolworth . . ."

Marsha Levine, N.Y.C.

Answer Game

Answer: Cold Duck
Question: What is the quickest cure for a person addicted to sparkling wines?

A. Abraham & Straus
Q. Who wrote the "Old Testament" Waltz?

Above, the Answer Game. Competitors were asked to supply an original answer/question.

Report: A. Read them and weep. **Q.** What does the competition editor do upon receiving more than 100 entries beginning "9 W" or "Washington, Irving"? For all I know, some of our honorable mentions may be, er, abrogated from Johnny (Carnac) Carson, to whom, along with Messrs. Allen and Arbogast, we are indebted for the concept of this contest. But the majority seemed original and fetchingly dopey. **A.** I'm sure I don't know, but while you're up, please get me some Poland Water. **Q.** What in hell is "fetchingly dopey" supposed to mean?

A. Lévi-Strauss.
Q. Who wrote the "Blue Denim" Waltz?

Herb Sargent, N.Y.C.

A. Airport '79.
Q. What wine is served on most domestic flights?

Anthony Ralph, Waterville, Maine

A. 4Q.
Q. Herr Wagner, do you spell your name with a "V"?
L. Tribe, Cambridge, Mass.

A. Mr. Green Jeans, Miss Piggy, and Suzy Chapstick.
Q. At the White House dinner for Vice-Premier Teng, who sat at Nixon's table?
Dr. & Mrs. John R. Driskill, Maryville, Tenn.

A. Woody Hayes.
Q. Who lost the 1978 Nobel Peace Prize?
Pete Carlson, Columbus, Ga.

A. Jack the Ripper, Vlad the Impaler, and Attila the Hun.
Q. Who have not yet been photographed with the First Lady?
Barbara Jerome, Oakdale, Pa.

A. No.
Q. "Mares eat oats and does eat oats and little lambs eat ivy. A kid'll eat ivy too; wouldn't you?"
Tim Hanley, N.Y.C.

A. Incisors, canines, bicuspids, and molars.
Q. What are four outstanding features of the Carter presidency?
Dr. Arthur S. Ash, Mt. Vernon, N.Y.

A. Movie Movie.
Q. Where do you want to go after din-din?
Barry Warner, Chicago, Ill.

A. Alexander Pope.
Q. What drink contains brandy, cream, and holy water?
Rob Cassie, Old Saybrook, Conn.

A. Bell & Howell.
Q. Describe Pavlov's experiments.
Gloria Hoffman, N.Y.C.

A. Pleh!
Q. What do you say when you dial 119?
David Toron, Woodmere, N.Y.

A. Gee, I could have had a V-8!
Q. What was Socrates' reaction to the hemlock?

Albert White, N.Y.C.

A. Plato's Republic.
Q. What is the most swinging form of government?

Anthony Gray, Closter, N.J.

A. Sansui.
Q. Who is the patron of pigs?

Trudy Littenberg, Snyder, N.Y.

A. The SALT talks.
Q. What happens when you dine with a ventriloquist?

Eleanor Paul, Brooklyn

A. Capsize.
Q. What's that funny little 7 1/8 label?

Alan Rubin, Delaplane, Va.

A. Polyester crêpe.
Q. What is the favorite gourmet dish on Seventh Avenue?

Betsey Potter, Los Angeles, Calif.

A. Times Square.
Q. What is the root of all evil?

E. Rose, Toronto, Ont.

A. R-O-L-A-I-D-S.
Q. How do you spell "Rolaids"?

Russ Rubin, Wayzata, Minn.

A. Plague, Famine, Pestilence, and Death.
Q. Name three deductible expenses and a capital loss.

Jim McDonough, Bronxville, N.Y.

A. Rula Lenska.
Q. What were the first words that my toaster oven spoke?

Robert M. Hunt, Cambridge, Mass.

A. Remember the Alamo.
Q. What were the last words of the customer who wanted ice cream on his pie?

Victor L. Cahn, Exeter, N.H.

A. ILGWU.
Q. Supply an acronym for "I love going without underwear."

Eve Thompson, Studio City, Calif.

A. Bernoulli's principle.
Q. Who monitors study hall at Bernoulli Junior High?

Sandi Saccocio, Waterford, Conn.

A. *Max Havelaar*—a large-scale, nobly intentioned Dutch film about the hypocrisies of colonialism in the East Indies in the 1850s.
Q. If you had to miss one film this year, which might it be?

Tony Lang, N.Y.C.

A. Twelve.
Q. What is meant by the expression "Six of one and half a dozen of the other"?

Ellis Schein, Reading, Pa.

A. A silver lining.
Q. What's on the inside of Sammy Davis's sport coat?

Candy Wolfson, Spring Valley, N.Y.

A. Bullpen.
Q. What's another name for a press agent's ballpoint?

Ted Berkelmann, Bronx

A. Shoo-fly pie and apple pan dowdy makes my eyes light up, my tummy say howdy; shoo-fly pie and apple pan dowdy—I never get enough of that wonderful stuff.
Q. *Et pour monsieur?*

Dan Greenburg, N.Y.C.

A. Glitter Rock.
Q. What's the capital of Glarkansas?

Michael J. Faems, Shaker Hts., Ohio

A. Two Gentlemen of Verona.
Q. What's the largest discount house in Italy?

Allan B. Smith, N.Y.C.

A. Mine Field.
Q. What's the name of the book written by a tyrannical German farmer?

Jonathan Abrams, Bklyn.

A. Mach Turtle.
Q. What's the best soup to serve in a fast-food restaurant?

John Hofer, Southborough, Mass.

A. Handkerchief pandkerchief.
Q. Why did Queen Victoria keep an apartment in town?

Maurice Klein Katz, N.Y.C.

A. To be or not to be.
Q. What is the question?

Eve Shafter, E. Brunswick, N.J.

A. Geritol.
Q. When you have your health, what have you got?

L. Garfunkel, N.Y.C.

A. Jejune.
Q. What is Porky Pig's favorite month?

Joel W. Darrow, White Plains, N.Y.

A. Rhythm and blues.
Q. What did the Pill replace?

Anna Brennan, E. Greenwich, R.I.

A. Scotch Tape.
Q. What did Mary, Queen of Scots refuse to turn over to Parliament?

Pericles Crystal, Bklyn.

A. I don't know, I couldn't see under their long coats.
Q. Were the male guests at the ball wearing tails?

Albert Miller, N.Y.C.

A. Beethoven's Ninth.
Q. Where is Ludwig in the batting order?

Lelia Vincent, Providence, R.I.

A. O.T.B.
Q. Name an Irish chest disease.

Bill Braydon, N.Y.C.

A. John-Boy.
Q. What was the Tydee-Bowl Man's childhood nickname?

Bunny Daniels, Hewlett, N.Y.

A. Morton and Delco.
Q. What is assault and battery?

Leonard Fass, Kew Gardens, N.Y.

A. Roast beef.
Q. What's Dean Martin going to do when there aren't any people left to honor?

Alan Levine, Copiague, N.Y.

A. Pullet surprise.
Q. What is the National Chicken Award?

Robert Rossner, N.Y.C.

A. A boy named Sue.
Q. Does Alice Cooper have any children?

Elsie Watkins, Graford, Texas

A. Tinker, tailor, soldier, spy.
Q. What jobs are presently open to college graduates?

D. P. Hauptman, S.I., N.Y.

A. Parsley, Sage, Rosemary, and Thyme.
Q. What did Mrs. Clooney call her daughters?

Emily Karp, N.Y.C.

A. Gloria Steinem.
Q. What is Gloria doing with those shoelaces?

Dodi Schultz, N.Y.C.

A. Personperson.
Q. Who delivers letters to Gloria Steinem?

Robert Rubin, Pittsburgh, Pa.

A. Post mortems.
Q. What do you call a popular breakfast cereal supposedly tainted with botulism?

Fred Fuller, Flushing, N.Y.

A. Jacks or better.
Q. What does it take to open a New York City bus window?

Michael Deskey, N.Y.C.

A. Groucho, Harpo, Chico, Zeppo.
Q. Name three Marx brothers and a cigarette lighter.

Gerald J. Levy, N.Y.C.

A. Venetian blinds.
Q. Where are you likely to find Venetian duck hunters?

Larry Laiken, Bayside, N.Y.

A. Ambience.
Q. What do you call that car with the siren?

Nita Schroeder, Bedford Vill., N.Y.

A. The garden of the Finzi-Continis.
Q. Where is Rover Finzi-Contini?

Aaron Stein, N.Y.C.

Fractured Names

Musical Star and Daredevil Aerialist—NONETTE FABRAY
Composer/Raconteur, regular at Budapest Tavern—BELA BARTALK
Child Star/Evangelist—SHIRLEY TEMPLE McPHERSON
Eccentric billionaire and private detective—JOHN BERESFORD TIPTOE
Self-absorbed Prussian porn king—OTTO EROTIC

Above, contrived nomenclature. Competitors were asked to devise one fanciful name-cum-occupation.

Report: These results are gleaned from five separate competitions, so the repeats are mostly *déjà* views. As, for example, ALFRED LORD TENNISANYONE. Or GLORIA SWANSONG. The latter was lovely in a heavenly blue caftan. She wore green the last time.

"GAUDY" AMOS IGITUR—Class show-off.

Mimi Cozzens, Hollywood, Calif.

J. PINPOINT MORGAN—Millionaire bombardier.

Thomas E. Gitto, Staten Island, N.Y.

IRA MUMBA APRIL—Songwriting African tax consultant.

Mrs. Anna Lambiase, Brooklyn

BRONISLAW REX—Polish dinosaur, closely related to Tyrannosaurus Stash.

David Klein, East Brunswick, N.J.

HERALDO RIVIERA—Spanish-language newspaper of Cannes.

Doris Lynn, Sausalito, Calif.

SAVANNAH PUMA—Southern belle, known for catty remarks.

A. S. Hayman, N.Y.C.

RICARDO MONTALBAN—Secret hiding place of actor Richard Mandelbaum.

Judith Klein, East Brunswick, N.J.

"HELL" O' DOLLY—Full-o'-the-devil Irish moving man.

Jacqueline Fogel, Jamaica, N.Y.

OZZIE MANN DIAZ—Husband of Harriet and obscure author of *Death in Venezuela.*

Alice M. Yohalem, N.Y.C.

TARA RABUM, D.A.—Bombay plantation owner and prosecutor.

Ellen Strano, Manchester, Conn.

CURTIS LAMÉ—Monty Python's favorite general.

Anthony Gray, Closter, N.J.

SEMIMODO—The halfback of Notre Dame.

Darius Leybold, Newton Centre, Mass.

OUIDA PEEPHOLE—Gossip-monger and writer of preambles.

Albert G. Miller, N.Y.C.

O'ERLANDO FURIOSO—Madcap pony express rider on the Rome-Naples run.

Jack Ryan, N.Y.C.

POX NABISCO—Cookie exorcist.

Oliver M. Neshamkin, M.D., N.Y.C.

QZLGPUISNZI BRZEZINSKI—Owner of renowned restaurant It's Easy for Me to Say (*spécialité de la maison:* Qzlgpuisnzi's quenelles sautéed in Fazi Battaglia).

Joshua Sigal, Freeport, N.Y.

HUGE GINO KNEEL—Titan of American religious playwrights.

James Fechheimer, Glen Head, N.Y.

MAIDA BEST-MANWYN—Pioneering female boxing referee, born in Brooklyn of English parentage.

John Ashbery, N.Y.C.

A-FRAME SYMBOLIST, JR.—Late-nineteenth-century French architect noted for conservatism.

Sara K. Alterman, Denver, Colo.

FAN DE SIÈCLE—Turn-of-the-century groupie.

Arnold M. Berke, Springfield, Mass.

CARP A. DIEM—Industrious Vietnamese fishmonger.

Joseph Schaffner, Wellsville, N.Y.

CHOU EN WOODWARD—Washington *Post* reporter, currently Peking bureau chief.

Dave Badger, Nashville, Tenn.

JACQUES WELLKNOWN ASSES—Custom *corsetière.*

Paul Jung, Ann Arbor, Mich.

HAUS BAYOU—Dean, Southern School of Architecture.

Ralph Gerald, Cleveland, Ohio

"BOSS" SILICA—Revered godfather (alias, the Sandman).

Alissa Abrams, Brooklyn

HECTOR BARELY OATS—Composer of the pop classic "Barely oats and dozey oats . . ."

Lou Grillo, West Hartford, Conn.

CARMEN VERANDAH—House painter specializing in red porches.

Louis B. Raffel, Skokie, Ill.

CASH-US KLEE—Swiss pawnbroker/artist.

Joel F. Crystal, Scarsdale, N.Y.

MICKEY "AMINO" MIMI—Acid-tongued Irish soprano.

Rosemarie Williamson, Basking Ridge, N.J.

JOCK GOOSE TOE—Famed underwater scuba coach, suspended for odd behavior.

Carol Rosenfeld, Great Neck Plaza, N.Y.

D. S. EERIE—Originator of the Black Mass.

Lewy Olfson, South Lyme, Conn.

ETHYL REDD (THE UNREDDY)—Singer, non-Australian.

Hugh Strangeways, Corff Castle, England

IVAN TOBY ALONE—Cosmetic saleswoman in business for herself.

Lillian Cherensky, Metuchen, N.J.

RUDE DOLPH, VAL, AND TINO—Ill-mannered singing trio.

Ruth Migdal, Brooklyn

SHIRLEY, GOODNESS, AND MERCY—Trio of singing nuns.

Allan G. Sperling, Rye, N.Y.

SCYLLA, MET EAGLE—Greek pet rock, baseball scout, and mascot.

Fran Ross, N.Y.C.

BENT TURBAN—Myopic Turkish hatter.

Msgr. A. V. McLees, St. Albans, N.Y.

FATHER NOSEBEST—Clergyman detective.

Dory Mathews, St. Louis, Mo.

A. "FORTE" GELATO—Manufacturer of Italian confections for Independence Day.

Lewis Ware, Montgomery, Ala.

LOW RENTS OF ARABIA—Saudi dealer in subsidized housing.

Helene B. Ellner, Richland, Wash.

MANNIE OCCULT—Prophet and author, *The Unchosen People.*
Eleanor Paul, Brooklyn

MEYER ANGEL LOO—Spiritual guardian of delicatessen washrooms.
Ken Pober, Rahway, N.J.

IVAN ITALIA—Bilingual comedian.
Jack Paul, Brooklyn

COSMO POLLY TAN—Star of *Topper* and inventor of Parrot Sun Oil.
Steven Dorfman, Southfield, Mich.

MARIA, ASPEN SKIER—Gypsy and downhill racer.
William S. Hicks, N.Y.C.

AMAPOLA DAY—Organizer of physicians' golf tournaments.
Hank Hartmann, Salem, Ore.

JOHN GREENLEAF WITTIER—Adam and Eve's favorite comedian.
Patchen Gallagher, N.Y.C.

F. STOP FITZGERALD—photographer of the Jazz Age.
Irwin Skenazy, Wilmette, Ill.

KINGMAN KONG—former Yale president, now British ambassador to the Empire State Building.
Gary Skenhardt, New Haven, Conn.

FLIP FLOP—unsuccessful black comedian.
Janet Blume, Sayville, N.Y.

CROQUE MONSIEUR—Parisian hit-man.
Murry Harris, N.Y.C.

THOMAS NOGUCCI—shabbily dressed Los Angeles County coroner.
Anita Oeschger, Los Angeles, Calif.

DARTH NADER—author of *Unsafe in Any Galaxy.*
Homer Schall, N.Y.C.

MRS. C. P. MUDD—downtrodden Bayou housewife.
Dan Kennedy, Chattanooga, Tenn.

YVETTE MIMEO—undistinguished starlet.
Eve Thompson, Upper Montclair, N.J.

MIFUNE VALENTINE—Japanese screen heartthrob.
Alex Vaughn, Old Lyme, Conn.

ST. THOMAS AQUININE—jungle missionary.
Clark Whelton, N.Y.C.

NOLA MAE TANGERINE—abstemious Orange Bowl queen.
K. B. Robinson, N.Y.C.

"TSOURIS" TRAPP—Austrian yodeler whose career was cut short by an avalanche.
William Schallert, Pacific Palisades, Calif.

EMILY POST MORTEM—author of *Gracious Things to Say at Funerals.*
Kathleen Duplantier, New Orleans, La.

JOHN HAVETHECHECK—generous basketball star, known as "the open man."
Stan Karp, N.Y.C.

J. EDGAR HOOFER—former head of Federal Bureau of Tap Dancing.
N. Riordan, Santa Ana, Calif.

HERMIONE GINKGO—British star of *Pacific Overtures.*
Richard Helfer, N.Y.C.

MOLLY CODDLE—wet nurse.
Larry Laiken, Bayside, N.Y.

HORACE COPE—barely successful astrologist.
Raymond E. Beneson, Niskayuna, N.Y.

MARSHA DIMES—physical therapist.
David Scoggins, N.Y.C.

CHARITY BALL—prostitute with a heart of gold.

Lenore Kaplan, New Haven, Conn.

SHANGHAI CZECH—Prague's attaché in mainland China.

Pericles Crystal, Scarsdale, N.Y.

LOLA CONTENDERE—Italian actress, candidate for an Oscar.

Nancy E. Ash, Washington, D.C.

MILLARD FILMLORE—undistinguished former president of the American Movie Trivia Society.

Roy Blount Jr., Mill River, Mass.

HARMON KILLABREW—pivotal character in Cooper's *The Beerslayer.*

Pete Morawetz, Minneapolis, Minn.

ALFALFA ROMEO—Neapolitan hayseed and backseat lover.

Charles Burlingham Jr., Boston, Mass.

J. PAUL GHETTO—billionaire social worker.

Mark A. Cohen, N.Y.C.

KENO SOBBY—Indian gambler and sore loser.

Virginia Feine, Hartford, Conn.

HERR TRIGGER—volatile co-star of *Achtung Roy Rogers.*

Chris Doyle, Reston, Va.

ROBERT DOUGHNUT—British actor/baker, star of *Good Pie, Mr. Chips.*

Elizabeth L. Kauders, Pittsburgh, Pa.

SANCHO PANDA—sidekick of Don Coyote.

Morey Filler, M.D., San Francisco, Calif.

ARTHUR PEDICK SHUE—undersecretary, Department of Correction.

Alice Wofford, Port Washington, N.Y.

"BUFFALO" CHIPS—western schoolmaster.

C. L. Mollott, Fairfield, Conn.

HENNY JUNGMAN—Swiss comedian noted for one-liners (e.g. "Take my alter ego, please").

Howard Kuperberg, N.Y.C.

VISCOUNT U. BEHAVE—imperial disciplinarian.

Shelly Stein, Falls Church, Va.

CURTIS LEMAYFIELD—reactionary rock star.

Teri Dale, Los Angeles, Calif.

ORSON BUGGY—Lincoln's secretary of transportation.

No signature, Cambridge, Mass.

VESCO DA GAMA—explorer of Costa Rican tax shelters.

Fritz Lamont, Lawrenceville, N.J.

VASCO DA GUMMO—proprietor, Marx of Mulberry Street restaurant.

Sam Klein, North Caldwell, N.J.

ABDULLAH OBLONGATA—brainy Arab potentate.

Sheila B. Blume, M.D., Sayville, N.Y.

KUBLA KHAN AND OLLIE—favorite children's show on TV-Xanadu.

Bill Detty, Austin, Tex.

LUCIANO PAVAROTISSERIE—opera star noted for roles in *Grill of the Golden West* and *The Barbecue of Seville.*

Reuben Tam, N.Y.C.

SLALOM ALEICHEM—Israeli ski instructor.

David Sacks, N.Y.C.

KLAUS ENCOUNTERS—Dutch manufacturer of space ships.

Maddy Krauser, Roslyn Estates, N.Y.

LOUISA MAY BOYCOTT—feminist author/activist.

Frank L. Visco, Latham, N.Y.

"SEMINOLE" VESICLE—Florida nurseryman.

Jim Stack, Berinda, Calif.

"MENTAL" BLOCK—H & R's smarter brother.
Arthur Barnett, Long Beach, N.Y.

MALA "PROP" POWERS—actress and author of *Usification of Words.*
Ted Berkelmann, Bronx

"GARTER" DAMMERUNG—Wagner aide from silk-stocking district.
Norton Bramesco, N.Y.C.

ANTONIA BRICABRAC—orchestra leader and collector of used batons.
David Girshoff, N.Y.C.

PUTANA RITZ—courtesan.
Charlotte Laiken, Bayside, N.Y.

JULIE YARD—vocal teacher.
Arthur Weller, Interlaken, N.J.

GALLO LEO GALILEE—alcoholic Israeli astronomer.
Ted Althole, Tallahassee, Fla.

CHIP 'N' DALE—vaudeville team/antique dealers.
Dan Gallagher, N.Y.C.

"BABS" BUSHKA—Russian child star.
Steve Hoyman, Memphis, Tenn.

THOMAS ALVA EDSELSON—inventor of the electric lemon.
Dr. Neil R. Power, Jamestown, N.Y.

EMMA NEMS—scientist who made chocolate safe for children.
Bill Sakolsky, Durham, N.C.

TEMPEST FUGIT—fading starlet.
Brenda Lindberg, Little Silver, N.J.

DOM DELLAREESE—Mel Brooks's favorite singer.
John Olesen, Stamford, Conn.

LARS POETICA—collector of Scandinavian verse.
Miles Klein, East Brunswick, N.J.

GERALDINE STRUTS—grand marshal of all Fifth Avenue parades.
Ellen Schor, Brooklyn

CHRISTOPHER UNDERWOOD—Author of *I Am a Typewriter.*
Karl Levett, N.Y.C.

CLOCK GHENT—Mild-mannered Flemish watchmaker.
Ovilia Levine, Phoenix, Ariz.

SAM PECKINPECK—Director of violent movies for overweight women.
Don Hauptman, N.Y.C.

WILLIAM OF LEMON—King of used-car lots.
Oliver M. Neshamkin, M.D., N.Y.C.

TORONTO—The Lone Ranger's faithful Canadian companion.
Pat Greensmith, Lancaster, Pa.

CASWELL MASAI—The tallest chemist and *parfumeur* in America.
K. B. Robinson, N.Y.C.

HAILE UNLIKELY—Perennial pretender to the Ethiopian throne.
Michael K. Stone, Kentfield, Calif.

MERRILL, LYNCH, PIERCE, FENNER, AND MANOLETE—Corporate toreadors.
Jack Conlon, Tenafly, N.J.

VICTORIA DE LOS ANGELES CALIFORNIA—Spanish soprano who missed her debut because of a freeway traffic jam.
John Markham, N.Y.C.

CYRUS VONCE—Secretary of state. Speciality: flea bargaining.
Geri Berg, Clarks Summit, Pa.

PRINCE P. GETTY—Guess who's coming to dinner on Wednesday?
Elsie Angell, Greenville, R.I.

HALSTON PURINA—Couturier and high-fiber-diet enthusiast.
Ellen Burr, New Paltz, N.Y.

LAURENCE DUCKINBILL—Actor and professional freeloader.
Mary Eileen Stephens, Fort Lee, N.J.

F. COTT FITZGERALD—American novelist and root-beer fancier.
Jan Leighton, N.Y.C.

BLARNEY BARUCH—Political adviser and Dublin talk-show host.
Alma Spinosa, Gallup, N.M.

MAURICE REVEL—Composer given to attending wild parties.
John C. Williams, Fairport, N.Y.

NATHAN HALE BROUN—Self-sacrificing sports commentator.
Jeffrey Loeb, Flushing, N.Y.

ABU BEN DOWDY—"Worst-dressed" OPEC minister and amateur pastry chef.
John Kolars, Ann Arbor, Mich.

JEAN-PIERRE RAMPALSTILTSKIN—Hitherto anonymous flutist.
Harold T. Ellner, M.D., Richland, Wash.

OSKAR "MEYER" WERNER—Hot-dog manufacturer and actor.
Lian Farrer, North Brunswick, N.J.

"CONTRIVED" NORMAN CLAYTURE—Artless French sculptor.
Stephen Dines, Hollywood, Calif.

DAN DWARFMAN—Business and finance editor for small press, the "Gnome of Geneva."
Missey Hartmann, Ogden, Utah

MORT DARTHUR—Professor of English.
Leslie Shapiro, West Newton, Mass.

ALICE ROOSEVELT WOOLWORTH—Daughter of president who said: "What this country needs is a good five-and-ten-cent cigar."
Ronald E. Ballard, Little Rock, Ark.

LATISSIMUS DORSEY—Swing bandleader, former Mr. Universe.
Alex Vaughn, Old Lyme, Conn.

MARGAUX FONTEYN—Six-foot ballerina.
Bettina Conner, Washington, D.C.

TAMMY WHYNOT—Nashville's number-one call girl.
Anne Bernstein, Bronx

SKIPPY O'AFRICANUS—Celtic peanut farmer and mercenary conqueror.
Pericles Crystal, Scarsdale, N.Y.

REGGAE JACKSON—Jamaican musician and ballplayer.
Howard Kuperberg, N.Y.C.

ETHAN ALLEN POE—Famous maker of fine American horror furniture.
Edward Shmunes, Columbia, S.C.

BUNNY BEARAGAIN—Monster rabbit, hornplayer, and stockbroker.
Jeff Urbanski, Toledo, Ohio

MICKEY ROONEY PLAZA—Actor and songwriter best remembered for "There's a Small Hotel."
Arthur Weller, Interlaken, N.J.

MELLOW DEEDA MOORE—Chanteuse.
Janet Lemkau, Plandome, N.Y.

IGOR SICKHORSKY—Russian veterinarian.
Scott Shugar, Nashville, Tenn.

EL SID—Legendary conqueror of Spain's ready-to-wear market.
Jeff Monasch, Brooklyn

MARIE-ANTOINETTE PERRY—Model for the famous headless statuette presented annually for the best performance by a French actress.
Adele Ahronheim, N.Y.C.

O. DANNY BOYD—The London dairy heir.
Douglas J. Hoylman, Chevy Chase, Md.

JOE WILLIE LOMAN—Coast-to-coast liniment salesman.
Esther Z. Magilow, Kansas City, Mo.

SRI LANKAWANA—Rail magnate from Ceylon.
Michael Trossman, N.Y.C.

SUN YAT SEN-SEN—Inventor of Chinese breath sweetener.
Mike Leifer, Lake Success, N.Y.

MOONLIGHT SONATRA—By evening a successful singer/composer.
Simi Kirschner, Bronx

DIETRICH FISCHER-DISCO—Baritone, Der Schleswig-Holstein All-Soul Band.
Larry Laiken, Bayside, N.Y.

RENATA SCOTT KEY—Soprano who often sings the national anthem before the start of bocci-ball games.
Ross Allen, Bloomington, Ind.

GERTRUDE EINSTEIN—Expatriate physicist, theorized that a mass is a mass is a mass.
George Bucciero, Detroit, Mich.

HAT TRICK HENRY—One of his three goals was liberty.
Linda Quirini, Greenville, R.I.

FRANCIS ALBERT SCOTT KEY—Singer and composer.
Lillian Panansky, Belleville, N.J.

"JEWELS" FIFER—Over-adorned flutist.
Shirley Boardman, Wayne, N.J.

HENLEY REGATTA—English/Italian opera star and yachtsman.
James Deming, St. Paul, Minn.

EDWARD VALHALLA—Heavenly Norse ballet star.
Louis B. Raffel, Skokie, Ill.

JOHN DOS PESOS—Mexican writer of cheap novels.
Penny Boardman, Wayne, N.J.

GEORGE WASHINGTON "JIMMY" CARVER—Twice president and twice peanut fancier.

John B. Powers, Monsey, N.Y.

HADRIAN BARBEAU—Imperial cocktail waitress.

Coleen Levine, Boston, Mass.

MADALYN MURRAY O'PAIR—Baby-sitter to prominent atheists.

R. Harvie, Ste. Julie de Vercheres, Quebec

EDWARD ALBEE DARNED—Naïve playwright.

Barbara Belen, Southfield, Mich.

PETER "TOUPEE" PAUL—Balding candy manufacturer, frequent robbery victim.

Jack Labow, N.Y.C.

JOHN UPDOC—Author of trilogy *Rabbit Run, Rabbit Redux,* and *What's.*

Carol Ann Lemkau, Port Washington, N.Y.

BETE MIDLER—The singing second wife of a thrice-married veterinarian.

J. Heaton, N.Y.C.

WILLY LO MEIN—Principal character in *The Killing of a Chinese Salesman.*

Alan Walker, N.Y.C.

SIMON BULOVA—South American watchmaker.

Karen J. Bergstrom, Arlington, Va.

GONER TED ARMSTRONG—The ultimate evangelist.

Todd D. Ellner, Richland, Wash.

SUN MYUNG HARVEST MOON—Spiritualist/ballroom dancer.

Sylvia Feinberg, Brooklyn

BABAR WALTERS—Newsperson with a strong bias towards the Republican party.

Toby Hecht, Silver Spring, Md.

VELVEETA CULP HOBBY—Secretary of Health, Education, Welfare, and Home Ec.

Arnold M. Berke, Springfield, Mass.

VALERY GISCARD M'USTANG—French government official accused of accepting bribes from Ford Motor Company.

Alex Vaughn, Old Lyme, Conn.

JOHN OF GANT—Noble shirtmaker, father of Bolingbrooks Bros.

Joel F. Crystal, Scarsdale, N.Y.

MARCUS WALLABY, M.D.—Australian G.P.

Bernard J. Schimmel, Bethlehem, Pa.

MOSHE DIANE—Transsexual Israeli leader.

Jay M. Tischenkel, North Miami, Fla.

JESSICA DRAGONATE—Heroine of fairy tale with unhappy ending.

James Elward, N.Y.C.

VIJAY ARBITRAGE—Tennis-playing securities speculator.

David C. Pollack, N.Y.C.

KING COMMUTE—Chief executive of Scandinavian Railways.

Karl Levett, N.Y.C.

BILL MAUDLIN—Oversentimental political cartoonist.

Jeff Monasch, Brooklyn

"SARGE" KOUSSEVITZKY—Conductor/volunteer policeman. Loved *A Little Nightstick Music.*

J. F. O'Connor, Silver Spring, Md.

CANTINFLASH—Comical exhibitionist.

Amy Kassiola, Brooklyn

MARGE NGOWA CHAMPION—Dancer who introduced the Watusi.

Byron Fink, Philadelphia, Pa.

NIKITA CRUISECHEF—Head cook aboard Russian excursion liner.

Lynn S. Ellner, Richland, Wash.

MINKY MOUTH—Animal character featured in first all-talkie cartoon. A failure.

William Millhollen, Philadelphia, Pa.

RONALD MCREAGAN—Some clown who wants to be president.

John H. Corcoran Jr., Chevy Chase, Md.

QUASI-MOTO—Ambivalent hunchbacked Oriental detective.

Nancy Gallanty, N.Y.C.

MILES STANDOFFISH—Pilgrim and stuffed shirt.

Bruce Tabakman, Mt. Kisco, N.Y.

JOKESON POLACK—Painter and president of the Anti-Ethnic Humor Foundation.

Gregory Baron, Fairfield, Conn.

GIAN-CARLO MONOTONOUS—Composer of *Banal and the Night Visitors.*

Nancy Dickinson, Waterford, Conn.

SIR WALTER ROLLEI—Gentleman photographer known for his street scenes.

Richard J. Hafey, Morningdale, Mass.

JOHANN SEBASTIAN BACHE—Organist and member of the Leipzig Stock Exchange.

Joseph Lisanti, N.Y.C.

JOHANN SEBASTIAN BALK—Left-handed hurler of the Munich All-Stars.

Jack Mutzabaugh, Ft. Myers, Fla.

LORETTA SWAT—Policewoman.

Mitchell B. Kramer, Evanston, Ill.

CHEETAH REVERER—Worshiper of abandoned discotheque.

Steve Tuttle, N.Y.C.

IGNORE STRAVINSKY—Composer/author of *The Waiter's Guide to Selective Perception.*

A. B. Ternoff, Kenmore, N.Y.

BURT BRICABRAC—Collector/composer; Oscar for *Junk Keeps Falling on My Head.*

Chris Tani, Lombard, Ill.

STANLEY COUGHMAN—Inconsiderate critic.

Eleanor Paul, Brooklyn

BERGDWARF GOODMAN—Snow White's fashion consultant/spiritual adviser.

Derek Dantry, Oakdale, Pa.

JERRY DELIFEMINA—Adman and proprietor of the N.O.W. food store.

Phyllis Jeacock, New Canaan, Conn.

GRETA GARBLE—Swedish actress who said "I to be alone vant."

Mimi Cozzens, Hollywood, Calif.
Bettina Conner, Washington, D.C.

DATSUN RAIDER—Japanese consumer advocate.

D. J. Morgan, N.Y.C.

EDGAR ALLAN POOH—Writer, author of *Christopher Raven.*

Robin E. Olesen, College Park, Md.

RUBY KEEBLER—Dancer/heiress to cookie fortune.

Judith M. Kass, N.Y.C.

NORMAN VINCENT PELE—Positive thinker/soccer star.

Margaret Rodgers, Massapequa, N.Y.

FIDEL CASTRATO—Tenor/specialist in Cuban lieder.

William E. Dickinson, Waterford, Conn.

JOHN KENNETH CALLBREATH—Economist/crank telephoner.

Michael Schreiber, Brooklyn

ELFIN JOHN—Rock star/actor in Tidy Bowl commercials.
Judy Mostowitz, Brooklyn

PETER BIGSONUVABICH—Hollywood's tallest director.
Alison Lemkau, Locust Valley, N.Y.

FREESTONE KOPS—Comedy stars of silent classic *The Fuzz.*
J-C Labowitz, Washington, D.C.

FRANCO HARASS—Fullback/vociferous critic of Spanish dictatorship.
Kenneth DeNeal, St. Louis, Mo.

OLSON AND JENSEN—Co-anchormen on the Hellzapoppin Evening News.
Peri Crystal, Scarsdale, N.Y.

FLASHER GORDON—The first man to wear a raincoat in outer space.
Thomas E. Noyes, Washington, D.C.

WILT CHAMBERMAID—World's tallest housekeeper.
Bruce Karp, Flushing, N.Y.

MOTHRA WASHINGTON—Japanese movie monster buried at Mt. Vernon.
Ken Bloom, Silver Spring, Md.

AGATHA CRISPY—Manufacturer of breakfast cereal with a surprise at the bottom of every package.
Alice M. Yohalem, N.Y.C.

ELMIRA VATICAN—The first woman pope.
Martin Kantor, M.D., N.Y.C.

POPE O'CATERPILLAR—Spiritual leader of the early Chrysalises.
Eve Jelof, Verona, N.J.

ATTILA THE HON—A real sweetheart of a Tartar.
Miles Klein, E. Brunswick, N.J.
Joel Mansbach, Forest Hills, N.Y.

ADOLFO HITLER—The Mad Hatter.

Erika Little, Chevy Chase, Md.

ADOLF HILTON—German hotelier.

M. G. Baeder, Bklyn.

COMRADE HILTON—Soviet minister of tourism and builder of détente hotels.

George Fairbanks, Nutley, N.J.

CONELRAD HILTON—Owner of a chain of furnished bomb shelters.

Stanley David Chess, N.Y.C.

BABY REBOZO—Richest child circus star in history.

Jack Limpert, N.Y.C.

LEONARDO DA VINSHIELD—Artistic owner of Renaissance car wash.

Leslie N. Wheeler, Howell, N.J.

WORDY ALLEN—Author/Star of *Play It Again, Zhivago.*

Anne Hamill, N.Y.C.

AGNUS DEI MILLE—Gamboler.

Henry Morgan, Truro, Mass.

JESTER ALAN ARTHUR—Famous comic impressionist who posed successfully as president of the U.S. for three years.

Edward W. Powell Jr., N.Y.C.

YESSUH ARAFAT—The Arabian Stepin Fetchit.

Joe Raskin, Jamaica, N.Y.

HAVALOOK ELLIS—Psychologist noted for research in visual stimuli.

Wendy R. Ellner, Richland, Wash.

PYRAMUS AND FRISBEE—B.C. Roman boy with his A.D. play toy.

Mary LeMieux, New Orleans, La.

TEUTON TONY GALENTO—German pugilist, wrongly thought to be Italian.

Lynn S. Ellner, Richland, Wash.

ROGER DE COVERLET—Inventor of strenuous dance performed in bed.

David G. McAneny, Upper Darby, Pa.

AL PACHINKO—Japanese pinball wizard.

Sam Harned, N.Y.C.

JOHN BERESFORD LIPTON—Eccentric billionaire who gives strangers tax-free gifts of 1 million flow-thru tea bags.

John H. Corcoran, Jr., Chevy Chase, Md.

ALEXIS DE TALKVILLE—Famous historian and late-night TV panelist.

Dan Greenburg, N.Y.C.

MOUNTY HALL—Canadian lawman who always gets his man—or makes a deal.

Elizabeth Ross, Washington, D.C.

KRISTOPHER KRISTOFFERSON—Discoverer of Nashville, Tennessee.

David Chaklai, Port Chester, N.Y.

HELEN GUERNSEY BROWN—Editor of *Cosmoopolitan.*

Felice Lesser, N.Y.C.

MICROAVELLI—Lilliputian philosopher, author of *The Little Prince.*

Robert L. McGowen, Tulsa, Okla.

ANDY WARHEIL—Favorite pop artist/filmmaker of Field Marshal Rommel.

Oliver Katz, N.Y.C.

FILIPPINO LIPPY—Loud-mouthed but artistic Pacific baseball manager.

Emily Koppell, N.Y.C.

BOLIVIA NEWTON-JOHN—Revolutionary Latin American singer.

Jeff Baron, Linden, N.J.

THOMASA BECKET—Ancestor of ethnic writer Samuela Beckett. A holy man. A pussycat. A saint.

Sal Rosa, N.Y.C.

MEL BROOKS ATKINSON—Zany drama critic.

Martin Blume, Sayville, N.Y.

JERRY ORBACHS—Actor who studied at Herbert Bergdorf's.

Lil Wilen, N.Y.C.

GEORGE GOEBBELS—Crew-cut Nazi leader.

Mitchell C. Bailin, Rockville, Md.

CLEAR BOOTHE LUCE—Graffiti remover for New York Telephone.

Jerome Abarbanel, N.Y.C.

GENERAL SIGNOFF—TV executive who decides which shows to cancel.

Terry Heines, Albany, N.Y.

BORIS DAY—Star of musical horror movies.

Peter Goldfarb, N.Y.C.

PABLUM CASALS—Cellist/Babysitter.

Vera Leeds, N.Y.C.

BILLY MONDAY—Latter day saint.

Jonathan Abrams, Bklyn.

TENACITY WILLIAMS—Author of *The Milk Train Never Stops.*

Hayden Freeman, San Antonio, Texas

BILLY THE KED—Sneaky outlaw of the Old West.

Elsie Angell, Greenville, R.I.

PRIVATE SANDERS—Restaurant magnate famed for unplucked chicken.

B. A. Zeman, Omaha, Neb.

MAUREEN STAPLEGUN—Actress/Set designer.

Anne Milton, San Francisco, Calif.

CHRISTOPHER WHEN—Architect noted for taking his time.
Joel Crystal, Scarsdale, N.Y.

ART BOOKWALL—Librarian in 700's section.
Baylor Bd. of Old Trustee, Chatt., Tenn.

USELESS S. GRANT—General who captured Miami instead of Richmond.
Ben Kessler, Bklyn.

JIMMY THE GEEK—Fowl-mouthed oddsmaker.
Elizabeth Cruthis, Milford, Conn.

IVAN THE TREBLE—Squeaky-voiced Russian czar.
Martha H. Freedman, Longboat Key, Fla.

ROBERT BROWNIE—Romantic poet, husband of the diabetic Elizabeth Barton Brownie.
M. Hossbacher, Bklyn.

THE THANE OF CANDOR—Patron saint of presidential news secretaries.
Albert G. Miller Fan Club, Laurel, Miss.

NORMAN VINCENT PIELS—Author, *The Power of Positive Drinking.*
James R. Dalin, Avenel, N.J.

FEDERICO FELONY—Italian director accused of stealing half of a competitor's screenplay entitled *17.*
Marilyn S. Wells, Bloomfield, N.J.

RHONDA PHLEGMING—Actress who appeared in 2,653 performances of *Camille.*
Margaret C. Clancy, N.Y.C.

BLAZE PASCAL—Torrid stripper billed as "the Easter Bunny."
Harry Jubelirer, Sharon, Pa.

SAMUEL F. B. MOROSE—Sullen inventor. (See Jonas Sulk, Alexander Grim Bell.)
Nancy Vernon, Greenlawn, N.Y.

SMYRNA LOY—Retired film star; "I don't give a fig for Hollywood."

David Dember, Jamaica, N. Y.

BURT BACKTRACK—Composer wondering how to get to San Jose from Shangri-la.

Charlie Laiken, N. Y. C.

JACQUES COUTEAU—Star of French underwater version of *The Threepenny Opera.*

Chas. Shoenberg, N. Y. C.

Redistributed Names

Tat um, one—Al—tentative instruction from Mr. Pacino to his lacemaker.
Pearl Dropstooth (Polish)—Inept Warsaw dental hygienist.
Buss top—In France, greeting accorded visiting heads of puppet states.

Above, redistribution. Competitors were asked to repunctuate and redefine a familiar name, product, title or the like.

Report: Repunctuation sent many of you off the shallow end. Conjoined with a redefinition, it inspired a grinding reliance on accents, jargon, argot, dialect, or what-you-will. Cockney. Tarzan talk. One good example: Lo! Hen grin!—Behold a smiling chicken. And a—well—a bad example: Rich, ar de Nix on?—Query from a basketball fan. Urgent repeaters: John N.Y.C. Arson. Women swear daily. Hippo crates. Frank's in a tra. Flee Bailey. Psycho the Rapist. Bet Ted—Avis. Chic Omar X. Er, ma bomb—eck! Beverly's ills. Hollywood lawn. Also duplicated, these redefinitions: Margaret's anger—The pill that failed. Henry K. is singer—Will debut in *Flying Dutchman.* Gorgon Zola—Emile's unattractive sister. Formal de Hyde—Dr. Jekyll's tuxedo. Ernes, the Ming way—Chinese seafood. R.I.P. to R.N.—Elegy to a nurse. Buff Erin—Dublin streaker. And so on.

Le chat eau mout on Roth's child—Literally, "the cat has passed water on young Philip."

Peter Slade, N.Y.C.

Yo semite—Shalom!

Martha H. Freedman, Longboat Key, Fla.

In her, it the wind—And they calls it Maria.

David Laiken, Bayside, N.Y.

"Joan's Uther Land"—Soap opera.

Anthony Gray, Closter, N.J.

Chim Pan Zee—The bridge connecting Central Park with the rest of New York State.

John E. Hirsch, Rego Park, N.Y.

Motoro la qua sart e Levis ions et?—Query by Roman dandy: "Is it my tailor or static cling that makes my pants look funny?"

C. E. Sherrick, Princeton, N.J.

Ire land—Ireland.

Stan Rulapaugh, Birmingham, Mich.

Hoover'd A.M.—Note left by a cleaning woman.

Jack Labow, N.Y.C.

"You Can Twin the Mall"—U.S. government horticultural cloning manual.

J. Bickart, N.Y.C.

Mild, red nat-wick—Humane insecticide invented by Ernest and Julio Gallo.

Bernard Lovett, Hillside, N.J.

Cors I Can Brothers—Autobiography by Sammy Davis III.

Louis B. Raffel, Phoenix, Ariz.

Ibm.—Footnote abbreviation: cited information recorded by computer, now unavailable due to accidental erasure.

Psyche Wilhelm, N.Y.C.

Mo? To? Ro? La!—Julie Andrews unable to remember the note that follows So.

Escape Committee, Lompoc F.C.I., Calif.

H.R.H. Al de Man—Island prince. Scutcheon bears cat with stunted tail.

Albert Miller, N.Y.C.

Noelc, O, ward.—Challenge from Professor Backward to Met outfielder.

Tim Hanley, Woodhaven, N.Y.

Bi Ble—Old Testament fellow who hung out in Sodom and Gomorrah.

Jay McDonnell, N.Y.C.

East Erbun, N.Y.—A hamlet in Warren County.

Frances Larson, Guilderland, N.J.

John mit Chell—East German television program similar to "Sonny and Cher."

Jane W. Gray, Albuquerque, N.M.

Redd Fox . . . . X—How to vote for Redd Fox.

William Cole, N.Y.C.

Wald or fast or I-A—Alternatives facing potential German draftee.

Jas. Fechheimer, Glen Head, N.Y.

Fear off lying—Presidential pardon.

Sam Bassin, Bklyn.

Easter Nair lines—Post-lenten depilatory sale.

George Rossi, Bronx

Petro celli—Arab pasta.

Sara Nickerson, No. Hollywood, Calif.

"Brother, the Odor"—E—The foot-spray song (and the original key it was written in).

Lydia Wilen, N.Y.C.

No Par King—Billie Jean.

Lee Glaser, N.Y.C.

Olive®!—Trademark for an exciting musical hors d'oeuvre.

Lee A. Davies, Douglaston, N.Y.

Madam, I'm a dam.—Palindromist horsing around.

Alan H. Kroker, Oak Park, Mich.

Ivorys Now—Radical piano organization.

Cookie Gray, Closter, N.J.

Thea, Lex, and Ria, quartet—Greece's entry in the World Barbershop Singing Competition.

Erna Lovett, Hillside, N.J.

Rabbi Tredux—The leader of France's Jewish community.

Mike Cohn, San Francisco, Calif.

Bon Witteller—A French comic.

Sara Feinstein, N.Y.C.

Bur lives—Inept newspaper account of Alexander Hamilton's duel.

Bruce Karp, Flushing, N.Y.

F. A. O'Schwarz—Founder of Irish toy company.

Richard Hauver, Rochester, N.Y.

He's per ides.—Pay rate of Caesar's soothsayer.

Anne Hamill, N.Y.C.

Catonahottinroof—Similar in origin to Faulkner's Yoknapatawpha County, this fictional Washington, D.C. suburb appears frequently in the social novels of Tennessee Buchwald.

John Hofer, Southborough, Mass.

"A Scent of Man"—The Compleat Bloodhound's Manual.

D. P. Hauptman, N.Y.C.

Harvey—Wall Banger—Calling card of invisible rabbit specializing in lease-breaking.

T. J. Greensmith, Lancaster, Pa.

A bébé a me—(Fr.) Give the baby to me.

Jack Ryan, N.Y.C.

Plane to Ft. Heapes—Now Western starring the 82nd Airborne Division.

Richard S. Hudes, Fresh Meadows, N.Y.

Jimcat "fish hunter"—John Boy's brother.

Harvey Fader, D.D.S., Merrick, N.Y.

The goo dearth—The oil shortage.

Mary J. Bohr, Arlington Hts., Ill.

I.R.A.—Le Vin—An item on a French shipping document.

Mark Wolfson, Spring Valley, N.Y.

Hankaaron—A pharaoh.

Johnny Randy, N.Y.C.

Che R—Founder of the Havana branch of Alcoholics Anonymous.

Emily Karp, N.Y.C.

Papal Nun C.I.O.—Women's labor union in Vatican City.

Thomas Cadogan, Glen Burnie, Md.

The ad ventures of Huck, LeBerry, Finn—Odyssey of an agency.

Don Frost, Fairfield, Conn.

U Sa—Burmese ambassador to Washington, D.C.

Edmund Lysek, Chicopee, Mass.

Chuck's Car Borough—Used auto lot.

David Greene, Montclair, N.J.

The carp enters—Announcement of a formal fish fry.

George Stephenson, Chicago, Ill.

Chi. coma Rx.—Windy City pep pills.

Mel Taub, N.Y.C.

Ultima Tum—New Revson cosmetic to beautify the intestinal tract.

Henna Arond Zacks, Bklyn.

Ed sel and Stu de baker—Southern mother describing her sons' careers.

Levy Children, Monsey, N.Y.

Am Eric, an ex-press card—Waggish self-description by Mr. Sevareid.

Paula Callan, N.Y.C.

Mar y Livingston—The Sea and Gull, popular Spanish restaurant, est. 1971.

Marshall Karp, N.Y.C.

Norton Bramesco—Trade name for the Norton Brames Company.

Miles Klein, E. Brunswick, N.J.

Ciné Qua Non

ADVENTURE/WESTERN: **"I know you have to face this thing alone, Sam."** ***(Sam goes to door)*** **"But darling—"** ***(Sam turns.)*** **"please . . . be careful."**

DISASTER: **". . . so as governor of this great state, I am proud to launch the first ultrasonic monorail in the . . . say, do you smell something burning?"**

Above, ciné qua non. Competitors were asked to invent random but indispensable lines from any one category of motion picture.

Report: "Don't shoot, I think it wants to be friends." "The battery is dead, we'll have to spend the night in the castle." "After this stinkin' war ends, I'm gonna take my goil to Ebbets Field and cheer dem bums." "Look, Dad, Pard is trying to tell us something." "Hello—what's this—a bit of cloth from a woman's dress—and an expensive one too, I'll wager." "The giant [lips move out of synch] aardvark is heading for Tokyo! No, professor! [lips stop]. No! Don't try to examine it!" "Don't nobody move, dis is a stickup!" And others. I thought this species had been extinct for a million years. Well, you learn something new every day here on my beat—the city. So long, guys, see you in a better snake.

WESTERN: "Kiowa. Fresh tracks. One, mebbe two day. This many pony. One paleface . . . woman."

Jack Ryan, N.Y.C.

TYCOON: "I've watched over you, rode with you, taught you, believed in you since you were a boy. You've done some foolish things, some brilliant things. I've tried to understand. I've watched your ambition. I've stood by while you grew big in power and small in humanity. I've see you make men tremble in fear, and women cry with shame. But never until this moment have I judged the full measure of your cruelty and madness."

David Buckley, Palos Heights, Ill.

GOOD MAN GONE WRONG: "Crying? I'm not crying, you old fool—I'm laughing! Ha, ha, ha, ha, ha! Ha, ha, ha, ha, ha! Ha, ha-arrgh!"

Kevin Hanlon, N.Y.C.

MEDICAL DRAMA: "The answer is here, Lionel, in one of these 300 livers. The answer is here, but I'm too blind to see it."

Beth Strode, Scarborough, N.Y.

MARX BROTHERS: "Don't point that thing at me—it might be loaded. *You* might be loaded. You might go off. As a matter of fact, I wish you would."

Bill Detty, Austin, Tex.

SCI-FI: "That's funny. My watch stopped, too."

Richard Tyce, Dayton, Ohio

MOPPET: "How do you do, Mr. Ambassador. My name is Betsy Miller. Do you like to play piggyback?"

Ilene McGrath, Leonia, N.J.

SOCIETY: "Never mind what the doctor says, darling. I'm sure in no time you'll be up and playing second fiddle again."

Walter Price, N.Y.C.

TEACHER BIO: "I didn't fail you; you failed yourself."

V. S. Perretti, Belle Vernon, Pa.

LOVE/MEDICAL: ". . . Visiting hours are up. You'll have to go now."

Jan Leighton, N.Y.C.

DETECTIVE: "Let go of me, you're hurting my arm."
Pia McKay, Washington, D.C.

JUNGLE/ADVENTURE: "You're describing killer ants, Martha—why do you ask?"
Jon Maier, Eugene, Ore.

DORIS DAY: "But I still don't understand what I'm doing in your pajamas."
Della Friedall, St. Louis Park, Minn.

WESTERN: "I hear you're pretty fast with a gun."
C. Robinson, Pittsford, N.Y.

LOVE: "Couldn't we talk it over? I know a little Italian place just around the corner. A hole in the wall, but Mama Nandini makes the best pasta this side of Naples . . ."
John Lapsley, Montgomery, Ala.

SCI-FI: "I know it sounds weird, sir, but the thing is afraid of its mother."
George Fairbanks, Nutley, N.J.

PRIVATE EYE: "Where to, mister?" "Follow that cab."
Jack O'Neill, N.Y.C.

MILITARY/WESTERN: "How can we stop him, General?" "Simply arrest him, Major. Arrest Sitting Bull."
Edward Zap, Coraopolis, Pa.

LOVE (UNREQUITED): "You'll never get a taxi in this snowfall. You . . . you could stay here. . . ."
James Elward, N.Y.C.

DETECTIVE: "Don't open this door for anyone."
Alan Levine, Copiague, N.Y.

JAMES BOND: "I wish I might stay to watch your slow death, but I must leave to detonate the Washington bomb. . . ."
Jim Drucker, Glenside, Pa.

CANINE: "I don't want a hundred dogs; I want Pal!"

Robert Patrick, N.Y.C.

MANHUNT: "He can't get far in these woods in the dark. We'll knock off for the night."

Teresa Gerbers, Glenmont, N.Y.

WAR: "I warn you, I want you to forget what you are about to see."

Barbara Broff, N.Y.C.

DETECTIVE: "Why, that's blackmail!" "Blackmail is such an ugly word."

Alan Theaman, Clifton Park, N.Y.

WAR/GANGSTER: "All right, let's synchronize our watches."

Candy Wolfson, Spring Valley, N.Y.

SCI-FI: "C'mon Susie, give me a kiss." "Wait a minute, Herbie. Something's wrong with the car radio."

Janet Blume, Sayville, N.Y.

GANGSTER: "Are you sure no one followed you here?"

Ms. Simi Kirschner, Bronx

ARISTOCRATIC MELODRAMA: "Whatever you may do to me, you'll never see a son of yours in the governor's mansion, because . . . Michael is . . . not . . . your . . . child."

John Gilman, N.Y.C.

ROMANCE: "You mean you're not my mother?"

Jean D. Brown, Bangor, Me.

OCCULT: "Mommy, Mommy. Come to my bedroom and see what some bad person did to Mrs. Lindquist."

Lil Wilen, N.Y.C.

WESTERN: "And keep running from town to town until they find me? No thanks."

Bill Wunder, Port Washington, N.Y.

DISNEY: "Ralph, there's an opossum in our bathtub." "Come on, Louise, how would he get past the doorman?"

Pat Gilleran, N.Y.C.

COWBOY: "Do you savvy white-man talk?"

Ruth Migdal, Brooklyn

TEARJERKER: "Nothing? It's been everything, Paul—just seeing you even once a year—even like this."

Helen Merrill, N.Y.C.

'30S MUSICAL (JACK OAKIE): "I'm gonna one-step, two-step. / Even gonna goose step. / HONK! HONK! / Into your heart."

David G. McAneny, Upper Darby, Pa.

SPORTS BIO: "First is first and second is nowhere."

Jack Schindler, Brooklyn Heights

HORROR: "The AMA has no listing for a Doctor Freiderich Mordor!"

Howard Pasternak, Brooklyn

COURTROOM: "I'll ask you one last question and remember you're still under oath. Are you in love with the defendant?"

William Lambiase, Brooklyn

SCI-FI: "These things you call diamonds—they are common stones on our planet."

C. Scott Harris, Tucson, Ariz.

NATURE: "A close call for the mouse, but all in a day's work for a hungry hawk."

Sheila Blume, M.D., Sayville, N.Y.

'30S COMEDY: "Listen, ya big palooka, do I have to spell it out? I'm trying to tell you that a bundle from heaven is on the way." "You mean—the stork's going to pay us a visit?"

Oscar Weigle, Whitestone, N.Y.

CAPER: "Don't worry, it's all been planned, down to the smallest detail. Nothing can go wrong."

Lu Gordon, N.Y.C.

LOVE TRIANGLE: "I don't belong in your world, Alice, and you don't belong in mine. I found that out today."

Shelley Hanson-Little, Lansing, Mich.

DETECTIVE/SUSPENSE: "I'd heard of Carbella's $200,000 mansion. I'd heard of his women, his yacht, his investments, and his reputation. Now, I'd heard of his death."

Gary Levine, Albany, N.Y.

1940'S PRIVATE EYE: "Have her come in."

Julius Hovany, Chicago, Ill.

WESTERN: "It's mighty quiet out there." "Too quiet." "That a coyote?" "I hope so." "I heard them Injuns never attack at night." "Injuns has heard that, too."

David Wright. Pt. Washington, N.Y.

VAMPIRE: "Why, yes, doctor, the bedroom window *was* open."

George Fairbanks, Nutley, N.J.

SCIENCE FICTION ABOUT MINIATURIZED PEOPLE: "Meow . . ."

Arthur Bona, New Milford, Conn.

WILDLIFE DOCUMENTARY: "But life is not always so amusing for our inquisitive bear cubs . . ."

Lyell Rodieck, N.Y.C.

COSTUME EPIC: "Guards! Guards!"

David A. Hutchison, N.Y.C.

ADVENTURE/ROMANCE: "It's too late, Chuck. I can't pull 'er out. I'm done for. But I—no, just blacked out there for a second—Chuck, listen, it's the stabilizer. You got that? The sta . . . *(static)* . . . up to you now. Tell Laura. . . ."

Dodi Schultz, N.Y.C.

GANGSTER: The Star: "You call this *food!!!*" Frank McHugh: "Watch it! He's got a gun!"

Mrs. Fredric Moshier, N.Y.C.

COMEDY/ROMANCE: "No, you don't mean—gosh, honey, gee, don't you think you should be resting in a chair or something?"

Karl Levett, N.Y.C.

WORLD WAR II: *(Image of marching boots superimposed over map of Europe.)* Narrator: "Austria, Poland, Czechoslovakia . . . but while the Dominion of Death marched ruthlessly on, at an Allied outpost on a forgotten isle secret plans were being laid . . ."

Henry Geller, N.Y.C.

SPORTS BIO: "Go ahead, kid—try a few pitches. *(Aside)* This oughta be good for a few laughs, Lefty."

David Klein, E. Brunswick, N.J.

BOB HOPE/DANNY KAYE/JERRY LEWIS COMEDY: "Honest . . . I don't know anything about any missing rubies, I'm just Joey Hansen, a lousy song and dance man . . ."

Gerald Nachman, N.Y.C.

FOREIGN (Bucolic): "Ah, Jean-Pierre, and why are you not in school today? And what is that you are hiding behind your back?"

Sophia Press, N.Y.C.

ARABIAN NIGHTS: "So! You dare prefer the slave girl to me, the caliph's daughter! Guards! Teach this son of a jackal a lesson! Kill the girl!"

Angelo Papa, Trenton, N.J.

WESTERN: "And one day, son, this will all be yours . . ."

Jeff Goldberg, Brighton, Mass.

CAPER: "Worried?"

Richard Pinsky, N.Y.C.

HORROR: "Lock the door after me."

Jonathan Abrams, Bklyn.
Elizabeth Reichert, Old Bridge, N.J.

MURDER: "We'd better not see each other again until after the trial."

Robert N. Ruda, Miami Lakes, Fla.

POW CAMP: "Your tunnel plan just might work, Cogswell . . . but what'll we do with the *dirt?*"

Jerome Coopersmith, Rockville Ctr., N.Y.

CARTOON: "With this new wifle I'll take care of that wotten wabbit once and for all."

John Blumenthal, Rye, N.Y.

DORIS DAY: *(Stomping her foot.)* "Oooooh!" *(Blows unruly lock of hair off forehead.)*

Stuart Greenberger, No. Hollywood, Calif.

TRAVELOGUE: " . . . is truly a land of contrasts."

Fred Blume, Sayville, N.Y.

MYSTERY: Detective *(looking at city below):* "He's out there . . . somewhere."

Alice L. Cochrane, Bloomfield, N.J.

MONSTER: "He was really two men—one good, one evil. It's a pity both of them had to die."

Fran Ross, N.Y.C.

ROMANCE: "Charles, darling, we heard you were dead. I missed you so . . . Oh, I'm sorry. Charles, this is Alex, my husband."

David B. Roth, Bklyn. Hts., N.Y.

SWASHBUCKLER: "Zis man you have just insulted—he is ze best swordsman in all of France!"

Amy Midgley, Raleigh, N.C.

JOHN WAYNE: "*Sick of this war?* Ya know what you're fightin' for? Popcorn. Little girls puttin' on frilly petticoats for their first dance, the sun rising big as a crackerbarrel over the prairie, freedom to come and go whether you're drunk or sober and the right to boo the Yankees . . ."

Scott Burnham, N.Y.C.

SCI-FI: "On their planet, *we'd* be the grotesque ones, Mona."

G. P. Kiss, N.Y.C.

CRIME: "Sure I hated him. I'm glad he's dead. But I didn't kill him."
James Copeland, N.Y.C.

RELIGIOUS EPIC: "You see, Padre, my daughter has a very vivid imagination."
Mary J. Bohr, Arlington Hts., Ill.

MUMMY: "This inscription over here—it seems to be some sort of curse."
Jean B. Hall, Rockville, Md.

GANGSTER: "My kid's not gonna grow up like me, she's gonna have the best—schools, clothes, fancy friends . . ."
David Yarnell, Los Angeles, Calif.

JOHN AGAR: "We must find a way to communicate with the beast."
Gerard J. Cook, Westbury, N.Y.

EPIC: "They're called Christians, sire, religious fanatics, but small in number and doubtless of no significance to the empire."
Gabriel Peller, N.Y.C.

ADVENTURE: "Shooting you would be much too easy, Mr. Bond . . ."
Gerard Dallal, New Haven, Conn.

WALT DISNEY (Live Action): "No wonder . . . it won't fly . . . you've got the candy cane in the wrong position."
Leslie H. Goldenthal, Hollywood, Fla.

ENGLISH MURDER: "Yes, madam, I'll need a quiet room where I can practice my violin without disturbing anyone."
E. B. Callahan, Pittsburgh, Pa.

JAZZ BIO: "All right, we'll try it once more—only this time we'll play it *our* way . . ."
Terry Keiser, N. Ada, Ohio

ROMANCE: "Wash and set, ma'am?"
Anne Carlin Gottehrer, Bala-Cynwyd, Pa.

Sanders, take Helen back to the ship. Move slowly and keep 'l cover you from here."

Joan Reyes, N.Y.C.

JAPANESE SCI-FI: "No father, no! Don't destroy Googolplex! He's our friend! He'll fight Mythma for us!"

T. D. C. Kuch, Vienna, Va.

SUSPENSE: "Bill, can you hear out there on the ledge? This is Mary, and Father O'Brien is with me."

J. B. Salomon, Forest Grove, Ore.

SCI-FI: ". . . *Safe?* We've just bought ourselves a little time. We've got to . . . convince the world . . . they're *coming back!*"

Alan Foster Friedman, N.Y.C.

GOTHIC: "That was *her* room, miss. The master had it locked the night—but never mind. You'll be wanting to see your room, I suppose."

Alexandra Isles, N.Y.C.

ROMANCE: "Two months—two years. Does it matter how long you live? It's *how* you live that counts!"

Mrs. Jerry Stiller, N.Y.C.

PRIVATE EYE: Doctor: "You've got four fractured ribs and internal injuries. You'll be out in a week." Hero: "Sorry Doc. I've got some unfinished business. Hand me my shirt."

Chris S. Connor, Madison, N.J.

WILDLIFE DOCUMENTARY: Narrator: "The [your animal here] is one of the most misunderstood creatures in nature."

Ralph B. Patterson, Little Rock, Ark.

GOTHIC: "I say, Hugh, your fiancée bears an uncanny resemblance to her ancestress, Lady DeFelina, who was burned at the stake in 1475. Lucky we don't go in for that nonsense today."

E. Thurston, N.Y.C.

BATMAN: "Batman! Watch out—behind y—"

J. Bickart, N.Y.C.
sp. mention: Jacobi Radiology, N.Y.C.

MUSICAL/WESTERN/HORROR/WAR/DETECTIVE/ROMANCE/ETC.: "Stop! You can't go in there!"

John Geraci, Manhattan Beach, Calif.

World's Longest Books

THE BEST OF TONIGHT: **Selected Monologues, Edited by Ed McMahon**

DRY CLEANING, **by Tom Wolfe**

THE COMPLEAT ACCESSORY GUIDE, **by Sammy Davis Jr.**

A COMPENDIUM OF THE WORLD'S SHORTEST BOOKS, **edited by James Michener**

Above, four selections from our shelf of the World's Longest Books. Competitors were asked for one appropriate title.

Report: SAMPLE TITLES FROM THE BEST OF THE REPEATS, edited by Snare & Delusion. WE WERE NOT AMUSED, by John Simon. A BACKWARD GLANCE: A MEMOIR by Methuselah. PEOPLE I LOOOK UP TO by Abe Beame. REMEMBRANCE OF THINGS PAST: PART II, by Marcel Proust. INTERPRETATION OF DREAMS, by R. Van Winkle. WHAT ELSE HAPPENED? by Joseph Heller. HYPNOTISM CAN CHANGE YOUR LIFE, by Calvin Coolidge. And, NO THANKS, I ALREADY HAVE A PET: AN ANTHOLOGY OF UNPRINTED COMPETITION ENTRIES. Edited by Force & Violence. Nihil obstat.

EVERYTHING YOU'VE ALWAYS WANTED TO KNOW BUT WERE AFRAID TO ASK, by Tony Randall.

Wallace Tress, Athens, Ga.

SHOW BUSINESS HAIRDRESSING
SHOW BUSINESS HAIRDRESSING
SHOW BUSINESS HAIRDRESSING
SHOW BUSINESS IS MY LIFE, by Monte Rock III.

Joseph E. Behar, Forest Hills, N.Y.

YOU CAN READ THIS IN AN HOUR! by Evelyn Wood.

Renée Kornbluth, N.Y.C.

LOOK WHAT THE MAILMAN BROUGHT, by Ann Landers.

Chester Alan Marshall, E. Meadow, N.Y.

RETIREMENT PLANNING, by Frank Sinatra.

Barbara Migdal, Bklyn.

WHAT TO DO WITH YOUR SHMOO.

Mobil Rm. 303, N.Y.C.

A GUIDE TO LEISURE ACTIVITIES, by Prince Charles.

Robin Mensch, Forest Hills, N.Y.

THESE ARE A FEW OF MY FAVORITE THINGS, by Jacqueline Kennedy.

Douglas Braverman, E. Meadow, N.Y.

MY PARTNERS, by Steve Rossi.

Joan Wilen, N.Y.C.
Buffy Kogen, Encino, Calif.

MONOGRAMMING IN YOUR SPARE TIME, by Lana Turner.

Charlotte Laiken, Bayside, N.Y.

FRENCH AND ITALIAN POLITICAL PARTIES.

Chas. L. Anderson, Sacramento, Calif.

THE CONDENSED PLAYBOY PHILOSOPHY, by Hugh Hefner.

similarly: Carolyn Rosen, Baltimore, Md.
Robert Shepherd, Tarrytown, N.Y.

THE COMPLETE WORKS OF ISAAC ASIMOV, edited by Rod McKuen.

Trexel W. Hennison, Joliet, Ill.

THE CHINA-INDIA CENSUS RESULTS 1965–1975.
Wendy R. Ellner, Richland, Wash.

GOOD TASTE ON A BUDGET, by Bette Midler.
Mrs. David Oltsik, White Plains, N.Y.

THE MOTION PICTURE CODE AND WHAT IT MEANS TO YOU, by Jack Valenti.
Richard J. Hafey, Morningdale, Mass.

CAMPAIGNING, by Harold Stassen.
Lynda Reamer, Randallstown, Md.

A BRIEF EXPLANATION OF CURRENT ECONOMICS, by John Kenneth Galbraith.
Raymond LeKashman, Phila., Pa.

MY CROWD, by Truman Capote.
Andrew Rubenoff, Bklyn.

HE'S LIVING, SHE'S DEAD, by Richard Lamparski.
Kathy Laiken, N.Y.C.

WHAT WE KNOW ABOUT YOU, by the CIA.
Ray Jessel, Los Angeles, Calif.

EVERYTHING YOU'VE ALWAYS WANTED TO KNOW ABOUT EVERYBODY BUT WERE AFRAID TO ASK, by Gerold Frank.
David Galligan, Los Angeles, Calif.

GROWING UP, by Orphan Annie.
John S. Palmer III, Baltimore, Md.

SELECTED EXTEMPORANEOUS REMARKS AND ADDRESSES FOR DIVERSE OCCASIONS, by Fidel Castro.
Leslie H. Goldenthal, Hollywood, Fla.

HOW I QUIT SMOKING, by Johnny Carson.
Joel Schechter, Bklyn.

CONVERSATIONS—A MEMOIR, by Shelley Winters.
William Marriott, Athens, Ga.

A GUIDE TO VACATIONS IN THE MEDITERRANEAN, by Ulysses.
P. Hayes, Westport, Conn.

HARE KRISHNA: THE COMPLETE LYRICS.
Mildred Volker, N.Y.C.

AFTERTHOUGHTS, by Harry Lorayne.
Oscar Weigle, Whitestone, N.Y.

THE ENCYCLOPEDIA OF KNOCK KNOCK JOKES.
Edith Schwartz, Closter, N.J.

TEN HEADLINES FROM THE NEW YORK TIMES, edited by Arthur Ochs Sulzberger.
Bruce Karp, Flushing, N.Y.

THE GUINNESS BOOK OF RUNNERS-UP.
M. E. Whelan, N.Y.C.

NAMING YOUR BABY, by Charles Dickens.
Margaret A. Ost, N.Y.C.

A GAZETTEER OF WELSH PLACE NAMES, edited by Richard Burton.
Fran Ross, N.Y.C.

MY SLOW YEARS, by Vaughn Meader.
Jill Kogen, Encino, Calif.

THE WIT AND WISDOM OF JERRY LEWIS, by Jerry Lewis.
Sue Kogen, Encino, Calif.

THE JOE VALACHI SONG BOOK.
Fernando Soto, N.Y.C.

THE COLUMBIA UNIVERSITY CATALOGUE OF COURSES, ACTIVITIES, AND SPECIAL SERVICES UNAVAILABLE TO BARNARD STUDENTS.
J. Zuckor, N.Y.C.

SYMBOLISM IN THE CINEMA, by M. Antonioni, F. Fellini.

Hal Samis, N.Y.C.
R. F. Howard, N.Y.C.

THE ANNOTATED WORKS OF T. S. ELIOT.

Robin Downes, Bloomfield, Conn.

PEOPLE I'VE DECKED, by Frank Sinatra.

Arnie Kogen, Encino, Calif.

OBSERVATIONS FROM THE PENALTY BOX, by Dave Schultz.

Mark Wolfson, Spring Valley, N.Y.

MAN'S SEARCH FOR HAPPINESS.

J. Bickart, N.Y.C.

Kangaroo Joke

A kangaroo walks into a saloon and hops on a stool. He puts ten dollars on the bar and orders a vodka martini. The bartender serves the drink, then gives the kangaroo his change: two dollars. "Pardon me for staring, "says the bartender, "but we don't see too many kangaroos in here." "Yeah," replies the kangaroo, "and at these prices you won't see too many more."

Above, a once-told tale. Competitors were asked to retell the anecdote in the style of a well-known individual.

Report: A formidable range: Hemingway, Shakespeare, Chaucer, Joyce, Salinger, Cummings, Vonnegut, Conan Doyle, Ogden Nash (readily mimicked, but you'd better be damned good). And others: Dr. Spock, Burgess, Hawthorne, Galbraith, Michener, Eliot, Runyon, Bunyan, Tolkien, Jack Webb, Jane Austen, Jane Curtin, Mickey Spillane, C. C. Moore, Hunter Thompson, J. Didion, Cosmo, Canby, Marlin Perkins, Sid Caesar, L. Hellman, G. García Márquez, M. Marceau, B. Furness, A. Robbe-Grillet, J. Carol Oates, Lardner, the Bible, Kazantzakis, Amory, Levene, Milne, Gilbert, Melville, Snoopy, J. Caesar, E. Jong, M. Python, G. B. Shaw, A. Cooke, Aristotle, Twain, B. F. Skinner, T. Hardy, Conrad, James, Spooner, Trillin, Christie, Reuben, Stengel, Kafka, O'Neill, Milton, Suzy, Loos, Fields, Lear, Coolidge, Coleridge, Freud, Uncle Remus, H. Van Horne, R. L. Stevenson, Brontës, R. D. Laing, Barthelme, Wodehouse, and Mia Farrow. *Go know.*

Le Joke Kangaroo—1965

"And there is another juicy story," Ina said, half closing her cracked-ice eyes, dipping lobster morsels into the silver lake of Gloria's Dom Perignon. "The kangaroo at the bar?" "Baba's current lover. Gives him ten dollars a day mad money. He can't afford it here but he must imitate us." "Poor Baba! Kangaroos aren't very good in bed." We watched him grudgingly hand the bartender his daily allowance. "If you complain about the price of eight-dollar drinks, you must be poor." "I wouldn't know." The candlelight was like melting butter.

—TRUMAN CAPOTE
Gerald Williams, Oklahoma City, Okla.

I was looking through the *Post* today and I saw this story about a kangaroo buying a drink that cost eight dollars. Where does the *Post* get these *fantastic* stories! So when the bartender says he doesn't have too many kangaroos as customers, the kangaroo says, "Not at these prices." ALL RIGHT! Well, it was boffo in the office this afternoon. Bruce McKay loved it, but what does he know? We'll be back with tonight's guests, Dave Kopay and Anita Bryant, in exactly two minutes and five seconds.

—TOM SNYDER
Ralph Gottlieb, Washington, D.C.

A group you'll see / A troupe you'll see / But an alien Australian marsupial see? / (Bewitched, Bothered, and Bewildered, is He) / Martini, please. / A blini, please. / And pass down a little brown wienie, please. / (Bewitched, Bothered and Bewildered, is He) / Look at this, charged me triple / Made me snort and say Ouch. / 'F kangaroos wanna tipple / They will pay through the pouch. / A flop in here / *De trop* in here / So Pop, we who hop, just won't stop in here / (Bewitched, Bothered, and Bewildered—is He).

—L. HART
John Meyer, N.Y.C.

I'm reminded of a story on this cocktail napkin, just handed to me. It seems that a zebra, no, it was a kangaroo, well anyway, he goes into a saloon and pays, let me see, pays ten dollars for a martini. The bartender, I think it was, the one who served him the drink, says to the zebra that he doesn't see many in the bar or words to that effect. So, the kangaroo, if I'm not mistaken, says, "Take off those striped pajamas." I think that's what he said.

—GERALD FORD
Jack Ryan, N.Y.C.

Kangaroo *enters, sits at bar, produces four pound notes.*
Kangaroo: (*To* Bartender) Vodka martini, please.
Pause
Bartender: *(From behind newspaper)* Eh?
Kangaroo: Vodka martini, please.
Pause
Bartender: *(Folds newspaper)* Vodka martini, then?
Kangaroo: Yes.
Bartender *serves drink, leaves one pound change, unfolds newspaper.*
Bartender: Kangaroo, eh?
Kangaroo: Yes.
Bartender: Thought so.
Kangaroo: Did you?
Bartender: Yes. *Pause.* Bloody rare.
Kangaroo: Yes. *Pause.* Yes.

—HAROLD PINTER
Warren Hansen, N.Y.C.

It was warm outside, but the bar was as cool as a Hollywood blonde. I took a stool and ordered a vodka martini. The bartender placed it before me, no napkin, and then went back to polishing a glass with a dirty dish towel. From two sunken eyes he studied me carefully. "You're Marlowe, ain't you?" he said. "The shamus." "You got me confused, bud, I'm a kangaroo." "Smart guy, huh." He went to the register and came back with two crumpled Washingtons. I'd given him a ten. "We don't get many kangaroos in here." "Yeah," I said.

—RAYMOND CHANDLER
Richard Grant, Denver, Colo.

Once upon a midnight beery / Waiting for the owner, Cleary / To return and take me Weary / From the place and lock the door. / In there came a hopping mammal / To the bar and lit a Camel / Then it ordered a martini / (Damnedest thing I ever saw) / "Vodka," (it said) "Stolichnaya. / Pile the ice a little higher. / Less vermouth, I like it dryer / And some olives—*por favor.*" / Thinking fast to make a few bucks, / Back from ten I gave it two bucks, / Saying, "You're an odd one, Mister / Never seen your type before." "At these prices? Nevermore."

—E. A. POE
Mark Kabat, N.Y.C.

A kangaroo walks into a saloon and hops on a stool. He puts ten dollars on the bar and orders a vodka martini. The bartender serves the drink, then gives the kangaroo his change: two dollars. "Pardon me for staring," says the bartender, "but we don't see too many kangaroos in here." "Yeah," replies the kanagaroo, "and at these prices you won't see too many more."

—MILTON BERLE
Philip Milstein, Amherst, Mass.;
Howard Kuperberg, N.Y.C.;
Susan Wolfson, Chicago, Ill.;
Leslie Rothkopf, Jericho, N.Y.;
Anthony Jerome, Troy, N.Y.;
A. Barry Levine, N.Y.C.;
Edward B. Davids, Media, Pa.

Tank you veddy much. There is kangaroo, from zoo, and he hop into the bar to buy a drink. He put ten dollars on the bar. Where does he get the ten dollars? He is kangaroo! Tank you veddy much.

—ANDY KAUFMAN
Robert M. Eich, Minneapolis, Minn.

The owner of the Kangaroos, a minor-league team, and I go into my favorite New York saloon. He puts ten dollars on the bar and orders a vodka martini. The bartender serves the drink, then gives the guy his change: two dollars. "Pardon me for staring," says the bartender, "but we don't see too many of the Kangaroos in here." "You will soon," I reply, "I just bought most of them."

—GEORGE STEINBRENNER
Matt Greenberg, N.Y.C.

When I was one-and-twenty, / I heard a kangaroo, / "Set them up, bartender, / A double shot and brew. / Here's a ten spot for them, / I carried in my poke." / The drink and two bills change / Came sliding down the oak. / When I was one-and-twenty, / I heard the barkeep say, / "We don't get many roos here, / At least not in my day." / The gray old duck retorted, / As he hopped toward the door, / "At eight bills for a drink, lad, / You won't get many more."

—A. E. HOUSMAN
John A. Ferner, Medford, N.J.

Consumer Beware: Local Saloon, vodka martini: eight dollars. Lackluster service. Occasional kangaroo at bar. 755 Second Avenue. Open

Mon. thru Sat. 4:30 P.M. to 3 A.M.; Sun. 8 P.M. to 2 A.M. (Do not phone.)

—LEONORE FLEISCHER
A. R. Gerald, New Haven, Conn.

Once upon a time, Corky the Kangaroo goes into a Times Square drugstore and orders a vanilla milk shake. The kindly old man behind the counter takes Corky's dime and gives him two cents change, then says, "Pardon me for staring, but we don't see too many kangaroos in here." "Yeah," Corky replies, "and at these prices you won't see too many more!" At this smart-alecky remark, the kindly old man gets highly upset and, pulling a loaded .45 from the folds of his dirty white apron, shoots Corky dead. The end.

—MICHAEL O'DONOGHUE (MR. MIKE)
Angelo Papa, Trenton, N.J.

Rabbi Morgel, the sage of Omsk, known for his clever parables, often told this tale: An old peasant woman who had very large feet and carried all of her belongings in her apron, ordered a vodka martini and paid with a ten-kopek piece. Taking her for a kangaroo, an animal rarely seen in the *shtetl,* the bartender gave her two kopeks change. She departed in a huff without leaving a tip. The meaning of this story is disputed by Talmudic scholars. It is said, however, that the rabbi was usually able to sponge a free drink.

—WOODY ALLEN
Martin Blume, Sayville, N.Y.

A kangaroo did not walk into a %$¢#@*#$£! saloon, and hop on a stool . . .

—RICHARD NIXON
Patricia Sierra, Marion, Ohio

In 1902 Father opened a saloon on Fairview Avenue in Yonkers, New York. It had a big front window and a large mirror behind the bar. Mother's Younger Brother was the bartender. One day Kangaroo walked in. "Here are ten dollars," said Kangaroo. "I would like a vodka martini." Mother's Younger Brother said nothing. He felt he should listen. President Theodore Roosevelt's third cousin was there. He said, "I have never seen a kangaroo here before." Emma Goldman stepped up to the bar. She said, "You never will again at these prices."

—E. L. DOCTOROW
Andrea Joline, Huntington, N.Y.

A pale yellow chicken, each feather catching and snapping light in ever-widening golden circles, wandered into the absurd little bar, gently lifted itself onto a stool rooted in the city beneath it, and, with a wan, weary smile, whispered, "D-d-darling, let me have a gin." The bartender, huge, contained in prison walls of bottles and leather, raised a heavy brow, smiled suggestively and said, "We don't get many chicks like you in here." The pale yellow chicken, poised, alone, different, unique in its chickenness, drawled, "Cluck."

—F. SCOTT FITZGERALD
Jane Garron, Knoxville, Tenn.

A kangaroo walks in

you won't see too many more.

—ROSE MARY WOODS
Marsha Caplin, Cincinnati, Ohio
Jack Rottenstein, Brooklyn

. . . "Parbleu," dit le kangourou, "C'est certainement vrai / Et, pour, çelà, je suis tellement navré / Mais à ces prix que tu augments à l'excès / Tu ne m'y verras plus, tu peux en être assuré."

—LA FONTAINE
Lewis Ware, Montgomery, Ala.

The Frugal Marsupial from *Imperfect Laughter,* a revue.
Barman: Pardon if I seem to stare, / But draped upon the barstool there / We see so few / Of kangaroo.
Kangaroo: Forgive me if I say I think / At what one's asked to pay for drink / You'll be the viewer / Of fewer.

—NOEL COWARD
Ross Allen, Bloomington, Ind.

From down in Auckland comes the tale of a kangaroo. A smart animal who turns out to be a humorist. The kangaroo, thirsty for drink, goes into a saloon. The bartender, willing to serve anyone, can't help but stare at his unusual customer. Seeing that gaze as he downs his drink, the kangaroo winks and remarks, "Prices are too high in this place, even for a rich kangaroo. I won't be back." And so long until tomorrow.

—LOWELL THOMAS
Martin Fass, Rochester, N.Y.

Ingmar Bergman presents *The Joke.*
The action takes place in a bar or any spiritual wasteland. The bartender is underlining a borrowed copy of Hegel when a kangaroo places a fifty-kroner note on the bar.
Kangaroo: An akvavit martini, please. (The bartender nods and fixes the drink.)
Bartender: Here we are. And your change. (He hands him a ten-kroner note.) Frankly, we don't see your type in these parts.
Kangaroo: Indeed. You have much to learn about economics!
(There is much laughter as the other patrons exchange private jokes at the expense of the bartender.)

Larry Laiken, Bayside, N.Y.

"Oh, my pouch and joey," murmured the kangaroo, propping herself tailwise against the pub's counter. "Quickly, potboy, a vodka martini." "I'm not a potboy," said Alice. "If you would turn countertailwise and mind your manners, you could see that quite clearly." "So long as you're not a potboiler," said the kangaroo. "And don't be mean with the pickled onions." "Just exactly what kind of creature are you?" asked Alice. "A marsupial, of course." "That'll be £8 including marsupial tax." "Boycott!" shrieked the roo . . .

—LEWIS CARROLL
Joyce Harrington, Brooklyn

KANGAROO TO BARTENDER: "DROP DEAD"
as told to Michael J. O'Neill, New York *Daily News.*

Jonathan Garlick, Riverdale

George: Once a kangaroo came with us. We ordered drinks and when it was his turn he put ten dollars on the bar and said, "I'll have bergin, bergin and water, please." Laughter spread throughout the saloon. The bartender served him a vodka martini and gave him two dollars. "Pardon me for laughing," said the bartender, "but we don't get many orders for bergin."
Nick: What happened to the kangaroo?
George: Soon after, with his driving permit in his pouch, he swerved his car to avoid a koala and drove right into a mimosa.

—EDWARD ALBEE
Mona Finston, N.Y.C.

Kang Snopes squinted through the cigarette-distilled Venetian blind-filtered five-o'clock light at the two moss-green wrinkled ones lying in what seemed like ridicule next to the newly served silver (although it, too, was jaundiced by the spent afternoon sun) eight-dollar vodka martini on the butt-scarred mahogany with an expected (unrehearsed, really, but ingrained by constant repetition) empty feeling and the memory of a tryst he had heard of involving a traveling circus and his cousin (the ogling bartender's uncle had owned the circus) and filled with a resigned resolution not to drink in town again.

—W. FAULKNER
Bob Peay, Montgomery, N.Y.

Perry Mason stood up at the defense counsel's table and announced, "I re-call Joe the Bartender. Now, sir," asked Mason, "tell the jury again about the last time you saw the deceased." "I was alone behind the bar when the deceased hopped in and ordered a vodka martini. I gave him his drink and his change, and then made a remark about not seeing too many kangaroos in there. He came back with a wiseacre crack about my prices." "Then what did you do?" "I shot him—he had it coming." "The defense rests." —ERLE STANLEY GARDNER
Joel Crystal, Scarsdale, N.Y.

STEWED KANGAROO
1 six-foot kangaroo
15 bunches carrots (diced)
6 fifths imported vodka
Seasoning
2 rabbits (optional)
Cut the kangaroo into 2-inch squares and add the diced carrots. Pour vodka over meat and carrots. Season and cook at 425 degrees for 8 days. Serves 150. If more are expected, add rabbits, but only as needed, as one does not like to find a hare in the stew. —JULIA CHILD
Cassie Tully, Monsey, N.Y.

One day out of a clear blue sea, this kangaroo saunters into a bar, pulls a tenor out of his pocket, and orders a vodka martini . . .

—SAMUEL GOLDWYN
Norton Bramesco, N.Y.C.

My Roo, my rue. She stood barely four feet high in her blue Adidas. Dark eyes, gray fur furrowed by the elastic of her boxer shorts; powerful, downy arms thrusting eight-ounce gloves—these stirred memories: adolescent evenings at my father's lambent, lost Outback Hotel.

I first saw my marsupial mistress when she leapt to the barstool . . .

—V. NABOKOV
T. Ban, N.Y.C.

The Kangaroo of Livinsk

Yasha Grobelnik, or the Kangaroo of Livinsk, as he was known everywhere but in his own village, sat at the end of the long wooden table and watched the workmen eat with gusto. "You want?" asked the table attendant. "Vodka," he said in Polish. "Vodka with the rich, foreign wine."

As he made his ablutions, Yasha conversed with God, Bless the Name, over 4-1 or 5-1 in the mixing. "Eight zlotys," demanded the attendant, placing the shimmering liquid on the table. "Payment in advance. Not every kangaroo from the provinces is seen here." "For eight zlotys, he'll suffer only fools from Chelm," Yasha lamented quietly to God, Bless the Name.

—I.B. SINGER
Stephen R. Sandler, Westerville, Ohio

We surveyed 100 people and the top six answers are on the board to this question: Name a comment a bartender might make to a kangaroo after serving him a vodka martini.

1. Pardon me for staring.
2. We don't get too many kangaroos in here.
3. That's a cute change purse.
4. No, but if you hop a few bars . . .
5. How come you're so jumpy?
6. I'm sure you won't like their prices either. Same to you!

—RICHARD DAWSON
Alan Levine, Copiague, N.Y.

One look at the titular marsupial in Disney's pernicious *The Last Kangaroo* and you know he is a mutant. Even less talented is Dean Jones as the inquisitive innkeeper . . .

—JOHN SIMON
Roger A. Gindo, Brooklyn

One day little Kimmy Kangaroo decided to leave home and seek Adventure. Klip, Klop! Hip, Hop! Pretty soon he came to Mr. McGregor's Bar and Grill. . . . —BEATRIX POTTER

Laura Cowman, Columbus, Ohio

Let us not forget that it is a joke we are expounding. Petitioner Kangaroo avers entering Respondents' drinking establishment and admits specifically . . . —CHIEF JUSTICE MARSHALL

Douglas L. Day, Washington, D.C.

She lifted the cool glass carefully with her tiny brown hands. "Eight." She started, spilling it. "What did you . . . ?" The bartender grinned. "Eight bucks. Say, we don't get many . . ." The glass fell onto the bar. "Damn you!" She rummaged in her pouch and drew out a handful of tissues, stamps, and paper bills. She threw it all onto the counter. "*Damn* you!" He laughed, "Say now, Brownie, don't . . ." The door slammed. Out on the sidewalk the sun made her feel a little better. At least she wouldn't have to go back. Not at those prices. She hopped to the curb. "Taxi," she called. "Taxi!" —DOROTHY PARKER

Bob Colonna, Philenda Stryker, Providence, R.I.

3:00 ⑤ *Mr. Roo*—Comedy (BW) Roo talks Wilbur into taking him to a bar, gets upset over prices. Wilbur: Alan Young.

Brian Plante, Staten Island

A man walks on an airplane, and the stewardess asks, "Hello, sir, would you like to sit by a window?" "No, thank you, I'm blind," he replies. "Oh, I'm sorry! Would you care for a magazine?"

—BOBBY VINTON

Frances Perkins, Columbia, S.C.

Fractured Fables

John James Audubon glanced through a sheaf of possible illustrations for the revised *Ornithological Biography.* In his haste, the drawing of a recently discovered sea swallow escaped his attention. Thus, inadvertently, did he leaf over a new tern.

Above, a Foolish Fable with a Mangled Moral. Competitors were asked to provide one example of same.

Report: Into each reign some life must fall. Repeats fell into four categories: **1. The All Too Familiar:** people in grass houses shouldn't stow thrones; don't hatchet your counts; a man's comb is his hassle; the squaw of the hippo; don't put all your Basques in one exit; and the bird-hater who left no tern unstoned. **2. Original, But Used in Previous Comps:** the matricidal Fritz: "Look Hans, no Ma"; the jungle chieftain whose reign was called on account of game. **3. New But Manifold:** pre-dinner romance, or putting the heart before the course; philosophy before philanthropy, or Descartes before the whores; the sea captain whose barque was worse than his bight; John P. Sousa fighting the band that heeds him; and sun oil leaving no stern untoned. **4. The Outrageous Pun:** the piano adjuster whose name is Opporknockity. *Guess what* he'll do only once. Give up? Tune in next week for surprise answer. And write when you find work.

Audubon was also interested in the genetic traits of birds, and one of his experiments was raising a colony of ravens, causing a friend he met on the street one day to inquire if he had bred any good rooks lately.

Michael Deskey, N.Y.C.

Jack the Ripper's grandmother, armed with a switchblade, often attacked visitors to a London lavatory. Terrified citizens referred to her as the old woman who shivved in a loo.

Albert G. Miller, N.Y.C.

Monday's dog is fair of face / Tuesday's dog is full of grace / Wednesday's dog never sheds / Thursday's dog sleeps on beds / Friday's dog always drools / Saturday's and Sunday's dogs need obedience schools. / As you can see from this canine log, / Every day has its dog.

Lydia Wilen, N.Y.C.

We were creeping through hostile jungle, well camouflaged. I was covered with vines. My wife wore twigs. And we pressed onward bravely with sod on our guide.

Anthony Gray, Closter, N.J.

If it isn't gasoline, it's rice. There's nary a grain in Scotch Plains. Little Italy? *Niente.* Even in Chinatown chopsticks go wanting. But as one might expect, there is arroz in Spanish Harlem.

Larry Laiken, Bayside, N.Y.

When a bill-poster developed an allergy to paste, he tried a rainbow of medicines. But they brought him little relief, and in desperation, he sought a faith healer. In no time at all he could boast no pills.

Philip D. Merwin, Great Neck, N.Y.

During a rare outside-of-the-Iron-Curtain tour a midget acrobat of the Prague Circus decided to defect. He presented himself to the American Embassy in France and asked: "Pardon, but can you cache a small Czech?"

Similarly: David Martin, N.Y.C.
Aaron Silver, M.D., N.Y.C.

An ogre who owned a flock of sheep lost them in a card game to a passing knight errant. A ghoul and his fold are soon parted.

Judith M. Kass, N.Y.C.

During the 1968 campaign, a pro-war candidate stooped to traveling from brothel to brothel. Thus, he became the first tart-to-tart hawk.

Bob Mead, Gautier, Miss.

Walter is having an affair with a sailor. He is having a difficult time keeping it from his wife. Thus, the sailor became known as the secret middy of Walter's life.

Harriet Moulton, N.Y.C.

A publisher read a manuscript about a famous fashion model. He especially needed a book on her fabulous hair style. But he had to reject the manuscript. While there was a lot about her jewelry, her cosmetics, a dress and a coat, there was nothing much about a do.

Don Wigal, N.Y.C.

[At a convention of] researchers into psychic phenomena [were] students of the supernatural and practitioners of the esoteric. Every country but Korea was well represented. Many occult but few Chosan.

Jack Paul, Bklyn.

Nixard Richon, the little old glassmaker, had a secret ambition. He therefore resisted every effort to retire him. Finally compelled to explain: "My fellow Americans," he said, "let me make one clear thing perfectly. . . ."

Michael Schreiber, Bklyn.

My husband has the same name as the star of *Hawaii Five-O,* but my husband's not an actor. He's a cattle rancher. In other words, the shepherd is my Lord.

Joan Wilen, N.Y.C.

George Gershwin, on a tour of Cape Cod with several musical colleagues, couldn't decide whether to rehearse a composition or spend the afternoon cycling along the beach. He asked: "Which shall it be—do we get down to work, or shall we bike up the strand?"

Joseph Gelband, N.Y.C.

Every time Sonny's boys threw away a corpse, his garbageman offered it to the police as evidence against them. As the evidence mounted, Rocco asked, "Papa, how do we throw this garbageman off our track?" Sonny responded, "We'll make him a refuse he cannot offer."

Michael Reiss, Bristol, Conn.

The coach turned to his assistant: "There ain't a man out there that can run the 40 in under six seconds. It looks like we will field the slowest team in the league again. Oh, well—these are the tries that time men's soles."

Sam L. Catter, Dallas, Tex.

Orfus, King of Canaan, sent his runners to seek out Nahum, for only Nahum could end the plague. He bid them go about it discreetly. But one runner, waxing impatient, yelled loudly for Nahum wherever he went. He was the only one running for Orfus to resort to Nahum calling.

Phyllis Taub, Bklyn.

This particular laboratory rat was extremely stubborn. No matter what the rewards, he would not conform to the laboratory-set patterns. After a while, lack of nourishment made him consider, so he wended his maze.

Nanette V. Jay, N.Y.C.
sp. ment.: John Hofer, Southborough, Mass.

It was a cold day in Reykjavik, and Boris Spassky and Bobby Fischer had completed their return match. . . . Their gracious hosts had built a large fire to keep the auditorium warm . . . the Icelanders wanted to have chess nuts roasting on an open foyer.

Richard Alan Polunsky, San Angelo, Tex.

A pair of hungry poets went into the speedy home furnace installation business, and advertised, "Two Bards That Heat in 3/4 Time."

Cookie Gray, Closter, N.J.

People felt sorry for the poor little Russian boy with his arms full of newspapers. But Ivan held his head high with pride, for after all, he did have a clutch of Tass.

Mary Ann Miller, Columbus, Ohio

Young Floyd signed up for the Golden Gloves as a middleweight. However, after the weigh-in, the judges decided to rank Floyd light.

Alissa Abrams, Bklyn.

Had not Magellan been pardoned he would have been forced to narrow the strait and walk.

Sheldon Clark, Kansas City, Mo.

Chevrolets were recalled last week, causing irate owners to question dealers about inferior workmanship. . . . Salesmen told their customers to blame it on the boss at Nova.

Marjorie Rothenberg, Merrick, N.Y.

After months of condemnation of the populace, the power-crazed head of government was finally forced to resign. On the happy day . . . the people rejoiced and the bells of the capital began ringing in the sane.

R. Galper, Dept. of Psych., C.C.N.Y.

When the president of South Vietnam was a boy, he was captain of a team of velocipede racers who frequently challenged a team that used scooters. The scooter racers always lost because they had Thieu's trikes against them.

Ruth Brewster, Hillside, N.J.

The millionaire playboy would light his cigars ostentatiously with five-dollar bills. Unfortunately, the burning currency imparted a bad fragrance to an otherwise fine cigar. "What this country needs," he complained, "is a good cigar-scented five."

Baylor Bd. of Old Trustee, Chatt., Tenn.

A certain man had a mania for eating cookies during a performance of "The Dance of the Sugar Plum Fairy." Irate members of the audience called him The Sweetcracker Nut.

Jane King, N.Y.C.

When his castle was completed, the king invited all the noblemen to the celebration, except the duke of Burgundy. To avenge the insult, the duke entered the castle by stealth later that night and set fire to the draperies in the grand hall. Thus did he bring the new castle to coals.

Janet Fire, Sunnyvale, Calif.

A gnu was donated to a local zoo and temporarily placed in an unfinished cage. The next morning it was discovered that the cage had been cleaned, the floor repaired. The zookeeper remarked, "We're lucky to have a typical gnu and tiler too."

David Kurzman, N.Y.C.

A certain politician was much beset with accusations of scandal concerning his cronies. Hoping to take the minds of the electorate off these matters, he embarked on a whirlwind campaign of cutting ribbons, launching ships, and, most of all, dedicating new hydroelectric plants. Thus did he win, by feigning with dam praise.

Michael K. Stone, Greenbrae, Calif.

Remembering that a personal friend of his had been most lavish with gifts of wine, Richard Nixon approached him for a sizable campaign fund contribution. Nor was the President surprised at how easily he was able to obtain the money. It was like taking chianti from a Bebe.

Norton Bramesco, N.Y.C.

John was a WHO epidemiologist studying diseases carried by freshwater organisms. His wife, Honey, hated him for never taking her to exotic places. "I'll do anything to help out if you take me." He made her a porter for his African trip. That's how Honey saw key Mali ponds.

Arthur Penn, Livermore, Calif.

Mind Reading I

1. "Or, we could just go to a movie and have a pizza . . ."
2. "Regine's? *Now* he asks—this dress is two years old, and my hair looks like a turkey shoot. . . ."

Above, Mind Reading, or 1. What was said, 2. What was thought. Competitors were asked to provide 1. a remark made aloud, and 2. the silent thoughts of the speaker.

Report: 1. "Mmmmm, delicious!" **2.** "What is it? Owl?" Much talk, heard and unheard, of dining, recipes, and the like. Also much to-do about shopping, gifts, etc. **1.** "I love it!" **2.** "Will they take it back?" or **1.** "Madame, that dress *is* you." **2.** "Large." Talk of mothers-in-law, refusing dates, admiring baby pictures, and sounding pompous while thinking pompous. All of that. Plus: **1.** "It is a far, far better thing I do. . . ." **2.** "*Somebody* stop this. . . ." And **1.** "25?" **2.** "41." Some holdovers here from ésprit d'escalier (what I said, what I should've said)—which contest this isn't. Among these: **1.** "Yes." **2.** "No." **1.** "NO!" **2.** "Yes." **1.** "I do." **2.** "Oops." Etc. **1.** Thanks to all who entered—this and all the comps—especially the patient unprinted. I understand. **2.** God, writing the report is the *worst.*

---

1. "Frankly, I've never done this on a first date either."
2. "Yeah, sure, and it don't rain in Indianapolis in the summertime."

Jack Rose, N.Y.C.

1. "Thursday? Just a minute, I'll check my calendar."
2. "One, two, three, four, five, six, seven, eight, nine, ten . . ."

Ira Avery, Stamford, Conn.

1. "I, James Earl Carter, do solemnly swear to uphold the Constitution of the United States. . . ."
2. "Boy, look at the legs on that woman. . . ."

John Falxa, N.Y.C.

1. "You know, I've never thought of it that way before. That's really incredible. No, I mean it. That's absolutely *incredible!*"
2. "My *God,* am I stoned."

Bob Colonna, Phyllis Stryker, Providence, R.I.

1. "The whaling prints are charming, I love that nautical wallpaper, and the bunk bed is just adorable."
2. "How could she have thought I meant the *actual* little boy's room?"

Norton Bramesco, N.Y.C.

1. "And this button summons Secret Service people."
2. "And this wastebasket is for your peanut shells."

Eugene Gramm, N.Y.C.

1. "No, you're not boring me at all."
2. "Does Bloomingdale's have them in blue? Or maybe red . . ."

Susan Bass, N.Y.C.

1. "What's *your* birth sign?"
2. "The Knicks should cinch tonight's game."

Mark Geier, N.Y.C.

1. "Mother, look who's here!!"
2. "Oh, God, who *is* this person?"

James Padnos, N.Y.C.
Bari Biern, Washington, D.C.

1. "Oh, sure I can Hustle."
2. "But I think I'll fox-trot myself right out of here."

Jerri Bazala, N.Y.C.

1. "He's kind, charming, and 'high-powered.' "
2. "And rich."

Hollie Bernstein, Sun Valley, Calif.

1. "I am not a crook."
2. "I am not a crook."

Barry N. Malzberg, Teaneck, N.J.

1. "Om mani padme hum.
   Om mani padme hum."
2. "Candice Bergen."

Robert S. Brown, N.Y.C.

1. "I'm so glad you could come to my dinner party!"
2. "I've told everyone to be sure to watch how you eat."

Mrs. Carl Brock, Columbus, Ohio

1. "35—64—92—Hut Hut Hut."
2. "46—84—9—Hut Hut Hut."

James J. O'Loughlin, Bloomfield, Conn.

1. "Just a party for a few 'fun' people from the office."
2. "No one from Personnel."

Norma Grahame, Mar Vista, Calif.

1. "Listen, he'll have time enough to think about settling down after he gets his practice established."
2. "I think my son is gay, and I think I'll kill myself."

Mimi Cozzens, Hollywood, Calif.

1. "I refuse to answer on the grounds that it might tend to incriminate me."
2. "In the cellar."

Sylvia Gassell, N.Y.C.

1. "It's a *'he'*—he's just a writer."
2. "I can't *believe* this jerk never even *heard* of Somerset Maugham."

Trudy Ship, N.Y.C.

1. "What a lovely baby. He looks just like his father. . . ."
2. "Whoever he is."

Pericles Crystal, Scarsdale, N.Y.

1. "I won't insult your intelligence. . . ."
2. "In fact, I doubt that I can."

Bill Wunder, Port Washington, N.Y.

1. "I'm surprised that an intelligent person like you could take astrology seriously."
2. "So Leos are distinguished and sexy, eh?"

J. Bickart, N.Y.C.

1. "Fat? You're not fat, you're just . . ."
2. ". . . fat."

Ken Olfson, Los Angeles, Calif.

1. "I really had something with larger diamonds in mind."
2. "This sure beats waiting out there in the cold."

Nancy E. Ash, N.Y.C.

1. "You were magnificently spontaneous in the part."
2. "Try rehearsing."

Raymond E. Benenson, Niskayuna, N.Y.

1. "Darling, you were absolutely fantastic. . . ."
2. "Act your little heart out, dear, but I'm doing the part in the movie."

Jay McDonnell, N.Y.C.

1. "Is that what you're wearing to the Junior League ball?"
2. "That's more 'Little League.' "

Carolyn Noah, Canton, Ohio

1. "Thanks, Mr. Silverman."
2. " 'Me and the Chimp'? **'Me and the Chimp'?** I should've done summer theaters. . . ."

Harry LaPlume, North Adams, Mass.

1. "I knew you were pretty last night. It wasn't until this morning that I realized you had *real* beauty. . . ."
2. ". . . two eggs, bacon. (Do you think she could make a pot of really strong coffee?) And I suppose I can't very well ask her to go out for the papers. . . ."

James Elward, N.Y.C.

1. "Well, if you insist, maybe I'll have just one—though I *never* drink this early in the day. . . ."
2. "I thought you'd *never* ask. . . ."

J. M. Riordan, Laguna Beach, Calif.

1. "No, I have no last words for the enemies of freedom."
2. "I want my mommy."

Jimmy Schlosberg, New Rochelle, N.Y.

1. "Sure, count me in."
2. "Let's see—if I skip lunches this week and walk to work and don't pay the phone bill till next month . . ."

Ruth Migdal, Brooklyn

1. "In this scene you play a simple, stupid, vicious peasant."
2. "That's right, just be yourself."

Michael Schreiber, Brooklyn

1. "And now—heeeeeeeeeeeere's Johnny!"
2. "$184,312.50 plus $55,832 plus . . ."

P. Howard Lyons, Toronto, Ont.

1. "And now, for our postgame interview with today's star. . . ."
2. "I wish these guys would shower before coming up here."

Edward Steinberg, Silver Spring, Md.

1. "Is that why you're so upset? Why, *everybody* has those feelings at some time or another."
2. "Weird! Weird!"

Lewy Olfson, South Lyme, Conn.

1. "I met your brother today. It's amazing how different you two are!"
2. "I *liked* your brother."

Ellen McMullan, Ames, Iowa

1. "Oh, what a terrible piece of luck for you!"
2. "If you weren't such an ass . . ."

Cynthia Harrison, McLean, Va.

1. "I've been trying to get up the nerve to talk to you all evening."
2. "You're the only girl left in the bar."

Candace Minnick, Hartford, Conn.

1. "No, I'm sure the alligator is not an endangered species."
2. "And if the question ever comes up, you'll have no trouble convincing people you had your shoes made from your own skin."

Arthur Weller, Interlaken, N.J.

1. "By the way—did you happen to see Competition 268 in *New York?* Oh, it's no big deal—they printed my entry—but of course the whole thing is really rather silly. . . ."
2. "WHOOPEE! YAHOO! They picked me! I'm published! I'm famous! Yay! Yippee!"

Deborah Loverd, Storrs, Conn.
sp. mention: W. Shakespeare, Stratford-on-Avon, England

Mind Reading II

1. "Actually, it needs a little polishing. I mean, it's *finished*—all but the final draft. I'll have it on your desk tomorrow morning."
2. "I wonder who else I can get to write this thing."

1. "I saw this darling dress today—just right for you. It has an uneven hemline. . . . Wait, give me that napkin, I'll draw it for you. Now, here's the sleeve, see . . ."
2. "Oh, God."

Above, the loud and the profane, or 1. what was said, and 2. what was thought by the *hearer.* Competitors were asked for a remark made aloud and the unheard thoughts of the addressee.

Report: Secret thoughts of (unemployment insurance, anti-medicine, and murder). During job interviews, physicals, and home movies. Also sexism. Both ways. *Bi-sexism?* Who knows? Hoping you the same. (God, I hate writing the report.)

---

1. "You've been working here three years now and in all that time you haven't produced a single usable idea or given any indication of *ever* having a single original thought. You're fired."
2. "I've been working here three years now and in all that time I haven't produced a single usable idea or given any indication of *ever* having a single original thought. I'm fired."

Angelo Papa, Trenton, N.J.

1. "My wife and I are, uh, separated."
2. "Sure you are. You're here and she's not."

Mary J. Lutton, N.Y.C.

1. "Because thou hast done this, thou art cursed above all cattle, and above every beast of the field; upon thy belly shalt thou go, and dust shalt thou eat all the days of thy life."
2. "Well—*exc-u-u-se* me!"

Michael Godwin, Austin, Tex.

1. "Sorry, darling—I know how you'd looked forward to going to the ballet tonight, but this problem came up at the office and then I had to drive Suzanne home and, of all the darned crazy things, I got a flat tire at her house and the jack was broken, so I got stuck there waiting for the AAA. . . ."
2. "Soon to be made into a major motion picture."

Miles Klein, East Brunswick, N.J.

1. "Hi. I'm Ed Koch, your congressman."
2. "Drat! I knew I should've used the other subway entrance."

Albert G. Miller, N.Y.C.

1. "I am not a crook."
2. "He's a crook."

Mark A. Sherman, New Paltz, N.Y.

1. "And in here, Mother, is the actual bedroom. Yes, I got a real bargain—$75 for a double bed. And you tell me guys don't know how to shop! Of course Mark isn't unhappy. We flipped a coin. Heads, I got the bedroom; tails, he got the living-room sofa. He figures he'll buy the rollaway next month; his heart is set on a stereo at the moment. . . . No, Mark tells me the couch really isn't too bad on the back."
2. "Oh, well. Who needs grandchildren anyhow?"

Michael Sinder, Aberdeen, Md.

1. "Ten cents a dance . . ."
2. "*Nine* cents a dance."

Ron Green, Yonkers, N.Y.

1. "Well, of course the third set of tests were just as inconclusive, and the doctors couldn't tell a thing from the x-rays. That's why they ordered the fourth set of tests, because at *that* point they still didn't know what I had . . ."
2. "I wish to hell it was lockjaw."

Douglas Braverman, East Meadow, N.Y.

1. "Now relax. This inoculation isn't going to hurt. . . ."
2. "Oh, my God, I am heartily sorry for having offended thee . . ."

Peggy Osofsky, Hilo, Hawaii

1. "Hey, you gotta try this coke! It's supposed to be 90 percent pure, crystal rock flake or something. It cost me a bundle, but . . ."
2. "Where the hell did he get that leisure suit?"

Davey Lubin, Brooklyn

1. "Enjoying myself? You have got to be kidding. This so-called party is absolutely the pits. I understand our hostess only gives these bashes because her husband is too stupid to make his own business contacts. Actually, I haven't met her yet, but I hear she's . . ."
2. "Shall I tell her now or let her go on?"

Barbara Allen, Ridgewood, N.J.

1. "Are you Jewish?"
2. "Oy, veh."

Richard Grossman, N.Y.C.

1. "I've got this really nice guy for you. He's kinda tall, well—very tall. And he's got a nice full head of hair—he's really got a nice full head of hair—he's really got a lot of hair, and he's real outdoorsy, y'know? And well, he, ah, oh yeah, he looks just like that movie star, what's-his-name. . . ."
2. "King Kong."

Bobbie Jean Patrick, Staten Island

1. "Bentley, I've been thinking."
2. "That's a first."

Alan Levine, Copiague, N.Y.

1. "They're doing the hustle."
2. "*Really?* I thought maybe it was the dance of death."

Jack Schindler, Brooklyn Heights

1. ". . . I really ought to stop by Mom's to pick up some T-shirts before we hit the Hamptons. Say, you've never met Mom, have you?"
2. ". . . champagne lace, I guess it's too late for pure white . . . Marion as my matron of honor . . ."

James Elward, N.Y.C.

1. "Is it true what it says on your folder—ten dollars covers everything, no tipping necessary?"
2. "Sure, if shaking hands with a girl is your idea of sex."

Richard Fried, Brooklyn

1. "If anyone knows why this man and this woman should not be joined in the bond of holy matrimony, let him speak now or forever hold his peace."
2. "The line forms to the left."

Larry Laiken, Bayside, N.Y.

1. "Harry and I went to extraordinary lengths to find this wedding gift for you."
2. "Yes, I go to the same bank."

Joel Schechter, Brooklyn

1. "Play it, Sam."
2. "Play it yourself."

Madeline Shikar, N.Y.C.

1. "Mother was right! She said when I was ready to settle down it would be with a wholesome, honest, natural girl like you."
2. "Thank you, Paine Webber; thank you, Ultrabrite; thank you, Miss Clairol; thank you, Erno Laszlo; thank you, Playtex . . ."

Abby Merrill, N.Y.C.

1. "You see, doctor, I have this dream—nightmare, really—where I'm standing on a corner, broke, asking for a handout . . ."
2. "Oh, dammit, I forgot to send the alimony check again."

Ruth Migdal, Brooklyn

1. "M—O.K.!"
2. "Yecch."

Margaret D. Dale, Longmeadow, Mass.

1. "Are you listening to me?"
2. "The one day I leave my umbrella home, and look at those clouds . . ."

Gregory Greenberg, N.Y.C.

1. "I'm thinking of having my sex changed."
2. "I thought you already had."

Walter Bossert, Chatham, N.J.

1. "Waiter! Bring me an order of canapés à la bayonnaise. Then I'll have the anguilles au vert followed by bisque d'ecrevisses. After that I'd like agneau rôti à l'arlésienne with cêpes à la périgourdine and pommes de terre savoyardes. I'll finish with tarte bourbonnaise and café filtre."
2. "One number three."

Jay M. Tischenkel, North Miami, Fla.

1. "I love you too, darling . . ."
2. "Willie Mays, Mickey Mantle, Whitey Ford, Tom Seaver, Pete Rose . . ."

similarly: Jeff Baron, Boston, Mass.
Grace Katz, Rutland, Vt.

1. "Take a deep breath and bear down hard."
2. "I wonder if it's too late to change my MIND."

Judy Disla, N.Y.C.

1. "On examining you, your uterus seemed a little enlarged and I think you need a hysterectomy. . . ."
2. "I wish I were *his* doctor . . ."

S. J. Vindekilde, Chicago, Ill.

1. "I saw the most fascinating program on PBS yesterday."
2. "*Sesame Street*?"

Peri Crystal, Scarsdale, N.Y.

1. "Gimme 'nother lil drinkie an'en I rrreally gotta go. Wha' time zit anyhoo?"
2. "About a fifth after one."

J. M. Riordan, Laguna Beach, Calif.

1. "Just saw a preview of that new mystery with the surprise ending. Had no idea the mass murderer was the priest."
2. "Thanks a lot."

Jeanne Remusat, Forest Hills, N.Y.

1. "Do you come here often?"
2. "Yes, and I wish you didn't."

Elsie Angell, Greenville, R.I.

1. "Yes, honey, I do think that Joyce is very cerebral."
2. "Who is she?"

Andrew A. Feeney, Old Greenwich, Conn.

1. "Dr. Aylesworth, this is Madge Brumling. You said to phone today about my ankle—you gave me some pills . . ."
2. "Brumling . . . Brumling . . ."

M. T. Lester, West Los Angeles, Calif.

1. "Look here, Buster, if you're not going to take me home, the least you can do is call me a cab."
2. "O.K. You're a cab."

Mark Gluckstern, Denver, Colo.

1. "This just in from the newsroom. Generalissimo Francisco Franco is still dead."
2. "I am?"

Carolyn Band, Newton Highlands, Mass.

Unusual Classified

PONCHO VILLA—**Raincoats**
PHARAOH FAUCET MAJORS—**Plumbing Fit for a King.**
ADIDAS ABABA—**Sporting Gear, All Sizes.**
COTS IN JAMMERS—**Bunks for Boats**

Above, candidates for our Unusual Classified Directory. Competitors were asked for one fanciful business listing.

Report: Some confusion here with Fractured Names—but was it not ever thus? Repeats, therefore, are both new and old. As which of us is not? Here now, those very repeats, and have some mysterious beauty fluid yourself, my good man: STAR DREK—Hollywood Memorabilia. CELESTE HOMES—Heavenly Real Estate. HAUT CUISINE—Grain & Feed. DONNY BROOKS—Boxing Couture. HAIR APPARENT—Toupees. SURELOCK HOMES—Alarm Systems. OEDIPUS WRECKS—Demolition. MARQUIS DE SOD, DAVE THE BUSHER, LAWN GREEN—Landscaping. SALVADOR DOLLYS—S. A. Toys. WARREN BURGER—Fast Food for Rabbits. AUDI MURPHY—Foldaway Car Beds. SAN SIMIAN—Luxury Retirement for Your Ape. HOUSE OF USHER—Falls. And, LONG JOHN SILVER—Underwear for the Affluent (see THE LITTLE LAMÉ PRINCE).

COAT D'AZURE—Police Uniforms—Imported From France.

Fred Berg, Boston, Mass.

TEARASS BULBA—Emergency Lighting Repairs.

Sol Maiman, Long Island City, N.Y.

CLOTHES BUT NO CIGAR—Antismokers Boutique.

Jack Rose, N.Y.C.

KATMANDU—Musicians' Credit Union.

Alan Kroker, Oak Park, Mich.

ARRIVEDERCI ROOMER—Hotel Foreclosures.

Amy Schreiber, Bklyn.

VIVALAH COMPANY—Paper Towels for Jewish Mothers.

Oscar Weigle, Whitestone, N.Y.

ALL THE KING'S MEN—Jigsaw Puzzles.

William N. Sanchez, Maplewood, N.J.

STRATA VARIOUS—Geological Specimens.

Margie Bond, Old Bethpage, N.Y.

APPAREL OF MONKEYS—Costumers, *Planet of the Apes.*

Don Hauptman, N.Y.C.

CAPTAIN & CHENILLE—Bedspreads to Order.

Dita Greene, Sayville, N.Y.

SOLOMON GRUNDY—Week-at-a-Glance Calendars.

Rebecca White, N.Y.C.

KELLY MOONTEETH—Space Souvenirs.

Eleanor Paul, Bklyn.

FADE ACCOMPLI—Prewashed Jeans.

Ed and Dodi Schultz, N.Y.C.

MACKEREL ON 34TH STREET—Fresh Fish in the City.

Due Losing, Montpelier, Vt.

PORGY & BASS—Sole Food.

Jim Baldassare, N.Y.C.
Iris Bass, Bklyn.

FORREST TUCKER—Sleeping Bags.
George Manley, Providence, R.I.

SPUR OF THE MOMENT—Latest Cowboy Fashions.
Michael Minard, N.Y.C.

RUIN ARLEDGE—Archaeologist.
Emma Kendzior, Cheshire, Conn.

HELLO YOUNG LOAFERS—Teen Shoes.
Oliver M. Neshamkin, M.D., N.Y.C.

REAL TORS—Mountain Land Sales.
Margaux McMillan, Orinda, Calif.

SUN AND LOUVERS—Venetian Blinds
Broad St. Law Library, Columbus, Ohio

NIGHT CRULLER—24-Hour Doughnut Shoppe.
Lee Edes, Washington, D.C.

ZERO MUSCATEL—We Carry *Almost* All Wines.
Donald R. Jacoby, Fair Lawn, N.J.

HUE DOWNS—Colorful Pillows.
Bruce J. Schachter, Bronx

O.K. CORAL—Polynesian Discount Jewelry.
Ellen Dawson, N.Y.C.

AD LIB—Employment Agency for Women.
Simi Kirschner, Bronx

PHOTO FINNISH—Helsinki Camera Shop.
Richard Fried, Bklyn.

STAR TRICK—Celebrity Escort Service.
David Jarrard, Atlanta, Ga.

TSAR TREK—Defunct. See *Intourist.*
Alex Vaughn, Old Lyme, Conn.

HEIR CONDITIONERS—Tutoring for Royalty.

Ernest Boehm, N.Y.C.

CHILL WILLS—Eskimo Estate Specialist.

Gary R. Claps, N.Y.C.

WONTONAMERA—Chinese/Spanish Restaurant.

Iris Goldstein, Bklyn.

MOPEY DICK—Private Detective.

Andrew Messetti, Flushing Meadows, N.Y.

COUSIN CUISINE—Family-Style Restaurant.

Pericles Crystal, Scarsdale, N.Y.

PERICLES CRYSTAL—Athenian Glassware.

Nancy Dickinson, Waterford, Conn.

HONORÉ DE BALZAC—Sports Trophies.

Joe Nalpin, Baldwin, N.Y.

PARAFFINALIA—Candle Works.

Todd D. Ellner, Shawnigan Lake, B.C.

CHEZ STADIUM—Lap Robes, Astroturf, Hot Dogs, Pompons.

Myrna Glick, Wayne, N.J.
sp. ment.: Dorothy Green, Yonkers, N.Y.

GATOR AID—Everglades Environmental Group.

Jay Hoster, Columbus, Ohio

SWINGING SHINGLES—Modern Roof Repair.

Jean Edes, Rockville, Md.

1. SOCKS FIFTH AVENUE—High-Class Hose.
2. SEX FIFTH AVENUE—Posh Massages.

1. *Shirley Rappoport, Piermont, N.Y.*
2. *Bob Boland, N.Y.C.*

WOMEN'S WEAR DELI—Garment-District Eatery.

Christy and Arnold Brown, N.Y.C.

HIC HAEC HOC—Loans.

J. Z. Melson, Bklyn.

ABE BEAM—Lincoln Logs.

Bob Colonna, Philenda Stryker, Providence, R.I.

CISTERN CHAPELS—Religious Reservoirs.

Joseph Brilla, Woburn, Mass.

MOANER LEASER—Professional Mourners.

Judith Klein, E. Brunswick, N.J.

JEAN-PIERRE RUMPLE—French Dry Cleaning.

Hanns Kolmar, San Francisco, Calif.

MARCUS WALLABY—Australian Veterinarian.

Diane Gentry, Norristown, Pa.

TOWED AWAY—Frog Removal.

Thomas M. Quinn, Carnegie, Pa.

PEAS AND QUEUES—Vegetarian Cafeteria.

Anita Greenberg, Flushing, N.Y.

ROUTES—Travel Agency.

Margaret D. Dale, Longmeadow, Mass.

CHUCK'S CAR BORROW—Auto Rental.

Alice M. Yohalem, N.Y.C.

NU HAVEN—Connecticut Home for the Jewish Aged.

Eve Thompson, Upper Montclair, N.J.

LEGGS BENEDICT—Socks for Monks.

George M. Jones, Elizabeth, N.J.

EL DOCTOROW—S.A. Medical Services Building.

Donna Cooper, Bellerose, N.Y.

EL DOC TORO—Specializing in Bull Shots.

Richard J. Hafey, Morningdale, Mass.

FRANKIE & JOHNNY'S BALLISTICS LAB.

Flora Boltz, Elizabeth, N.J.

TINKER BELLES—Handy Persons.

Ethel Jacobson, Lynn, Mass.

EAVES ST. LAURENT—Designer Roofs.

Joel Goldstein, Cincinnati, Ohio

PANORAMA—School for Critics.

Tony Crea, N.Y.C.

BUMPER CROP—Used Auto Parts.

Vic Rizzo, Levittown, N.Y.

RUDY VALET—Gentlemen's Gentleman.

J. P. Ackerman, Forest Hills, N.Y.

THOMAS PAINE CO.—Sensible Plate Glass.

Ellen Schor, Bklyn.

NOUVEAU RICCI—*Parfumeur* to Arrivistes.

Raymond E. Benenson, Niskayuna, N.Y.

DEUS EX MACKINAW—Outerwear for Atheists.

Jerry Weinberg, Passaic, N.J.

ALIEN CORN—Tapes of BBC Sitcoms.

James Fechheimer, Glen Head, N.Y.

ELVIRA CARDIGAN—Sweaters.

Joel Frome Crystal, Scarsdale, N.Y.

LAUREN BAA CALL—Shepherd Instruction.

Dr. George Friedman, Bethesda, Md.

GRIME 'N' PUNISHMENT—S-M Laundromat.

J. Bickart, N.Y.C.

ARMY SURPLICE—Chaplains' Vestments.

Alice Wofford, Port Washington, N.Y.

BEOWOOF—Old English Sheep Dogs.

Ellen Burr, New Paltz, N.Y.

MARY PICKFJORD—Norwegian Guided Tours.

Ron Luzenberg, Philadelphia, Pa.

BALLET RUSSE DE MONTY PYTHON—Fools, Russian.

Grace Katz, Rutland, Vt.

Oppress Clippings

Gentlemen: While most people do not take an active interest in such matters, I, for one, should like to comment favorably on your *New York Times* Magazine cover picturing the water buffalo . . .

It is midnight. Shortskirts (as we'll call her here) has been hustling since 4 P.M. and Dude won't like it if she turns up with less than two hundred . . .

Above, oppress clippings. Competitors were asked for the opening sentences of a feature, profile, letter to the editor or what-have-you of a similarly unengrossing nature.

Report: Among the uninviting, the following repeats: Arcane data correcting obscure misstatements or misprints. Pols denying candidacy. Baseball stats. Profiles of dismal persons easily lacking a frontal view. Boring reviews of boring-er works. Furious editorial replies: "Your unfair attack on aphid extermination struck me . . . please cancel, etc." And, to the Competition Editor: "Were sublety rather than favoritism your forte, perhaps the nuances of my entry to Comp. 254 would not have eluded . . ." As Pirandello remarked, when you're right, you're right.

Of course she's a star. Friendly, but wary at first, she sits on the large orange velvet sofa in her suite at the Sherry Netherland as she declaims, "I really *hate* to give interviews unless I'm sure I'm talking to someone on my intellectual level—you know what I mean? . . ."

Rosemary Bascome, Shelter Island, N.Y.

"*Tomorrow and tomorrow and tomorrow* . . ."

—WILLIAM SHAKESPEARE

For 89-year-old Matilda Laird, like thousands of other senior citizens who live alone, there will be no more tomorrows.

Norm Bloom, Ottawa, Canada

The 200th birthday of the United States will be here in just a few weeks, and Maple Grove, Idaho, will be ready for it.

Richard Fried, Brooklyn

When we arranged to meet Marjoe Gortner for breakfast, we didn't know what to expect.

Barry M. Brooks, Chicago, Ill.

The year was 1925. Scott and Zelda were scandalizing Europe again. Bathtub gin was the national drink, some say even in the White House. Weimar was struggling to survive. Meanwhile, in Plains, Georgia, Miz Lillian felt life stirring inside her. . . .

Al Dale, Chicago, Ill.

Capturing insects in this part of Africa does have its lighter side. At *n'umba* (daybreak), as I took my *trekka* (stroll) through the *gambogambi* (tall grass), I glimpsed the *b'windayumba* (head man) of the neighboring *kraal* (village). He greeted me thus: "*Lamgourna!*" ("Good morrow sir or commendable person!").

Jack Ryan, N.Y.C.

He's not attached to any church; the streets are his congregation. Kids. Out of the rubble of their rumbles he has heard their cry, "Yearning to be *Me!*" His office? "Just a store-front rumpus room for raps," he shrugs. The kids call him Father Hep.

Webb R. Marris, Pacific Palisades, Calif.

He sprawls on the ornate sofa in his Plaza Hotel suite, blue work shirt half unbuttoned, Levi's tight, Gucci boots resting on the edge of the coffee table. A pretty blonde enters and disappears into another room. He fixes his famous blue eyes on mine. . . .

Dan Williams, N.Y.C.

Breaker one-nine, breaker one-nine. You got Wallingford Fats here, proceeding north into Hartford town on I-91. Is it clean and green up ahead, or is it Bear Country?
The above may sound like gibberish, but in fact it's the lingo of a craze that is sweeping . . .

Chilie Vaughn, Manhasset, N.Y.

A series of recent discoveries has linked prehuman primates of half a million years ago with stone tools.

Bruce Karp, N.Y.C.

Myrna Smith keeps a lion in her Sheridan Square apartment. Along with a cobra, rhinoceros, elephant, and dozens of other animals. But her neighbors don't mind a bit because the menagerie isn't flesh and blood, but fashioned out of cloth and cotton batting. . . .

Charles Librizzi, Atlantic City, N.J.

Who has not been awed by the dazzling insouciance of the fly who, endowed by Nature with exquisite sensibility, elegantly eludes the assiduously computed aim of a murderous attack?

Barbara Bassett, Alexandria, Va.

The average person has twenty of us. Even though we're dead, we get cut, trimmed, adorned, lacquered, bitten, and filed. Who are we? We're Joe's nails. . . .

Miles Klein, E. Brunswick, N.J.

Elizabeth Taylor, Richard Burton, Princess Margaret, Margaux Hemingway, Barbara Walters, the Loch Ness Monster . . .

Larry Laiken, Bayside, N.Y.

Whatever anyone might say about Ben Bradlee, even his worst enemies admit he has style. He uses it, abuses it, flaunts it, contradicts it—it's made him what he is. Roommate Sally Quinn agrees. . . .

Barbara R. Weiss, Pleasantville, N.Y.

In this so-called Democracy, where Individual Rights are daily trampled underfoot by the Authoritarian Establishment, it doubtless comes as no surprise to your readers that in nearly every Worker-exploiting Restaurant in this City there are separate Lavatories for Men and Women but none for . . .

Fred Berg, Boston, Mass.

This would be his twelfth performance in eight days. At 38, the charismatic Tartar is in a grueling race against time. Pushing his body to the limits of . . .

Susan Weinstein, N.Y.C.

Dear Doctor: Are fallen arches hereditary? My husband and I both suffer from this condition and now that I am expecting our first . . .

Iris Bass, Brooklyn

Few who pass her cash register at Ace Foods on Bellevue Avenue recognize the lady with the graying hair and matronly figure, but if they did, they'd realize that Mrs. Pietropinto was once Priscilla Sweet, in 1944 one of the brightest starlets on the MGM lot.

Nancy Dickinson, Waterford, Conn.

Editor: The next time I hear someone say that your town is a cold, unfriendly place, I'll tell him of my experience last night on a deserted highway: a woman from out of town, alone in the rain with a flat . . .

Priscilla G. Osborne, Boston, Mass.

Stephen Sondheim, often called the theater's greatest composer, sips his chilled Chablis and talks about his score for the new Hal Prince-directed *Shrouds,* a musical look at the influence of death on contemporary urban society. . . .

Gladys Wolff, N.Y.C.

She lives in a neat house that sits upon a well-trimmed lawn. Her father is a promising bank executive. Her mother is pretty and active in the arts. Her life seems ideal. Yet Judy is a teenage alcoholic.

Rebecca V. Rosenthal, Alexandria, Va.

The Pittsburgh Community Theatre Players, who now and again come up with something really special, hit the mirth jackpot last night at the Downtown Parish House with their production of the laff riot, *Judy Makes a Mistake.*

Lewy Olfson, South Lyme, Conn.

Dear Ann: Please settle this argument for us. My husband and I have had what I thought was a happy marriage for twelve years. I recently found a collection of ladies' undergarments (in his size) tucked beneath his old socks. . . .

Paula Drechsler, Palisades, N.Y.

To the Restaurant Editor: We couldn't possibly have been to the same restaurant. On our visit, we found no waiting line, the salad was crisp . . .

Debbie Markwitz, University Heights, Ohio

Every morning petite, blue-eyed Mary Lou Harper rises at 5 A.M. She styles her platinum hair and applies her makeup with the skill of the fashion model she once was. Now the driver of a twenty-ton rig . . .

Robin Mensch, Westfield, N.J.

Fred Johnson wasn't the type of person who'd normally go down to the corner grocery at night to get a pack of cigarettes. Fred didn't like walking at night. In fact, Fred was trying to quit smoking. . . .

Newsroom, the Times, *Trenton, N.J.*

"No two days are the same. I'm meeting thousands of people. There's tremendous responsibility." Stockbroker? Public-relations executive? Actually, Arnold Quigley is a toll collector at the George Washington Bridge. At 43, he's one of the best in his field. With six children, he has to be.

Peter Burkard, New Rochelle, N.Y.

To the Editor of the *Times:* How are you? I am fine. . . .

David Ross, Highwood, Ill.

Unconventional Greeting Cards

CONGRATULATIONS ON BEING READMITTED TO THE BAR.
HAPPY BIRTHDAY TO THE NONAGENARIAN—DON'T STAND TOO NEAR THE CAKE.
SO YOU'VE BEEN ELECTED MAYOR OF CASTERBRIDGE!

Above, unconventional greeting cards. Competitors were asked for an imprudent greeting card message for an impudent occasion.

Report: Greetings from pale horse, pale writer. This group, large but unwieldy, at once provided mirth and revulsion. (As what, these days, does not?) The dubious taste of congratulatory cards for tubal ligations, vasectomies, and sex-change operations dimmed considerably beside the hilarity of abortion and legionnaires' disease. Further favored topics: congratulations to the divorced priest, the hijackee, letter bombee, plea bargainer, *Titanic* passenger, defector, closet emerger, candidate for exorcism, and welfare recipient. To the attempted suicide—better luck next time. Many happy returns on your IRS investigation. Congrtlatns on gradtng fr spd ritng skl. Congratulations on your lobotomy.

SO YOU BOYCOTTED YOUR FIRST OLYMPIC GAMES!

Ronald Weinger, Valley Stream, N.Y.

CONGRATULATIONS FROM HALSTON ON YOUR FALL COLLECTION

Ed Millard, Los Angeles, Calif.

wElcom 2 thE Conggressionnle Typnmg POOL froM you r NEW ColllеaGUEs

Bette McLaughlin, Brookline, Mass.

CONGRATULATIONS ON BEING CONSIDERED FOR VICE-PRESIDENT

Stephen Gelb, Brooklyn

ELATED BIRTHDAY WISHES TO MY TWIN!

Daniel J. Moriarty, Hollywood, Calif.

THANK YOU FOR THE ONE-NIGHT STAND

Lee Powell, N.Y.C.

VALENTINE, I'M NOT SURE HOW I FEEL ABOUT YOU

Christine Barber, Kennett Square, Pa.

SO YOU'VE JUST FOUND OUT YOU WERE ADOPTED!

Jeff Monasch, Brooklyn

CONGRATULATIONS ON YOUR RESERVATION AT WINDOWS ON THE WORLD

Celia R. C. Mandel, E. Meadow, N.Y.

SO YOU DROVE TO FLORIDA AND DIDN'T STOP IN PLAINS!

Denise Accardi, Huntsville, Ala.

"ON YOUR 50TH WEDDING ANNIVERSARY . . . I SAID ON YOUR 50TH WEDDING ANNIVERSARY . . ."

R. Drezen, Metairie, La.

WE ARE PROUD TO KNOW WEST POINT'S GRADUATING SENIOR

Anthony Gray, Closter, N.J.

SO YOU'RE OFF TO SEE THE WIZARD

Oliver J. Dembling, N.Y.C.

CONGRATULATIONS ON YOUR WEDDING TO HIS MAJESTY HENRY VIII

Ann Maricle, Sweet Briar, Va.

HEAR YOU MADE IT INTO THE GUINNESS BOOK OF WORLD RECORDS

Edith Berman, Bellrose, N.Y.

CONGRATULATIONS ON BEING TRANSFERRED TO WAUWATOSA, WISCONSIN

Michael Deskey, Wauwatosa, Wis.

IN APPRECIATION OF YOUR THANKS FOR MY RESPONSE TO YOUR BEST WISHES AFTER MY EXPRESSION OF GOOD LUCK FOLLOWING YOUR CONGRATULATIONS ON MY ANNOUNCEMENT

Joel Schechter, Brooklyn

THANK YOU FOR SENDING US YOUR RESUME

Nikki Rosa, N.Y.C.

SO YOU DANCED FOR HEROD!

Everett S. Joline, Huntington, N.Y.

SO GLAD YOUR OPINION WAS SOLICITED BY YANKELOVICH

Michael Agress, M.D., N.Y.C.

CONGRATULATIONS ON OPENING IN "EQUUS"

S. Pombo, Haines City, Fla.

MUGGED? UGH!

Carol White, N.Y.C.

WELCOME, EARTH WARRIORS, TO THE PEACEFUL PLANET, MARS

Walter S. Boone, Valdese, N.C.

HAPPY ANNIVERSARY! IT WOULD HAVE BEEN A YEAR TODAY!

Lori Pearson, Woodcliff Lake, N.J.

CONGRATULATIONS ON BEATING THE MORALS CHARGE FROM ONE WHOSE LIFE YOU CHANGED IN THE CLOAKROOM AT P.S. 141

John E. C. Taylor, N.Y.C.

SORRY I MISSED YOUR BIRTHDAY—I THOUGHT YOU DIED YEARS AGO

Marion Huber, Fredonia, N.Y.

CONGRATULATIONS ON YOUR APPOINTMENT. WELCOME TO SAMARRA

Mary Lambert Maricle, St. Louis, Mo.

CONGRATULATIONS ON YOUR FIRST PUBLICATION BY A VANITY PRESS

Hannah Craven, Washington, D.C.

CON-GRAT´U-LA´-TIONS ON YOUR AC-CEPT´-ANCE BY A COL´LEGE

Milton Bass, Brooklyn

SORRY I MISSED YOUR WAKE

J. Hawkes, Poughkeepsie, N.Y.

CONGRATULATIONS. YOUR T-SHIRT SAYS IT ALL

Jacqueline Scott, N.Y.C.

A NOTE OF THANKS FOR THE MUSHROOMS YOU SENT UNCLE PAUL AND THEN THE FLOWERS

Joseph Falk, E. Elmhurst, N.Y.

NICE TRY

Allan Herman, Downsview, Ont.

BEST WISHES FOR A HAPPY AND SUCCESSFUL FIRST MARRIAGE

Marc Rosen, Pompton Plains, N.J.

CONGRATULATIONS ON GETTING THE CHILDREN

Mark Sherman, New Paltz, N.Y.

BEST WISHES FOR YOUR SPEEDY RECOVERY. GLAD IT WAS HERPES SIMPLEX

H. D. Forester, Phoenix, Ariz.

BORN AGAIN! MAZEL TOV!

Ellen Conford, Massapequa, N.Y.

CONGRATULATIONS STAR! LOOKING FORWARD TO SEEING YOU IN THE (choose one: TOURING, MOVIE, SHOWCASE, HOME BOX OFFICE, COMMUNITY PLAYERS DINNER THEATER, STATE FAIR, HIGH SCHOOL, CHURCH LEAGUE, JONES BEACH, ALL-MALE) COMPANY OF "A CHORUS LINE"

Bob Kocheck, Perth Amboy, N.J.

SORRY YOU'VE LOST YOUR READING GLASSES

Debbi Sherwood, Titusville, N.J.

BLESSINGS ON YOUR UNSTRUCTURED RELATIONSHIP

Virginia Feine, Hartford, Conn.
sp. mention: Ethel Jacobson, Lynn, Mass.

DEEPEST SYMPATHY AND BELATED BIRTHDAY WISHES

Stephen Sadowsky, Vassar College, Pa.

SORRY TO HEAR ABOUT YOUR PAROLE VIOLATION

Jonathan Abrams, Brooklyn

GOOD LUCK ON YOUR SUBWAY RIDE

Sissy Cargill, Southport, Conn.

CONGRATULATIONS. A VOODOO DOLLY HAS BEEN NAMED FOR YOU. BEST OF LUCK

Rosemary Bascome, Shelter Island, N.Y.

OUR SYMPATHY ON THE DEATH OF YOUR GIANT SEA TORTOISE

Len Elliott, Auburn, Wash.

CONGRATULATIONS ON GETTING YOUR ENTRY PRINTED. WANTED TO BUY YOU "THE FINAL DAYS" AS A GIFT, BUT IT WOULD BE WRONG

Joel Lind, Alexandria, Va.

Conversation Openers

"See that waiter? I could have sworn he was doing thirty-to-life at Leavenworth. . . ."

Above, a Conversation Opener. Competitors were asked for one-liners to tempt a stranger into further colloquy.

Report: "Hi. I'm Father Damian. Put 'er there." The repeats as follows: "Hello. My name is Michael J. Anthony, and I have a cashier's check for one million dollars tax-free." "Didn't you used to be a woman?" "Is that a twenty-dollar bill under your shoe?" "As I was saying to Truman and Bianca . . ." "I can get that for you wholesale." "So, what do you think is wrong with this city, cabbie?" "Anyone find half a bikini?" "Hi, I'm with Masters and Johnson." "Don't move, I just dropped my contact lens." And, "Do you speak English?" Maybe. What did you have in mind?

"It should be called the New York Bank for Waiting."

Stuart Schwartzberg, N.Y.C.

"My uncle, the casting director, is looking for an attractive housewife for a couple of love scenes in a new Redford-Newman flick."

Jack Rose, N.Y.C.

"Hey Mac, I found the rectal thermometer—what should I do with it?"

Jack Ryan, N.Y.C.

"Excuse me; my name's Goodbar, have you been waiting long?"
Debby Lambert, McLean, Va.

"What's this I hear about Jackie Onassis marrying Jilly Rizzo?"
Norman Dickens, N.Y.C.

"Knock, knock."
Lee A. Davis, Douglaston, N.Y.

"Hi there, stranger—care to have some colloquy furthered?"
Miles Klein, E. Brunswick, N.J.

"Oh, by the way, did you know I'm wearing Hitler's old shoes?"
Pat McCormick, No. Hollywood, Calif.
Arnie Kogen, Encino, Calif.

"Excuse me, your shoes are on fire."
Joseph L. Streich, Bklyn.

"Hi! I'm Stanley Friedman . . ."
Sam N. Lehman-Wilzig, N.Y.C.

"My occupation is Urban Guerrilla."
Joel Schecter, Bklyn.

"My name is Asher Lev."
L. Neukrug, Bklyn.

"Madam, I'm Adam."
Jack Paul, Bklyn.

"Hi, I'm Leon, an accountant from Rego Park. During a previous life I was queen of Holland."
Buffy Kogen, Encino, Calif.

"Hello, my name is Howard Hughes."
H. Hughes, Nassau, Bahamas

"Hi. I'm Arthur Ash."
Arthur S. Ash, Mt. Vernon, N.Y.

"You know that's the very stool Ray Milland sat on when they shot *The Lost Weekend* here."

Mark Wolfson, Spring Valley, N.Y.

"Pardon me, but don't you think you've had enough to drink?"

Steven B. Black, Philadelphia, Pa.

"If you don't talk to me, I'll pour my drink on your head."

Major Fred Sims, Washington, D.C.

"Which one do you think is the male?"

Mrs. Fran Weiss, White Plains, N.Y.

"Are you a boy or a girl?"

Sandra Birdsong, Washington, D.C.

"Want some pancakes, little girl?"

Kathleen Krumm, Dayton, Ohio

"Did you happen to see a small vial marked 'Shellfish Toxin'?"

Larry Laiken, Bayside, N.Y.

"Everyone in *our* department got a raise."

Harry M. Schwalb, Pittsburgh, Pa.

"Would you happen to know the Suicide Emergency Hot Line number?"

Marilyn Shafer, N.Y.C.

"Why don't you let me heat up your orange juice?"

George Gallego, N.Y.C.

"Drinks are on me."

Diane Gentry, Norristown, Pa.

"I've found that people who say nothing are generally ignorant."

Judith Herzen, N.Y.C.

"Can you read my lips, Mr. Marceau?"

Michael Schreiber, Bklyn.

"See? Right there, next to the mailbox. A Martian."
Jean D. Brown, Bangor, Me.

"Are you the owner of this bridge?"
Marilyn Conti, Summit, N.J.

"Pardon me for yawning, but I was up all night proofreading J. D. Salinger's new novel. . . ."
William Steinkellner, Hollywood, Calif.

"Turning lead into gold isn't as tricky as it looks."
George Malko, N.Y.C.

"That's the lieutenant governor over there. His wife's got an eighteen-inch neck."
David G. McAneny, Upper Darby, Pa.

"Oh, no, there's Frank Sinatra. What'll I do if he starts bothering me again?"
Terry Heines, Albany, N.Y.

"In all fairness, you are entitled to know how much is in the envelope you just saw me pick up from the sidewalk."
Helen J. Gilman, Ocean, N.J.

"Don't ever go into that store and ask for pajamas. It's a signal!"
A. Almet, Riverdale, N.Y.

"I'll give you $50 for that old T-shirt."
Anne Hamill, N.Y.C.

"WHAT?"
James Ewing Murray, Greenwich, Conn.

"Just drop one of these in your gas tank and then fill it up with water."
Gene Nichols, Spring Valley, N.Y.

"Don't look now."
Mrs. E. M. Weyer, Westbrook, Conn.

"Pardon me, but that's *my* rice pudding you're sitting on."

Wexler, McCarron & Roth, N.Y.C.

"That's funny, I've been to bed with everyone in this room."

Tom Morrow, N.Y.C.

"Which one's the Druid?"

Alan Jorgensen, Newton, Mass.

"Okay, Mac, pull over."

Sidney Abrams, Bklyn.

"I found a way of cheating Con Ed. . . ."

Sal Rosa, N.Y.C.

"Did you happen to see a monkey pass by in the last few minutes?"

Phyllis Kelly, Locust Valley, N.Y.

"Is this the dog that talks to Jesuits?"

Robert Fabian, N.Y.C.

"I guess you aren't interested in discussing the Patty Hearst case either."

T. Incantalupo, Woodside, N.Y.

"You know, you've got to hand it to Charlie Manson."

Mark W. Johnson, Bethesda, Md.

"Now that this car is stuck between floors I think you should know that I was hurrying down to the men's room."

Albert G. Miller, N.Y.C.

"They sure keep the urinals clean here, don't they?"

T. D. C. Kuch, Vienna, Va.

"Did they capture it yet?"

Ms. S. Kirschner, Bklyn.

"Congratulate me. My wife had a baby girl."

Joel Frome Crystal, Scarsdale, N.Y.

"Am I on 'Candid Camera'?"

Linda Quirini, Greenville, R.I.

"Do you know what's in the center of Kojak's lollipops?"

Louis B. Raffel, Phoenix, Ariz.

"Columbus not only didn't discover America, she never actually left Genoa."

D. D. Heines, Albany, N.Y.

"I understand our pilot has an almost perfect record."

Teddy Huxford, Skaneateles, N.Y.

"Gee, you make a gifted lifeguard. . . ."

Ms. Agnes Molnar, Morristown, N.J.

"Take it from me, the Dalai Lama is an all right guy."

Levy Children, Monsey, N.Y.

"I'm looking for a tennis-lover to housesit for me in Martinique."

Walter L. Olesen, Westport, Conn.

"Miss, on what floor would I find silver stakes to put through vampires' hearts?"

Oliver M. Neshamkin, M.D., N.Y.C.

"Would you believe it? I've just come from surgery. They can't find a heart."

Paul Weiss, Washington, D.C.

"Would you mind talking to me for a minute? There's someone I'm trying to avoid."

Marcia Amsterdam, N.Y.C.

"When they cut back service on this line, how will anyone know the difference?"

Bruce Karp, Flushing, N.Y.

"See that escaped felon? I could have sworn he used to be a waiter."

Pericles Crystal, Scarsdale, N.Y.

Conversation Stoppers

"Would you believe that I had cosmetic surgery only last week?"

Above, a Conversation Stopper. Competitors were asked for one line guaranteed to doom further colloquy.

Report: "Hi, I'm Danny Thomas's plumber, and here's what's goin' on." The repeated themes: Therapy or diet news. Facts about, or pictures of, the kiddies. Lengthy plot descriptions of films or books. Lengthier jokes with forgotten punch lines. Home movies. Travelogues. Unappetizing food discussed post, or during, consumption. As to which, much talk of communicable diseases (leprosy was big) and abnormal appearance, personal or otherwise. For no reason, a proliferation of comments about socks. Yes, socks. Sample remarks: "My cousin's brother-in-law is Morty Gunty's agent." "I just happen to be of Polish extraction myself." "My broker is E. F. Hutton, and E. F. Hutton says . . ." "I think this room is bugged." "Meet Erwin—he's the funniest person." "This is a recording." And, "I just won that contest thing in the back of *New York* Magazine." Listen. What can I tell you?

"Hi, my name is Margaux—Yippie Skippie! M-A-R-G-A-U-X!"

Isabel J. Will, St. Matthews, Ken.

"That is what *I* call hide and seek."

Andrew A. Feeney, Old Greenwich, Conn.

"I'm Henry Marcotte and this is an NBC-TV editorial."

Tom Russell, Ft. Ogden, Fla.

"Who left this in the bathroom?"

Linda Quirini, Greenville, R.I.

"Got interesting mail from a publisher the other day—seems I have six chances to win $100,000 . . ."

Murray Frey, San Jose, Calif.

"Hi, I'm Bill Bruner, grew up in L.A., graduated from Princeton in '56, now write copy for J. Walter Thompson and live with my wife and three kids in Greenwich, love tennis and sailing, who are you and what do *you* do?"

Terry Gross, Kerhonkson, N.Y.

"Open wider, please."

Barbara A. Huff, N.Y.C.

"I don't think I've ever seen a U.F.O."

A. B. Callahan, Pittsburgh, Pa.

"Not necessarily, I never finished high school either."

Jack Levine, Long Beach, N.Y.

"My husband plays chess, Mr. Fischer."

Amy Schreiber, Bklyn.

"I do the London *Times* crossword in ink."

Dodi Schultz, N.Y.C.

"Let's all tell each other what we *really* think of each other."

Julie Swiler, Hayward, Wisc.

"I don't know, it looks like chicken."

Larry Laiken, Bayside, N.Y.

"Hi, I'm Larry Laiken of Bayside."

Judy Schwartz, N.Y.C.

"Did you catch this morning's 'AM America'?"

Pericles Crystal, Scarsdale, N.Y.

"But I *like* men to open doors for me, don't you?"

Pauline Dubkin, Phoenix, Ariz.

"I do."

Jules Schumacher, Rockville Centre, N.Y.

"Nothing is any good any more."

Peggy Bussey, Greenwich, Conn.

"You describe a nice investment opportunity, but I should have told you I have no money."

Janet Ellner LaRossa, Bronx

"I'd like to borrow $100."

Mrs. Arlene Goscinski, Woodside, N.Y.

"You remember Helen, don't you, the girl who solders so beautifully?"

Arthur Weller, Interlaken, N.J.

"That's okay—it's wooden."

G. R. B., Hollywood, Calif.

"Breaking my leg playing Ping-Pong was only the beginning . . ."

B. R. Cohn, Sherman Oaks, Calif.

"So I broke his nose."

Alex Thomas, Fort Clinton, Ohio

"Hitler was right about a lot of things."

Thomas Van Steenbergh, Bergenfield, N.J.

"Bear in mind that I've just completed a course in assertiveness training."

Lora A. Asdorian, Springfield, Va.

"Paul here can whistle the entire score of *Oklahoma!*"

Corinne Gillick, N.Y.C.

"Will you look at that getup?"

Sally Laiken, Whitestone, N.Y.

"Well, I've always wanted to be a fashion designer."

Edward G. Galligan II, E. Hampton, N.Y.

"Can you believe I once wore a size 7?"

Carlene Toron, Woodmere, N.Y.

"What kind of fool do you take me for?"

Elsie Angell, Greenville, R.I.

"My broker told me that Patty Hearst bought 100 shares of IBM before being kidnapped."

Kurt Beron, Greensboro, N.C.

"Where are the snows of yesteryear?"

Terry and Barbara Migdal, Bklyn.

"We had to have our septic tank pumped out."

Al Gorisek, Cleveland, Ohio

"Maybe after I practice, we can go dancing again."

Barbara Egan, Bklyn.

"Hey, Jock! How's your game?"

Dick Howell, Pittsford, N.Y.

"Vietnam? Let me tell you about Anzio . . ."

Hank Volker, N.Y.C.

"I'd like you to meet my ex-husband David, and my new husband, Jonathan."

Beryl Downey, Newark, N.J.

"I don't care what you say, I'm going to have him stuffed."

Judy Crichton, N.Y.C.

"Listen, could you do me a *really* big favor?"

Steven B. Black, Phila., Pa.

"Don't ask questions; you'll only embarrass yourself."

William Marriott, Athens, Ga.

"I was *born* in Iceland."

Margaret Clark, Lafayelle, Calif.

"I think my colostomy bag just broke."

Jack Ryan, N.Y.C.

"Surprise!"

Teddy Huxford, Skaneateles, N.Y.

"But seriously, do you think Dreyfus was innocent?"

Daily Princetonian Newsroom, N.J.

"Twenty-five years ago I didn't believe in civil rights but now I do, a little."

Emily Barnhart, Pittsburgh, Pa.

"You must be a Libra or else I simply never would have walked up to you like this."

John Walsh, Oakland, Calif.

"Do you think you could eat another human being?"

C. Bruce Gordon, Bronx

"Oh, then you're not a real doctor."

Janet S. Slifkin, Pittsburgh, Pa.

"Sixty years is a big chunk out of a man's life."

David G. McAneny, Upper Darby, Pa.

"I can spell every character in every Russian novel."

Alan Levine, Copiague, N.Y.

"I think Francis Bacon wrote all of them."

Tom Smith, Cleveland, Ohio

"Who are you?"

Stanley Stone, Oceanside, N.Y.

"I'm Anastasia, daughter of Nicholas II."

Sal Rosa, N.Y.C.

"Watch me drop my pants."

Hal Rothberg, Hollywood, Calif.

"We are pregnant."

Scott Burnham, N.Y.C.

"Now that you're finished, may I introduce you to Richard Nixon's brother Donald?"

Richard Baer, Beverly Hills, Calif.

"I can't understand why a country that can put a man on the moon can't straighten out the mess in the cities."

Martin W. Helgesen, Malverne, N.Y.

"I'm trying to stop smoking; do you have a cigarette?"

Nathan W. Blumenfeld, Flushing, N.Y.

"Your centerpiece reminds me of a story . . ."

JoAnn West, Cheverly, Md.

"I have to go to the bathroom."

Carolyn McMonegal, N.Y.C.

"Tell me, do you like string?"

Walter L. Olesen, Westport, Conn.

"My seven dogs and four cats always sleep with me."

Tom Morrow, N.Y.C.

"My wife is Jewish, so, naturally, I make every effort to understand her faith, and, each year, I mail cards to celebrate both Christmas *and* Yom Kippur."

Don Wigal, N.Y.C.

"This is my wife, she's part Chinese."

Earl A. Titman, Portsmouth, Va.

"Hi, Harvard, Class of '72."

Holly S. Kennedy, Cambridge, Mass.

"Look—I can see myself in this plate!"

Janet Chioffi, Woodstock, Vt.

"I'm pretty sure it's Limoges, but would you mind turning your plate over and checking?"

Felice Berney, N.Y.C.

"Don't mind me, I've just dropped some acid. . . ."

Jonathan Crespin, Cincinnati, Ohio

"You used to be able to get a nice green-bean-and-egg-casserole at the Exchange Buffet."

Martin Gross, N.Y.C.

"Have you consummated your marriage yet?"

K. E. O'Donnell, Milwaukee, Wis.

"You know, I've been in New York for three months now and I haven't seen any so-called beautiful people. . . ."

Mimi Cozzens, Hollywood, Calif.

"I find a piquant *je ne sais quoi* in this gazpacho, *nicht wahr?*"

James Fechheimer, Glen Head, N.Y.

"Do I seem depressed to you?"

Dennis Brite, N.Y.C.

"I've been bored all week. . . ."

P. J. Sweeney, Woodside, N.Y.

"Maybe I shouldn't tell this joke while you're eating, but it seems . . ."

Edmund Hartmann, Beverly Hills, Calif.

"You know you're the only person in this room who hasn't asked for my autograph yet."

Bella Israel, N. Miami Beach, Fla.

"That diamond isn't *real* is it?"
Marcia Grees, Philadelphia, Pa.

"I wish I had hands like yours—I bite my nails right down to the quick—LOOK!"
Leslie H. Goldenthal, Hollywood, Fla.

"It's amazing what a little bit of makeup will do for you. . . ."
Mrs. Edward P. Kennedy, Yardley, Pa.

"I hope you share my passion for *Star Trek* re-runs."
Joel Frome Crystal, Scarsdale, N.Y.

"Isn't that the place where it rains all the time?"
Alene Faveluke, Portland, Ore.

"Let me tell you how I gave up smoking those dirty things. . . ."
Sal Rosa, N.Y.C.
Nancy Joline, Huntington, N.Y.

"We just got back from a weekend marathon marriage-encounter and we've never been so much in love."
David Bakken, Arlington, Mass.

"You're not a Ms. are you?"
Elaine Anderson, N.Y.C.

"What is it that you people want, anyway?"
S. Fallon, Grand Island, N.Y.

"It might surprise you to learn that I enjoy being a housewife."
Barbara Bernstein, Los Angeles, Calif.

"She thinks like a man."
Anita Greenberg, Flushing, N.Y.

"The pattern on this china certainly makes a strong statement."
Jay McDonnell, N.Y.C.

"Hi! I'm a young filmmaker, what do you do?"
R. B. Brown, N.Y.C.

"I'm typing my autobiography."

Alan Levine, Copiague, N.Y.

"My friends call me 'Scoop.' "

Rena Turoff, N.Y.C.

"You may be interested to know that I'm a copywriter on the Black Flag roach-spray account."

Norton Bramesco, N.Y.C.

"I'm a writer for *Vending Times,* a trade magazine on vending machines."

Judy Mostowitz, Bklyn.

"Did you hear the news this morning 'bout Billie Joe?"

R. Chiappetto, Hartsdale, N.Y.

"Hi, I'm five and I just learned how to count to 100—1, 2, 3, 4 . . ."

Carol Runyan Fuchs, White Plains, N.Y.

"You're lucky that kinky hair is in."

Sidney Abrams, Bklyn.

"Excuse me, but did you just lose something?"

D. D. Ryan, N.Y.C.

"My Aunt Amelia, who is going on 88, always wipes her lipstick off on her napkin."

Mabel H. Ward, Kingston, N.Y.

"Would you go to bed with a complete stranger if it involved a matter of national security?"

Lloyd D. Uber, San Diego, Calif.

"How much does a watch like that go for?"

Eric Stevens, Newton, Mass.

"Could you cut my meat for me?"

Charlotte Laiken, Bayside, N.Y.

"I prefer sitting next to a left-handed person."

Nancy Pastor, Pittsburgh, Pa.

"Do you know where the gluttons go in Dante's *Inferno?*"

Miriam Weiss, N.Y.C.

"Isn't it disgraceful that at a big dinner like this they don't have the American flag on display somewhere?"

Alex Vaughn, Old Lyme, Conn.

"I wonder why she gave us three forks?"

P. Vajda, White Plains, N.Y.

"I've just returned from a tour of France and I'm no expert but I think that California wines are every bit as . . ."

Carlyn Huddleston, Los Angeles, Calif.

"I'm trying to think which Dick Tracy character you remind me of."

Bill Wunder, Port Washington, N.Y.

"I hardly recognized you; how did you gain so much weight?"

Bill Phillips, Lookout Mountain, Tenn.

Two for the Opening

It was a time when refinement languished, when blood ran in the gutters, when venal ambition was everywhere regarded as the talisman of princes, when simple dignity had no champion, and honor lay stillborn on the threshold of yesterday's decaying moral flesh. Alice Gracewell slept dreamlessly: She was eighteen and her future opened before her like a peony.

Above, two for the opening of *Lucky Alice,* a novel of the Middle Ages. Competitors were asked for the opening two sentences of a bad book; the first flavorful, the second deflating.

Report: The high cost of deflation included adroitly rotten writing, sexism, racism, and a soupçon of enviable bad taste. A day like all days. Many variations on "Call me Ishmael." Also, amorous letdowns, lust in the sandbox, Fear of Dentist and Love of Pet. Ye are wondrous strong, yet lovely in your strength, as is the light . . . have a Sealy Posturepedic morning.

Fay was just the type of dame that drives chumps like me crazy—tall and sleek, with liquid gray eyes, lush red lips, a soft, smoky voice, and long, silken, honey-blond hair that gracefully clung to her supple, tan shoulders. But, of course, that was before the accident.

Neal Leader, Norman, Okla.

Morning light cascaded over the porcelain roof tiles on the Imperial Palace at Peking, filtered in through the inlaid lattices of the Audience Hall, and bathed the Dragon Throne in the soft shimmer of early day. Then, in ran the little yellow people on tiny feet, all talking funny.

Elizabeth Happy, Kansas City, Mo.

The great army waited: Duke Robert, The Fearless; Duke Rollo of Brittany; Hugh of Montrose; Roger de Montgomery; Guy of Amiens; The Count of Flanders, he of the noble mien, his barons and housecarls; many true knights; brave rustics in leather jerkins—all waited in the dusk of St. Martin's Day for the king's call to arms. Then a guy in a real nice suit got up and said, "Ahem, ahem, er, let's go."

Jack Ryan, N.Y.C.

Tangier: hooded, ophidian eyes regarding one from the baleful darkness of beaded entryways; an ineffable sense of menace, present even in the unidentified smells that assault the nostrils, and in the strangled, glottal obligato of the muezzin calling the faithful through labyrinthine fly-spattered streets to prayer. "Eeeeee," squealed Kiki Westhoving, flinging one of the Tangier Hilton's whitest pillows at Muff and Binky, her roommates from Miss Porter's, "it's *marvy!!*"

Alex Vaughn, Old Lyme, Conn.

The sea churned and salt spray pooped the foredecks, soaking the mizzen; while sailors scrambled up the rigging, the first matey yelled, "Make ready all battens!" from the brass wheelhouse: The *Sea Lily* hove to, spars creaking, while maelstroms whirled about and boiling black waves broke over the bowsprit. "Looks like a storm," said Blind Hank.

David Ambos, Amherst, Mass.

The black limousine pulled up in front of the large house with the high iron fence, and out stepped a small man in a somber black suit who had been sent to deliver an important message to Don Genovese. "Are you home, Donald?" he shouted as he knocked on the front door.

Richard Fried, Brooklyn

It is a truth universally acknowledged that a single man in possession of a large fortune must be in want of a wife. Unless he's gay.

Mimi Cozzens, Hollywood, Calif.

Telling a tale, it is paramount for the first sentence to expose as much as possible of one's charisma by capturing it in a flavorful flight of words. Win a few, lose a few.

Jay Dantry, Pittsburgh, Pa.

She opened the door slowly and, as the white winter light filled the entrance hall, her mind raced back to another time when this narrow corridor was filled with galoshes, canoe paddles, polo mallets, tennis sweaters, picnic hampers, and other mementos of a childhood that now, she alone had survived. "I bet I can get a hundred thou for this place," she thought to herself.

Arthur Weller, Interlaken, N.J.

"Every man owns a corner of history," was the gist of the legacy which El Gran Señor de Barcelona, my father, left hidden in the hilt of his *hidalgo*'s rapier. I did not find it.

Thomas C. Rosica, N.Y.C.

The first time I gazed upon Jennifer, her mysterious and exquisitely, achingly beautiful face was bathed in an eerie, misty light. The maid invariably forgets to dust the bulbs in the entrance way.

Dan Williams, N.Y.C.

Once upon a time there lived a Mother Bunny who had three little bunnies who were very good bunnies, and one little bunny who was a very bad bunny indeed. Betsy Bunny was good because she always washed her ears, and Bambi Bunny was good because she always did as she was told, and Bobby Bunny was good because he always remembered his manners, but Benjy Bunny was a bad, bad bunny because he picked his nose.

Nancy Dickinson, Waterford, Conn.

Last night I dreamt of Manderwyck. This morning when I woke it seemed silly.

Ira Avery, Stamford, Conn.

Young Martina Levesque peered through the window of the clattering stagecoach at her looming journey's-end—isolated, mist-shrouded Château Grave, Breton residence of the mysterious Chandelière family: brilliant, brooding St. Juste Chandelière, stalker of Pasteur's reputation; his elegant, epileptic wife, Chesley; and their young ones—Martina's unmet charges—Jacques and Jacqueline, of whom there were only dark whispers. "Hurry, *mes chevaux,*" quietly urged Martina, who had to go tee-tee.

John Hofer, Southboro, Mass.

"Only a mind like Jorgensen's," thought Sir Wilfred, "an intellect choked by its own near-Kierkegaardian enigmas, could have brought such disgrace to the traditions of the Academy. Boy, am I upset."

Fred J. Abbate, Moorestown, N.J.

As Farris adjusted his specially tailored cashmere jacket over the kid-leather shoulder holster, he looked into the mirror and liked what looked back—brown, gold-flecked eyes set deep in a handsome face, all crowning a six-foot-two frame that had the chicks talking to themselves. Now, he thought, as he dialed the phone, if only dad can let me have the car tonight.

David Kritchevsky, Bryn Mawr, Pa.

His first memories of childhood were of long, lazy walks with his mother in her garden, where tarragon, sweet basil, chives, rosemary, mint, mustard, and a salt lick for the wild animals all tumbled in gay profusion. But he was leaving that sheltered life behind him now, and her sturdy little body was becoming smaller and smaller as she waved to him crying, "Come down from that balloon, Herb, you're breaking your mother's heart."

Joanie Rogers, Snowmass, Colo.

At about noon Long Arrow changed his stride from the tireless lope that had carried him 30 miles since sunup to a lung-bursting sprint. "O Wind Kachina," he gasped, as his rock-thewed legs pumped pistonlike and his feet drummed the baked plains earth, "make my speed as the wild stallion's or I shall be late for din-din."

Susan Burfoot, New London, Conn.

John Walker was, in every sense of the word, a winner: Phi Beta Kappa and football all-American; self-made millionaire by the age of 30; presidential adviser and confidant; international sportsman; the lover of several of the world's most renowned beauties. But now he had been rendered impotent by death.

J. M. Riordan, Laguna Beach, Calif.

"Before we set off on this expedition across unknown territory," said the gray-haired man, peering from beneath his broad-brimmed hat, "I want you to know that we'll meet up with Indians and grizzly bears and ferocious heat and killing cold—folks, it ain't gonna be no picnic!" Fifteen of the twenty-two wagons pulled out of line and started heading back East.

Paul Skaggs, River Edge, N.J.

"The study of nicotinic acids and their various stains on the human epidermis is an oft-neglected area of scrutiny," remarked my illustrious friend Sherlock Holmes after breakfast one morning in November, "yet I fancy that it is precisely that particular phenomenon that will lead us to unravel this baffling matter of Lady Hartescue and the seven golden prune pits." To which I replied, "Who cares, Hockey Puck?"

Ken Olfson, Los Angeles, Calif.

Five women murdered, all in their twenties, all with the first name of Belinda, all strangled with a navy-blue stocking. It's a good thing he transferred from homicide to robbery, thought Lieutenant Daton as he threw down the newspaper, or he would have had the inglorious task of tracking down yet another crackpot.

Teresa Gerbers, Glenmont, N.Y.

The sunlight squeezed its way through the dense foliage of the thicket of trees surrounding the pond, danced shimmeringly along the ripples on the surface, and alternately caressed and abandoned the tall figure strolling slowly and silently through the grove. Jackson Smith stroked his chin reflectively and pondered the futility of training frogs.

Charles G. Sonnen, Oak Ridge, Tenn.

Across the dimly lit lounge she stared, captivated, at the face of a once-beautiful woman, a face not etched by time or disappointments but molded by experience, a face which, by displaying the knowledge it had acquired, unknowingly mocked the ignorance of her own countenance. She stood up, and the face across the lounge in the mirror rose with her.

Scott Burnham, N.Y.C.

In the village the urchins jigged and suckled treacle humbugs: Lacking the delicacy to reseal the grave which yawned in the miasmal moonlight, a pair of slack-jawed miscreants, Messrs. Burke and Hare, trundled their creaking barrow through the bat-befouled churchyard to deliver to their surgical customer for the sum of ten pounds, ought and six, a grisly commodity. It chanced to be the bloated cadaver of a certain Millicent ("Muffy") Hays.

Albert G. Miller, N.Y.C.

Months of diligent, often frantic, digging, probing, snooping, investigating—even a bit of palm-greasing—and finally I had enough information to nail both the speaker and governor on kickback charges on the front page of my newspaper, the *Record.* Here's how the *Knickerbocker News* scooped me.

Eric Freedman, Averill Park, N.Y.

The townspeople had tried to burn down the cathedral twice; they had tried flooding and bombing, and finally desperate night-long praying for a miracle that would take the evil building from their town as abruptly as it had appeared. But Douglas, the magic duck, was determined not to reroute his home until he had made at least two new friends.

Caroline Leavitt, Pittsburgh, Pa.

The whole sky was bathed in a terrible light as the firestorm instantly leveled giant office buildings, sudden huge fissures swallowed whole city blocks, the tortured earth writhed in its terrible agony, and radioactive ash covered the now-silent countryside. All Rio was asking: Could young Francisco de Rosas overcome his playboy image?

Physics Bldg, SUNY, Albany, N.Y.

Some stood, some sat, but most knelt in silent prayer in the hushed locker room. "O.K., guys," our quarterback yelled, "let's go out there and show them this is a given day."

Richard Hafey, Morningdale, Mass.

Added Attractions

Thou Shalt Not Get Caught—The Eleventh Commandment.

Piggy—The Sixth Toe or Finger. Useful for counting, often adorned by a rhinestone piggy ring.

Pursiflage—The Eighth Deadly Sin. Pickpocketing.

Above, Added attractions. Competitors were asked to invent and describe an Eighth Dwarf, or Wonder of the World, Seventh Sense, Tenth Muse or any addition to a well-known group.

Report: But there *were* four Musketeers. Anyway. Repeats (in most cases one-day service): The Eighth Dwarf: Sleazy, Smelly, Squatty, Shorty, Lefty, Rooney or Bruce. The Fourth "R": Remediation. Ripoff. On the Thirteenth Day of Christmas my true love gave (or returned) to me: a pet rock. The Fourth *(sic)* Musketeer: Pathos, Amos (token), Canöe (after Aramis), Ethos (a character), Blunderbuss, Pantyhos, and Ruth. The Fifth Marx Brother: Karlo, Boozo, Uglo, Dumbo, Ringo, Zero and Jell-O. Donald Duck's fourth nephew: Screwy. The Eighth and Ninth hills of Rome: Sophia Loren. (I don't make these up, I just work here.) The Fifth Estate: San Simeon. Beethoven's Tenth: "The Erotica." Schubert's Tenth: "The Unstarted." Madden's Next: The Unprintable.

Cpl. Erwin "Lucky" O'Toole—601st Member of the Light Brigade.

Gerrit Graham, Los Angeles, Calif.

Remember—Thirteenth Month. Celebrities born this month include Jerry Lucas, Marcel Proust, Mama. Holidays: Pearl Harbor Day, Battle of the Alamo. Zodiac Sign: Jumbo the Elephant.

Mark Wolfson, Spring Valley, N.Y.

Rana the Frog—The Thirteenth Sign of the Zodiac. Those born under Rana are gregarious, passionate, inquisitive, and given to catching flies with their tongues.

Sunny Vaughn, Old Lyme, Conn.

NBS—Fourth Network. Based in Nebraska with very small but effective art and legal departments.

Russ Leland, Los Angeles, Calif.

Both—The Fourth Little Word.

Vee Busch, Tucson, Ariz.

Jalapeño—The Sixth Little Pepper.

Mrs. Sam S. Klein, No. Caldwell, N.J.
Gail Golladay, Rocky River, Ohio
David K. Little, Water Mill, N.Y.

Moola—The Fourth Gabor Sister.

Ken Olfson, Los Angeles, Calif.

DaDa—Gabor Sister who looks like father.

Gene Schinto, Greenwich, Conn.

The Gospel According to Norman—The Fifth Gospel. Long puzzling to Biblical scholars for its lack of substantive facts and the narrator's habit of referring to himself in the third person.

Janet Lemkau, Plandome, N.Y.

The Four Virtues—Faith, Hope, Charity, and La Verne.

J. Carter Joseph, Atlanta, Ga.

April 15A—The 366th Day of the Year.

Roberta Kohn, Bklyn.

Linkletter—The Eighth Lively Art.

Rina Mimoun, Bklyn.

. . . and they call the smog Dolores.

Pamela Blanc, Woodside, N.Y.

South Orange—The Fourth Love of Prokofiev.

Mariel Bossert, Chatham, N.J.

CCCCI—First Plebeian to crash the Roman Social Register.

E. B. Callahan, Pittsburgh, Pa.

Goldibear—The Fourth Bear. Product of a mixed marriage.

Debbi Glassberg, Forest Hills, N.Y.

Jerry—The Fourth Stooge. Dropped from the act because of his resemblance to Edgar Kennedy, and because he was always hurting himself.

Len Pronkine, Roslyn, N.Y.

Hear No Evil, Speak No Evil, See No Evil, and Not to My Recollection.

Kathleen A. Clifford, Camden, N.J.

Sid's Place—The Forum of the Thirteenth Caesar.

Irwin Rosen, Topeka, Kan.

$—The Twenty-Seventh Letter of the Alphabet.

Anita Bring, Hewlett, N.Y.

"I need the money"—Henry Block's Eighteenth Reason.

Valerie C. Samuels, Bronx

I've seven honest serving men / (They taught me all I know) / Their names are What, Why, How, and When, / And Where and Who and Joe.

Lucia Stell, South Salem, N.Y.

The Stella—Fourth Ship of Christopher Columbus. Headed toward Warsaw, got lost, and fell off the earth.

Adrienne Gusoff, Allsten, Mass.

Dusk—Fourth Member of Tony Orlando and Dawn.

Teddy Huxford, Skaneateles, N.Y.
Alan Levine, Copiague, N.Y.

Felix the Cat—Thirteenth Sign of the Zodiac.

John Lannen, Bronx

The "Shock" symphony—Haydn's 105th. More powerful than his "Surprise" symphony.

Cookie Gray, Closter, N.J.

Kasha—The Fourth Sister, who dreams of opening a restaurant in Moscow.

J. Bickart, N.Y.C.

Olga & Marsha & Irina & Gale Paige: The Four Sisters.

Jay Dantry, Pittsburgh, Pa.

"It is written that the motorcycle is more dangerous to ride than the camel"—The Eighth Pillar of Wisdom.

Thos. Van Steenbergh, Bergenfield, N.J.

Secretary of UGH—Cabinet Member in charge of opposition candidates.

Eleanor Paul, Bklyn.

Santini Claus—The Eighth Semi-Retired Brother. Now living in a Florida condominium.

Paul Bloom, Wayne, N.J.

OH—104th Member of the Periodic Table of Elements. Element of Surprise.

Leon Flesdrager, Yonkers, N.Y.

Euburpe—The Tenth Muse. Goddess of Radishes.

Albert G. Miller, N.Y.C.

Boog—Fourth Brother of the Alou Baseball Family.

Gary Levine, Merrick, N.Y.

Freedom of Joyce—The Fifth Freedom. The right to read *Ulysses.*
Kathie Coblentz, N.Y.C.

Quadruble—Fourth Coin in the Fountain.
Mrs. Rowann Gilman, N.Y.C.

You don't send in your entry unless you think it is best. If it is best, you will win first prize—a book you don't want. The best prize, a free subscription, is for the second-best entry. But if you don't think your entry is best, you don't send it in—Catch 23.
David Silliphant, Old Greenwich, Conn.

Famous Line, Flawed Tag

1. "To be or not to be, That is the question."
2. May I have the envelope, please?

1. "Bobby Shaftoe's gone to sea/Silver buckles on his knee."
2. He's very popular on the ship.

Above, familiar lines and flawed follow-ups. Competitors were asked for a famous line and a frivolous, invented tag.

Report: More of Anita Bryant than we cared to hear. And largely unencumbered by charm. A popular follow-up line was "Your place or mine?" First line could be anything and often was. Other repeats: " 'Twas brillig . . ." Thank you, Mr. President. "Love means never having to say you're sorry." I'm sorry. "Where are the snows of yesteryear?" Buffalo, I think. I am in love with the first-prize entry.

---

1. "Good night, sweet prince."
2. Have a good day.

Bruce B. Winters, Sarasota, Fla.

1. "When did your sparkle turn to fire, and your warmth become desire?"
2. Do you want another hit?

Meg McAleer, Washington, D.C.

1. "Give me liberty or give me death!"
2. *C.* None of the above.

Roslyn Spiegel, Flushing, N.Y.

1. "One if by land, two if by sea."
2. Three's a crowd. Giddyap!

Abraham Ellenbogen, Flushing, N.Y.

1. "Lo! I am become Siva, the destroyer of worlds!"
2. Would you like to see it again?

John Gilbert, Great Neck, N.Y.

1. "Thanking you for your time, this time until next time."
2. My time is up, and so it's time for me to say it's time to go.

Brian Plante, Staten Island, N.Y.

1. "Walk on through the wind,/Walk on through the rain . . ."
2. I'm afraid it's both pneumonia and total exhaustion, Mrs. Raitt.

Jo-Ann Padnos, Hewlett Neck, N.Y.

1. "Life is for the living."
2. Mikey likes it.

Jeff Baron, Boston, Mass.

1. "The little toy dog is covered with dust, but sturdy and staunch he stands."
2. Stella, cancha run a rag around this joint once in a while?

W. Fredrickson, Homewood, Ill.

1. "No man is an island. . . ."
2. No *person.*

Eve Merriam, N.Y.C.

1. "I am he as you are he as you are me and we are all together."
2. What did you say your name was?

Tina Feldman, Brooklyn

1. "I come to bury Caesar, not to praise him."
2. It's about time you showed up!

Ms. Marcia Cohen, Bayside, N.Y.
C. Rodosh, Arlington, Va.

1. " 'Tis better to give than to receive."
2. . . . then I must have it too.

Richard V. Coppolino, Brooklyn

1. "It is an ancient mariner/And he stoppeth one of three."
2. The Mariners never were strong on defense.

J. Freitag, Canton, N.Y.

1. "Is this a dagger which I see before me,/The handle toward my hand?"
2. No, that's VEGEMATIC! Slices, dices, makes coleslaw in seconds.

Michael D. Johnson, N.Y.C.

1. "Datta. Dayadhvam. Damyaya. Shantih shantih shantih."
2. The roof is so slantih/It touches the ground.

Miriam Weiss, N.Y.C.

1. "Void where prohibited."
2. Well, that might be carrying civil disobedience a little too far.

Alan Minkoff, Princeton, N.J.

1. "Hickory dickory dock, the mouse ran up the clock. The clock struck one. . . ."
2. The other was uninjured.

Anita Grien, N.Y.C.
R. Higgins, Syosset, N.Y.

1. "You must pay for your sins."
2. If you've already paid, please disregard this notice.

Jeanne Remusat, Forest Hills, N.Y.

1. "When the moon is in the seventh house/And Jupiter aligns with Mars."
2. Sell.

Joel S. Lind, Rochester, N.Y.

1. "Multi sunt vocati, pauci vero electi."
2. Stavros, read him his rights!

1. Jack Ryan, N.Y.C.
2. Leonard S. Meranus, Cincinnati, Ohio

1. "She was a worthy woman al hir lyve,/Housebondes at chirche dore she hadde fyve."
2. They don't write 'em like that anymore. (Haha! Joke!)

David G. McAneny, Upper Darby, Pa.

1. "If you were the only girl in the world . . ."
2. . . . and there were a paper bag over your head. . . .

Bill Wunder, Port Washington, N.Y.
sp. mention: Diane C. Hemmes, Rye, N.Y.

1. "Give me a place to stand and I will move the world."
2. Give me a place to sit and I'll watch.

Mariel Bossert, Chatham, N.J.

1. "Four score and seven years ago . . ."
2. Our fathers went into the half-size dress business together.

B. L. Freedman, N.Y.C.

1. "Baa, baa, black sheep,/Have you any wool?"
2. Yes, one size fits all.

Sylvia Ellenbogen, Flushing, N.Y.

1. "She was a day tripper."
2. And at night she handed out exploding cigars.

William Lambiase, Brooklyn

1. "I'm as restless as a willow in a windstorm, I'm as jumpy as a puppet on a string."
2. If that's the way you've been feeling lately, Dr. Art Ulene will be along in a few minutes to tell you . . .

Becky Boardman, Wayne, N.J.

1. "Down in the valley, the valley so low,/Hang your head over, hear the wind blow."
2. And do it fast, because the Army Corps of Engineers is coming tomorrow. . . .

J. Bickart, N.Y.C.

1. "He's just my Bill, an ordinary guy."
2. Yet today he's the president of a multi-national conglomerate.

Alexandra Schwartz, Boston, Mass.

1. "It was the best of times, it was the worst of times."
2. Details at eleven.

S. M. Santarelli, Harvey's Lake, Pa.

1. "The quality of mercy is not strained."
2. Use only as directed.

Steve Kotchko, East Hartford, Conn.

1. "A loaf of bread, a jug of wine, and thou . . ."
2. Not necessarily in that order.

Frank Di Palma, N.Y.C.

1. "Who knows what evil lurks in the hearts of men?"
2. Helen Gurley Brown.

Norman Stewart, Hickory, N.C.

1. "How do I love thee? Let me count the ways."
2. 1. Missionary . . .

Ed Boardman, Wayne, N.J.
Dora Ullian, Newton, Mass.
D. P. Parrish, Grosse Point Farms, Mich.

1. "I met a traveler from an antique land."
2. He shot fourteen rolls of film.

T. B. Adams, N.Y.C.

1. "First-prize winners will receive two-year subscriptions to *New York* and runners-up will receive one-year subscriptions."
2. Or is it the other way around?

Maria Conti, Warwick, R.I.

Jacket Copy

Maxwell Falloon was born in the Bronx. He was graduated from the University of North Dakota and worked as a bartender, oculist and goatherd before serving in the Korean navy. His first novel, *Priscilla Remembers,* received unanimous critical acclaim: ". . . good . . ." *(Kirkus Reviews).* A collection of short stories, *Double Fault and Whither Douglas Kiker,* appeared in 1972. Nearing completion, a nonfiction book, *Cow Pies,* is a study of the recurrence of death in modern society. Mr. Falloon lives in Manhattan with his second wife, Urethra, and her children, Dawn.

Above, hic jacket. Competitors were asked for biographical data à la "Who's Who in the Cast," album liner notes or book cover copy.

Report: Previous to writing this report, the author served as a cigar cutter, competition editor and patient. Fewer album-liner notes than writer or actor bios. For "Who's Who in the Cast," lists of past performances in *Kelly, Home Sweet Homer* or *Breakfast at Tiffany's.* "Ms. Smith, who has studied acting with Ty Hardin, made her debut in the Ferndale Country Day School production of *Trees Are Friends.*" Authors' prepublication jobs ran from landish to out. Album notes relied upon obscure instruments, peculiar titles and more peculiar techniques. As which of us does not?

MARY-JO BARNES began her singing career at the age of ten, when she made her own guitar from a cigar box. Married at twelve to Billy-Bob Barnes, a muscular Mack truck driver, she has found time between the births of their fifteen children to write such hits as "I'm a Total Woman," "Where Do Babies Come From?" and "Divorce Is a Four-Letter Word." Mary-Jo says singing comes as naturally to her as scrubbing a floor—and Billy-Bob agrees.

Iris Bass, Brooklyn.

MS. DEBBIE-SUE FITZ dispenses King Lear himself in our all-female rendering of Shakespeare's extravaganza. Ms. Fitz, a thunderstriking high-school freshwoman, has been digesting her role, to cite her, "by running around in the rain and yelling." Her long white beard will be artificial.

Keith Reagan, San Francisco, Calif.

GEOFFREY SMATHERS-FOSGATE has been a professional soldier. Born at Church Crookham, Hants., in 1889, he attended Wellington and R.M.A., Sandhurst. Gazetted to the 14/6th Lancers as subaltern, "Smathie" was very soon seconded to the greater demand of staff duties. During the dark days following Ypres, he led his horsed cavalry against massed enemy machine guns defiladed behind wire. Cited for "unmistakable zeal and élan, but questionable discretion," the author played no active part in W.W. II. Smathers-Fosgate has authored one previous book, *There Away,* acclaimed by the Manchester *Guardian* as "a impressive first effort."

Suzanna Tenenbaum, M.D., Queens

ANNA SICKWELL has, in her first novel, fictionally documented her own madness. As a child, her apparently normal upbringing concealed a many-faceted interplay of rejection and conditional behavior. At the age of fourteen her insanity manifested itself in dramatic outbursts of necromancy. Trundled from one institution to another, her condition worsening, she, at 23, finally encountered a doctor in whom she could implicitly trust. Here is the triumphant story of her illness, her treatment, and her bitter struggle toward health and the ability to truly live.

Laurie Winogrand, N.Y.C.

COLIN ST. BROWNE-BLACKBURNE comes to the Los Angeles Philharmonic after three seasons as concertmaster of the London Symphony Orchestra. His favorite color is aqua. His favorite car is the '72 Mustang. His favorite food is anchovy paste. His favorite material is shantung. His favorite nursery rhyme is "Little Jack Horner." His favorite shape is rectangle. His favorite facial feature is eyebrows. His favorite appliance is a toaster. His favorite greeting card is "Congratulations on Your Confirmation."

Anne Brett, Los Angeles, Calif.

SIR JOHNNE WYCKLIFFE (Puck) returns to *A Midsummer Night's Dream* in the role he created in the original [British] version. Sir Johnne, said to be the oldest member of Actors' Equity—he became a naturalized citizen in 1864—made his U.S. stage debut in the touring company of *Our American Cousin* (the play did not reach Broadway). Renowned for his ingenious makeup, Sir Johnne has portrayed the father in *The River Niger,* Danny Zuko in *Grease* (his only musical), and the boarder in *Come Back, Little Sheba.* Millions of TV viewers know him as Aunt Bluebell.

Gary Gobetz, N.Y.C.

KRIS KRINGLE (Santa Claus) has played the kindly benefactor for more years than he cares to remember. His unforgettable role as Pelz Nichol, a hairy imp, in Germany, and as Sinterklaas, in the Netherlands, led inevitably to the big time on this side of the pond. Between engagements, he is active in demography—compiling lists and finding out who's naughty or nice. ("It's not without its titillating side," he admits with characteristic jollity.) He resides not far from the Alaska pipeline with his wife, a contingent of elves, and domesticated reindeer.

Oscar Weigle, Whitestone, N.Y.

ALOIS PEMBROKE needs no introduction whatsoever. Authoress of more than 160 romances which have been translated into sixteen languages, she began her career in 1916, when *Now and Forever* appeared. Besides fiction, Dame Alois has written a book of verse, *Crudités,* which won her the coveted Guinness Prize in 1959, and *Brief Candle,* the well-known biography of Mary Shelley. A founding Member of the Royal Society of Venerable Persons, Dame Alois lives with her sister Eglantine at Dunmere, a rambling cottage on the Isle of Wight, where she raises border collies and maintains the world's largest collection of branched candelabra.

Robert Culicover, Palo Alto, Calif.

Waters of the Heart is the third album in Borborygmus Records' "Unheard Music" series. A blend of systolic and diastolic rhythms with the hauntingly mysterious pulse of the T-wave, *Waters* appeals to even the most unsympathetic nervous system. The reassuring regularity of "Pacemaker" and the honkytonk vivacity of "Plastic Valve Slam" and "Tachycardia" build beautifully to a shuddering climax in the finale, "Arrest." Recorded with double-catheter mini-mike and phase-locked transducers, this sensitive performance by the late Guido Mortali is in the great tradition of *Rumble* (BR-2121).

Paul Bickart, Princeton, N.J.

ALLEN DURST (the Wee One) made his debut at Harkness Pavilion in September, 1974, and appeared four months later on Broadway as Baby Alice in *And Baby Makes Three,* Costanza's adaptation of *Ménage à Trois.* In June, 1975, he left *And Baby*. . . with critical unanimity that he had outgrown the play. The role of Junior in the ill-fated *Junior's Miss* followed. As *Variety* put it, "Allen Durst provided a touch of verity in a fiasco posing as a farce." His characterization of the Wee One establishes Allen Durst as a force in contemporary theatre. He will be two next month.

Jane M. Ash, Scarsdale, N.Y.

JAMES JAMES ("T.J.") JAMES was born Shab'doo Shonga (literally, "one who dislikes veal") in Detroit. Previous to his present role in *Hey Ofay!,* Mr. James was best known for writing the lyrics to *Bad Boogie Baby,* an instrumental. Though born in August, Mr. James claims to be a Scorpio.

Grant Smith, Toledo, Ohio

NATHAN PRITKEIN, director of the Longevity Research Institute, Mineral Wells, Texas, has published his second health book. His first, *Lay Off the Health Foods,* sold well, according to a spokesman.

Bill Emery, Oklahoma City, Okla.

Although this is his first acting role, KEN KORNBUSH is no stranger to show business, having played his piccolo in front of most of the theaters on Broadway. He commutes daily from Pittsburgh ("My whippets hate to travel") and still finds time to be a Freemason. Ken is continuing his studies as a cryptographer and is currently encoding *The Final Days.*

Daniel Sachs, Brooklyn

American by birth in 1946, European by temperament, the author is currently developing a new form of the novel to be set against the socio-economic-political-religious confrontation which is Pittsburgh today. The trilogy is to be titled *Gulag Ohio, Gulag Monongahela,* and *Allegheny Archipelago.* The author is a slave to the written word.

Thomas M. Quinn, Carnegie, Pa.

ZELDA ANTWERT-HEMP, author of *Learn and Use Your Language,* is a graduate of Harvard University where she earned a master's degree in English Language. Her first books, *Master a Stunning Vocabulary* and *Creative Speaking,* are credited with crafting the art of conversation into millions of readers. Zelda Antwert-Hemp now lives in Boston with her husband, Lars, and their three children. She describes her home life as "fine."

Beverly Salter, Southfield, Mich.

"*Hermeneutics: An Inquiry into Pedialgia*" is S. P. Q. R. ROMAINE'S second attempt to articulate a philosophy of life while backpacking across the North American continent. His first attempt, the moribund *Vulture,* while more transparently autobiographical, lacked both focus and page numbers. In *Hermeneutics* the author has abandoned the formalism of the ecological monologue in *Vulture* and has opted instead for the looseness of his earlier *An Inquiry Into Diphthongs.* Romaine and his three-year-old boy live in Aetna, Louisiana. Romaine inhales freon and follows flies with his eyes.

Robert Schwartz, Charlottesville, Va.

PRINCESS ALABASTER'S newest recording, *Showstoppers for Sackbut,* is the first quadriphonal solo sackbut recording. Ps. Alabaster's distinguished lineage includes a great-great-great grandfather who was first sackbut in the Royal Distemper Fusiliers (1732–1748). She first learned to sackbut at her father's knee in the '30s while he wrote anti-union tracts set to baroque airs. Although his success was limited, she is enjoying great popularity with the burgeoning legions of sackbut and shawm players. Ps. Alabaster appears infrequently in public performance. A "must own" for all show-tune buffs!

Sylvia Cassell, Art Rubin, N.Y.C.

At twelve, LEONARD STONE's "Why I Want to Be a Doctor" won the National Essay Competition. Thereafter, his life had a mission: Ohio president of Tomorrow's Healers, undergraduate valedictorian at Hopkins, and five summers as an emergency-room attendant. When unfair grading precipitated his departure from Columbia P&S, Stone became determined to expose the chicanery of the medical profession. His earlier books, *Your Doctor the Crook; Cough, Please;* and *For an Arm and a Leg,* were condemned by the AMA. This new work, *Normal Practice,* will rattle skeletons in some very high closets.

Joel S. Lind, Alexandria, Va.

JIM "OUTBACK" ROBINSON walked into my office one day and said, "I know I can't sing, Sport, but I need a chance to try." That was the start of a singing career that is unparalleled to this day! I'm just happy to say, "I knew him when. . . ." —Peace, *Don Prophet,* FBN Records.

M. P. DiOrio, Milwaukee, Wis.

GRISCOM ROSS (Francis Scott Key) makes his Broadway debut in *Long May It Wave* after touring with the company in a lesser role. He was also understudy for ten of the original thirteen stars. Mr. Ross began his career singing in a tavern in Baltimore. He has played the role of the prisoner in *Surprise* and with his bride Betsy collaborated on the novel *Ana Creon in Heaven.* A strong believer in a home and a country, in his spare time Mr. Ross is active in several causes which he believes just.

Frances Glick, N.Y.C.

SOLOMON GRUNDY was born on Monday, and was baptised on Tuesday. After a seemingly brief courtship, he married on Wednesday. The marriage, it turned out, was to be short-lived, and he was divorced on Thursday. Following a sudden and unexpected illness on Friday, he died on Saturday and was buried on Sunday. His main work, an autobiography, was *The End.*

Thomas Van Steenbergh, Bergenfield, N.J.

Random Lines from TV

"Get in the car, the boss wants to see you."

"What is so funny about a woman wanting the same respect, the same salary, as a man—*listen* to me, I'm *talking* to you."

". . . lest we alarm these once-hostile creatures, our crew withdraws quietly; we will film no more today—the monkeys seem tired, and besides, we're losing the light."

Above, the results of television channel-hopping. Competitors were asked for a random extract from one popular category of TV program.

Report: I am consolable that no one thought to quote the Sports Colorperson saying: "He really comes to play." Thanks to all, and I advise you not to leave town.

"It's interesting that you brought up the subject of Eskimos, because I understand you just finished starring in a movie about them. . . ."

Harvey Salter, Southfield, Mich.

"Can the camera get a close shot of that?"

Don Brockway, Oyster Bay, N.Y.

"Put out an A.P.B. and let's hope we get to him before they do."

Lil Wilen, N.Y.C.

"Here's a couple of C-notes. Go get yourself some decent clothes. I like my boys looking sharp."

Andrew Cutrofello, Matt Goodman, Lake Success, N.Y.

". . . the jackal and the hyena are not, in truth, scavengers, but rather the housekeepers of the animal kingdom. . . ."

David Mimoun, Brooklyn

"We want to thank our guests, the Amazing Kreskin, the lovely Charo, and Doctor David Reuben. Sorry we didn't have time for Will and Ariel Durant. Goodnight."

Jay Dantry, Pittsburgh, Pa.

"A hundred a day plus expenses—O.K. take this, it's all I have, but I'll get more—just find Joey!"

Mark Wolfson, Spring Valley, N.Y.

"Thank you, Don Pardo. . . ."

Mike Lesker, Springfield, Mass.

SOAP OPERA: "Hello?"

Norm Bloom, Ottawa, Ontario, Canada

"Hi, honey I'm home . . . Ethel, what's Lucy doin' in the horse costume?"

Psychacoustics Lab, Purdue Univ., Ind.

"There *must* be a picture for Ricky in there *somewhere.* How about SEVEN BRIDGES FOR SEVEN CUBANS? THE RICARDOS OF WIMPOLE STREET? A STREETCAR NAMED RICARDO? RICKY, SON OF FLICKA? . . ."

Wesley Cauthers, Marvin Shabus, N.Y.C.

"Can you see some drunk turning on the set *just now?*"

Gerard J. Cook, Westbury, N.Y.

CABLE TV: "Which camera is on?"

Paul Noble, N.Y.C.

"Burt, does this film clip that we're going to see need any explanation or should we just roll it?"

John Torre, Secaucus, N.J.

"Milk Sugar!"

Edmund Hartmann, Beverly Hills, Calif.

Officer (rubbing substance between his fingers): "It's the real thing, all right. Book 'em."

Susan N. Klein, Pittsburgh, Pa.

"No, really. After my last appearance on this show, I'm recognized all over, the jobs are coming in, my price is going up and, uh, I owe it all to you. No, really."

Lydia Wilen, N.Y.C.

"Does he believe in marriage? Of course. He's married!"

Joan Wilen, N.Y.C.

"All my years on the force I never seen anything like this."

Sal Rosa, N.Y.C.

"I never expected the famous Dr. C. G. Snyder to be such an attractive woman."

Michel Novey, Alison Dray-Novey,
Highland Park, Calif.

"And now, for a replay of that injury!"

Cookie Gray, Closter, N.J.

". . . performance this reporter has ever seen . . . while we await the judges' scores, let's take another look at the spots where Mitzie fell out of her routine. . . ."

Walter S. Boone, Valdese, N.C.

"Since you're going to kill me anyhow, why don't you tell me how you did it?"

Charles F. Johnson, Valley Stream, N.Y.

". . . me and officer Wojciechvsk apprehended the alleged perpetrator and attempted to interrogate him, but when he begun discharging a firearm it was every man for themselves."

Norton Bramesco, N.Y.C.

"And special guest star, Cloris Leachman."

Chip Chapin, N.Y.C.

"I haven't read our next guest's new book yet, but I hear it's a grabber. Let's give a warm welcome to . . . uh. . . ."

Jack Rose, N.Y.C.

"Indira Gandhi in the Apple; The Knicks top the Bucks. Separate stories, after this word."

David C. Pollack, N.Y.C.

"He's got to hold his serve if he wants to get back into this match."

Anthony Gray, Closter, N.J.

"We just want to ask you a few questions—you can answer them here or downtown."

Eric W. Black, Little Rock, Ark.

". . . . and that's the way it was, April 19, 1776. I'm Chevy Chase and there is nothing you can do about it. Never mind."

Joseph Emanuele, Pittsburgh, Pa.

"Just as birds build their nests for protection, so Mutual of Omaha can protect *your* family in time of. . . ."

R. S. V. Carter, Oxford, Ohio

"Yeah? Well, I got a riddle for you, Augie. When is a fox a pig? And I'll tell you the answer. That broad you been seeing is really the *fuzz.*"

Lou Grillo, Middletown, Conn.

"You can't tell me on the phone? Meet you? Alone on the pier at midnight? No, I won't tell anyone. See you then."

Alice L. Johnson, Valley Stream, N.Y.

"Johnny, tell us what our lovely ladies have won so far. . . ."

Miles Klein, E. Brunswick, N.J.

"Hey man, you can't prove anything, I've been clean for three years."

Ginny Horvath, N.Y.C.

"We watch your show every day."

Fernando Soto, N.Y.C.

"The reason I don't practice my religion any more, meathead, is 'cause I already know it by heart."

Vincent Borgese, Bronx

"Dee-fense!"

Fran Ross, N.Y.C.

"Look out—he's got a gun!"

Mary Osborn, Ada, Mich.

"Thanks, but no thanks, Tom was more than my partner, he was my friend. I'll tell her."

David Yanes, Briarwood, N.Y.

". . . Lieutenant, it's for you."

Mark J. Jacobs, Kearny, N.J.

"Now, breathing regularly, and sitting in a lotus position, slowly lift your left arm straight in front of you with the palm open. . . ."

Ms. S. Kirschner, Bronx
Albert G. Miller, N.Y.C.

"I think you'd better sit down for this. . . ."

Wendy Stevens, New Rochelle H.S., N.Y.

". . . declined to comment, other than to call the charges politically motivated."

Edward Steinberg, Silver Spring, Md.

"*How cold was it?*"

Barry Black, Newton, Mass.

"He's dead, Jim."

Barry Edelstein, Fair Lawn, N.J.

"There appears to be a slight shadow in the X-ray but I think we've caught it in time. . . ."

Nancy Horvath, N.Y.C.

"What business is it of yours? You don't own me."

J. Bickart, N.Y.C.

"Grace, how many times do I have to tell you? Life doesn't *come* with a set of instructions." "Waiter, another round."

Larry Laiken, Bayside, N.Y.

"Oh, my gosh! I've never won anything before!"

Gary Levine, Merrick, N.Y.

"Here's Ronald McDonald with another check for you, Jerry."

Dr. Harry Choron, Hackensack, N.J.

"Do nothing to alarm the ladies—but join your regiment immediately."

Alex Sahagian-Edwards, N.Y.C.

"If *that's* his M.O., he's no hired gun."

Judith R. Goldsmith, Woodmere, N.Y.

"In basketball the Lakers swamped the Celts 91 to 89. The Bulls gored the Sonics 102 to 101. The Blazers burned the Colonels 126 to 124. In hockey the Sabres knifed the Kings 7 to 6. The Penguins nipped. . . ."

Beatrice Brailsford, Brooklyn

"The basket counts and he's fouled!"

Oliver Neshamkin, N.Y.C.

"Oh, no, Googum. Fluffbunny just meant that you must always be considerate of the feelings of others. Let's sing a song about it."

Alex Vaughn, Old Lyme, Conn.

"And you think it's been easy for me?"

John Horvath, N.Y.C.

". . . been sitting out here watching that house for three and a half hours, Elliott, and *nobody* has gone in *or* out."

Ted A. Carlin, Kew Gardens, N.Y.

Near Misses

THE ANTEPENULTIMATE MOHICAN
GUYS AND PLAYTHINGS
"There are more things in heaven and earth, Horatio, than you could possibly imagine."

Above, More Near Misses. Competitors were asked to provide a title, aphorism, or what-have-you of a similarly just-off-the-mark nature.

Report: For "Report" read "Repeats." For "Repeats" read these: MOBY RICHARD. LIEUTENANT KANGAROO. MRS. BUTTERFLY. "Eighty-seven years ago . . ." THE SUN COMES UP, TOO. DEATH OF A MANUFACTURER'S REPRESENTATIVE. The United States of Vespucci. MANDIBLES. LADY CHATTERLEY'S VERY GOOD FRIEND. WAR 'N' PEACE. START THE BEGUINE. HERE COMES THE ICEMAN. MAN AND SUPERPERSON. CRIME AND PLEA BARGAINING. WAR AND DETENTE. "It was the best of times, it was the pits." PIMIENTO. THE STAR-SPATTERED FLAG. 6Up. "I'm Bethesda, and you're not." THE CATCHER IN THE BOURBON. STAR TRIP. Ms., I'm Adam. The Ten Requests. NEBRASKA! ZHIVAGO, M.D. "Who is that bell ringing for anyway?" MY SO-SO LADY. "Frankly, my dear, I don't care." BREAKFAST AT FORTUNOFF'S. A miss is as good as 5,280 feet. Bison Bill Cody. Billy the Youngster. MARY HARTMAN. And President Udall. As Strunk and White point out, soulwise, these are trying times.

"Alas, poor Yorick, we were once introduced at a party, Horatio."
Miles Klein, E. Brunswick, N.J.

FEAR GROUNDS INTO A DOUBLE PLAY
Larry Laiken, Bayside, N.Y.

HELLOWATHA
Cliff Bareish, N.Y.C.

"Old MacDonald had a farm F-J-F-J-P."
Harvey L. Gordon, M.D., Houston, Tex.

SLAP THAT HADDOCK
Ulla Schnell, N.Y.C.

How Are Things in Loch Gomorrah?
Barbara Dunne, N.Y.C.

YANKEE DOODLE FOP
Edith Pearlman, N.Y.C.

"I've got the horse right here, his name is Nathan Hale."
Al Ward, Elizabethport, N.J.

LOOKING FOR SNICKERS
Mr. M. S. Secat, N.Y.C.
Len Elliott, Auburn, Wash.

HOW TO BE YOUR OWN CASUAL ACQUAINTANCE
Marcia Grees, Philadelphia, Pa.

"Stop in the name of the rules of conduct enforced by a controlling authority!"
Alan Levine, Copiague, N.Y.

THOSE KARAMAZOV BOYS
Michael Tolkin, Beverly Hills, Calif.

"Où est le ballpoint de ma tante?"
Albert G. Miller, N.Y.C.

"Those Wedding Bells Are Breaking Up That Old Peer Group of Mine"

Lora W. Asdorian, Springfield, Va.

IN THE FOYER OF THE MOUNTAIN KING

Richard M. Weissman, D.D.S., N.Y.C.

"It's always acceptable air quality when good fellows get together."

John F. Geer, N.Y.C.

THE CRACKPOT OF CHAILLOT

Benjamin A. Fairbank Jr., El Paso, Tex.

"Some enchanted evening, you may meet an alien."

MDI Art Dept., M. Dekker, Inc., N.Y.C.

ST. FRANCIS IS MY COPILOT

Florence W. Roberts, Providence, R.I.

"Well, if it isn't Dr. Livingston!"

Alice C. Martinson, N.Y.C.

"Friends, Romans, countrymen, may I have your attention, please."

Jean H. Nolan, Stamford, Conn.

"His is as the strength of ten because he's a really nice person."

Dr. Richard Burke, Ho-Ho-Kus, N.J.

THE 'ZARD

Carol Greenberg, Syosset, N.Y.

"Sufferin' Indian corn kernels and lima beans!"

R. Joe Heisler, Charlotte, N.C.

THE PHILLIES OF PENZANCE

Joel F. Crystal, Scarsdale, N.Y.

"Though I've belted you and flayed you / By the livin' Gawd that made you / You're a better man than I am Gunga Noise."

Bernard Katz, Plainview, N.Y.

"If it were done when 'tis done / Then 'twere well you got it over with."

Mrs. S. K. Fisher, Longmeadow, Mass.

"Roses are red / violets are violet . . ."

Margaux McMillan, Orinda, Calif.

THE PHANTOM OF AVERY FISHER HALL

Michael Deskey, Wauwatosa, Wis.

"I shot an arrow into the air / But I don't know where it fell down."

Rosmary Moran, Teaneck, N.J.

"Oh to be in England now that March is over."

Anne Salzano, Brooklyn

ENCORE, SAM

Paula Schwartz, Annadale, Va.
Dita Greene, Sayville, N.Y.

ANIMAL COOKIES

E. Schaffer, Baldwin, N.Y.

SIX CHARACTERS SEEK WRITER

Hortense Wolf, Corinth, Ky.

AMERICA, THE GOOD-LOOKING

Bernetta Nelson, N.Y.C.

Amateur Keds

Michael Conford, Massapequa, N.Y.

PAINT YOUR CONESTOGA

Pam Dunton, Boca Raton, Fla.

SEE YOU AROUND, MR. CHIPS

Dennis Pendleton, Roanoke, Va.

BLACK BECOMES ELECTRA

Steve McFarland, Brooklyn

Doc, Dopey, Sleepy, Sneezy, Happy, Bashful, and Annoyed.

Hilda Delfin, Valley Stream, N.Y.

"Take my wife, for example. . . ."

Capital Systems Group, Rockville, Md.

I'VE GOTTEN USED TO HER FACE

Murray L. Nolte, Merriam, Kan.

WHO'S AFRAID OF EDNA ST. VINCENT MILLAY?

James Rugirello, Encino, Calif.

"Discretion is more than 50 percent of valor."

Gordon Bear, Ramsey, N.J.

SYMPHONY WITH A COUPLE OF MOVEMENTS LEFT OUT

E. Rubinstein, N.Y.C.

"Tell it as it is, Baby!"

Jack Rose, N.Y.C.

TRELAWNY OF THE RESERVOIRS

David Greene, Montclair, N.J.

"Years from now, when you speak of this, and you will, for God's sake, don't mention my name."

Karl Levett, N.Y.C.

"No man is a body of land entirely surrounded by water."

Sal Rosa, N.Y.C.

"Sing a song of sixpence, a bottle full of rye. . . ."

Bea Adams, St. Louis, Mo.

Dressed to the eights

Joshua Daniels, Hewlett, N.Y.

"What the heck's Cuba to him, or he to Cuba / That he should weep for her?"

Jane M. Ash, Scarsdale, N.Y.

Plain, Georgia

Gwen Pettit, N.Y.C.

Literary Limericks

Meg, Jo, Beth and Amy (friend Laurie):
Meg's bland, Amy's vain, Jo's a Tory.
As for Laurie, their flame, he
Loves Jo, married Amy.
Beth dies. That's enough of that story.

Above, a small plot containing *Little Women.* Competitors were asked to encapsulate one literary or dramatic work in a limerick.

Report:
Competition Two Thirty and Eight
Came in cartons, two baskets, a crate.
Read each one. They were slick.
Loved each one. Made me *sick* . . .
Or it might have been something I hate.

I'm coolest when faced with a threat,
Too calm and decisive to fret.
Six crises to date
(I'm trying for eight)
And I'm not even president yet!

T.D.C. Kuch, Vienna, Va.

A young lady of candor and wit
Loved a lad she called Preppie (a twit).
And as she lay dying,
Instead of just crying,
She muttered "Oh. . . ." quite a bit.

Jack Rose, N.Y.C.

Now Jonathan flies like a comet.
His soul's part Thoreau, part Mahomet.
He is free and secure.
He is noble and pure.
(Excuse me. I'm going to vomit.)

Nancy Dickinson, Waterford, Conn.

Their mission in space takes five years:
Captain Kirk, brave and strong, has no fears;
"Bones" McCoy is soft-spoken,
Uhura's the token,
And Spock is the one with the ears.

Bunny Daniels, Hewlett, N.Y.

On an island for just a brief stay
Are ten guests who get killed, one a day;
It was done by the judge
Who had carried a grudge—
Oops!—I've given the ending away.

Ruth Migdal, Bklyn.

This prince, on advice from a ghost,
At a fête kills his uncle, the host.
Stabs a bore. The bore's daughter
Goes mad underwater.
And his mummy dies drinking a toast.

Paula Callan, N.Y.C.

In a manner befittingly gory
The *Pequod*'s whole crew goes to glory.
Now hold on, what gives?
Oh, well, Ishmael lives,
'Cause otherwise who'd tell the story?

Doug Cassie, Old Saybrook, Conn.

The Tyrone Clan—like the O'Neills—
Can bore you to death with their spiels;
Their Journey has got
A not-so-hot plot:
Four saints in four acts and three meals.

Eve Blake, N.Y.C.

A Florentine followed his nose
Through hell to the heavenly rose,
With Vergil his guide,
And Beatrice beside;
He saw all there was, I suppose.

Miriam Weiss, N.Y.C.

Well, Rome really needed the money;
And, further, the Gauls got too funny.
So we sent out our legions
To conquer those regions.
J. Caesar? Yep, he was there, sonny.

Morrie Ryskind, Beverly Hills, Calif.

A friendly imbiber named Dowd,
Who was neither rambunctious nor loud
Had a pal rather funny,
A seven-foot bunny
Who never stood out in a crowd.

Charles S. Morris, San Francisco, Calif.

Mobs of Russians, both guys and their dames,
With quite unpronounceable names,
Make a book that you need
A whole summer to read:
And once, Moscow goes up in flames.

Fred Berg, Boston, Mass.

Captain Ahab had queer mental flaws.
Moby Dick (got his leg) was the cause.
Harpooned in the flank
Dick and Ahab both sank.
I think it was better than *Jaws.*

Paula van Aken, N.Y.C.

They were lost for they hadn't a shrink. So
In Paris, Pamplona they'd drink so.
"Lady Ashley," said Jake, "It
Would help if we make it."
Said Brett: "Ain't it pretty to think so?"

Edna Blanchard, N.Y.C.

Miss Channing, née Lorelei Lee,
Hopped the old *Ile de France* to Paree.
There, the Little Rockette
Found the world's her baguette,
And a part to play permanently.

Carleton Carpenter, Warwick, N.Y.

An old man of Hebrew extraction,
Created the world. Some attraction.
It never was tested
'Cause Sunday He rested.
We're waiting for Nader's reaction.

Harry LaPlume, N. Adams, Mass.

Poor Crusoe, alone on an isle,
Found footprints near his domicile
Where he hadn't trod—
"It's Friday, thank God!"
He cried, and thus started a style.

Msgr. A.V. McLees, St. Albans, N.Y.

John Alden was Standish's proxy,
But Myles got the sharpest of knocks; he
Lost any scintilla
Of chance with Priscilla—
The price of his unorthodoxy.

Lynn S. Ellner, Richland, Wash.

The saga of Oedipus Rex
Is actually very complex:
He murders his dad,
Who's the king; then the cad
Blindly marries his mom. (Rated X)

Richard Des Ruisseaux, Louisville, Ky.

One-Sentence Book

Had Mara not departed Shadowcroft that night, that awful night, she would not have met Geoffrey; she'd not have loved him, died for him, and I would not now be writing these barren words before my final act of revenge.

Above, a whole in one. Competitors were asked to compose a one-sentence mystery, novel of manners, spy thriller, Gothic or science-fiction tale, biography or any other genre of prose.

Report: Favored topics included: transsexuality, abduction by space critters, the Eyress, time machines, cryogenics, murder at the manor, end of the world/universe, Nixon memorabilia, 007, Holmes & Watson, war and cease-fire. Thanks to all, and don't be fooled by imitations.

Is he one of ours or one of theirs, this toad-eyed, unsmiling Herr Glöckler, who got me seated on the Zagreb flight beside cynical, available Nadia the *Zeitung* stringer, and who led me to the brasserie in Zurich where vulpine, dyspeptic Kulyagin nearly offed me before I recovered the microdot: ours or theirs, I wonder, as I shoot him in the stomach—but it doesn't matter. . . .

Janet Lemkau, Plandome, N.Y.

Roosevelt in his shirtsleeves, laughing out loud at my Ickes impression; Ike angling away on my private pond . . . surely nothing could have been further from my thoughts as the midwife upended me and I squalled a lusty-lunged greeting at the lamplit laborer I would learn to call dad, a man destined never to relax in the rarefied air of Bel Air, of Belgravia—let alone the rough-and-tumble world of network TV comedy.

Fritz Steinegger, Beverly Hills, Calif.

Solving the apparent suicide required entrance as an earl into British society, forsaking the double-agent assignment in the CIA, which finally exorcised the demon battling for control of his body, the abandoned spaceship circulating forever in the time warp, thus adding significant details to this account of John Anderson's life which may be called murder mystery, novel of manners, spy thriller, Gothic or science-fiction tale, biography, or what you will.

Michael Schreiber, Bklyn.

My father danced the Paddington frisk ere I was born; had she not pleaded her belly, my mother would have joined him in that grisly dance and I would ne'er have seen the light of dusky day filtered through the crevices of Newgate Gaol, whence I received my introduction to a world of knaves and felons and my name, Gallows O'Farrell, which was the start of my undoing.

Robert McHaffey, N.Y.C.

The universe began when man learned to reason; the universe ended when man failed to communicate; and in between there was Lilo: half-Martian, half-goddess.

David McDonough, East Hampton, N.Y.

Little did I realize when Smoky Eyes ankled her shapely self into my cluttered office seeking my services on that sultry (and hungover) September morning that the next week would find me being bushwhacked comatose eleven times while scurrying a gamut from the squalor of L.A.'s skid row to the squareness of Pasadena's *haut monde* before finally discerning that it had been she who had scragged her missing elderly, but very wealthy, spouse.

J. M. Riordan, Laguna Beach, Calif.

It's crazy, I suppose—but I can't help wondering if I'd have married four of the world's greatest lovers, become the toast of Rumania at seventeen and a drug-riddled derelict at 22, or lost the most famous child-custody case of the century if the man sitting next to me on the Pullman out of Chicago on that grim August afternoon in 1937 hadn't been Howard.

Lewy Olfson, South Lyme, Conn.

As I departed from Gweneth's newly acquired Mercedes I stood in the chilly morning sun of Kensington and looked up to investigate what matter of life was dripping onto my face—an icicle, *an icicle*—Smedley was stabbed with an icicle; that explains the varied circumferences of puncture wounds from flesh to ventricle, *and* why a puddle but no weapon was found, *and* the poor bloke's frostbitten nipple—and what about Gweneth's perpetually gloved hand?

Charles Almon, Bklyn.

Ever since the accident, I'm told, that gave me amnesia, my search, I think, for who knows what has led to nobody existing on my memory, nor to any place evoking a sense of déjà vu (a phrase someone used), nor, for that matter, to any recovery that would have enabled me to flesh out this work with specifics with which it is perhaps just as well that I did not bore you.

Jack Paul, Bklyn.

Shelby tried to smile as her father clumsily muttered words of consolation that tripped over each other like a half-shod mare: yes, there would be other gymkhanas, other horses; besides, that young man next door, the boy entering Princeton, seemed quite taken with her; but for Shelby there could never be another gymkhana, and no Princeton freshman could ever replace the beautiful dish-faced pony with too much heart—the Alhambra!

Martin Gross, N.Y.C.

Delayed in traffic, the vice-president arrived late at the meeting of the National Security Council and found all of its members shot dead in their seats; he dashed to the Oval Office, streaking past the startled Secret Service agent, and burst in shouting, "They've shot everyone but me"; the president looked up, pulled a .38 from his desk, and replied, "I know."

Pericles Crystal, Scarsdale, N.Y.

Some might think it a familiar story, twice scorning a love in impetuous youth to spend the remainder of one's days in its idle pursuit, and I am among them.

Larry Laiken, Bayside, N.Y.

Here I was, 40 years old, I'd lost Alice, and what was worse, my big serve was deserting me; but I was beginning to learn that there was a kind of winning that had nothing to do with tournaments, and that maybe—just maybe—this sweet, crazy kid could teach it to me.

E. S. Joline, Huntington, N.Y.

Ace Brannigan nervously approached the high wall surrounding the Carlyle Mansion, flung a rope over the top, quickly scrambled over, ran up to the house, broke through the double French doors, and was startled by the sight of Colonel Rostonoff facing him in a green velvet club chair with a revolver in his hand.

A. M. Haluka, N.Y.C.

"My dear inspector, you were quite correct in your deduction that the pistol was held high, and in the left hand, but these four small indentations in the carpet suggest that the victim's jealous wife was too short to have fired the fatal shot, for I noticed in her bedroom a small footstool which I believe you will find fits the indentations exactly."

Skip Livingston, Hopewell, N.J.

As we stood there in the men's room of the Cine Palace, our usher's uniforms a sharp contrast to the gleaming white tile, I felt as though, perhaps for the first time in my life, I could say something that would prevent the pain and misery *I* had suffered, "Let me tell you something, kid, don't ever go to L.A."

Stephen Maynard, N.Y.C.

"Don't be an ass, Bunny," drawled Lalique, as she slathered on the Bain de Soleil, "there are plenty of reasons for coming to Acapulco out of season besides tracking down one's first husband. . . ."

James Elward, N.Y.C.

Even as Kate Darby took her bows to thunderous applause, she could see that grand lady of the theater, Margaret Manning, sitting in a wheelchair in the wings, a tight smile around her mouth and a fresh plaster cast around her leg; while handsome Mark Blenheim, the show's moody director and—miraculously—her husband-to-be, stepped forward and handed her a bouquet of red roses, the kind a chorus girl never gets to see.

Dorothy Lisee, Tenafly, N.J.

Figure your tax on the amount on line 47 by using Tax Rate Schedule X, Y, or Z or if applicable the alternative tax from Schedule D, income averaging form Schedule G or maximum tax from Form 4726 or take up arms against a sea of troubles as I do now.

Dorothy Green, Yonkers, N.Y.

Shadows swallowed Groansea near the Isles of Mordranth as vengeful dragons unleashed their spells of darkness, fear, and evil on the star-wise, wind-wealthy Sealords of Falmor, and Haebeeth the enchanter summoned the powers of the mages to save Falmor's destiny in numinous battles, but the wizard Geontuane named the dragons' powers, vanquished their evils, and sank the loathsome lair into the resounding silence of the seareach.

Dorothy Atkins, Lincoln, Neb.

As Nell stole a glance at her handsome, highborn bridegroom whose solemn gaze was fixed upon the bishop intoning their marriage vows, she thought of her sot of a husband who would never know of the dazzling future which now lay before her.

Judith R. Goldsmith, Woodmere, N.Y.

Melissa's marriage to bold, blond, handsome Frederick was spoiled only by his growing obsession with the emerald—looking like some idol's eye—which brought to her mind for a fleeting second dark forebodings of murder, rape, arson, fratricide, dope addiction, infidelity, parricide, assault, fanaticism, kidnapping, witchcraft, human sacrifice, suicide, psychosexual fetishism, and mysterious missed appointments; and yet—strangely—she intuitively felt the dark, intense, lonely Carlton would somehow be her savior.

W. S. Payton, Englewood, N.J.

Sir Peregrine Plum, having just finished his latest animal story for children, "Miss Piggywig Goes to Brighton," congratulated himself and lifted the hot Bovril to his lips, never suspecting that his favorite bedtime drink contained enough cyanide to kill ten of him or that his plump, pugnosed housekeeper, Miss Molly Coddley, would soon be slurping her last blancmange, outsmarted by Achille Parfum, the brilliant egg-shaped sleuth.

Ms. Freddi Bell, Hackensack, N.J.

It was a cold March afternoon, outside Philpitts, when I finally spotted the Denebian—a ghastly, horribly bloated, six-legged creature with one enormous eye and covered with a concretelike skin that chattered as it walked; I stunned the unspeakable horror with my remaining blaster charge, and muttered, "When will these aliens learn that they must, by law, register with the Solar Federation by 31Ja?"

Len Elliott, Auburn, Wash.

Had Marty Wagner not shown Mrs. Greer the *New York* Magazine, had we not written etymologies for an assignment, had Mrs. Greer not sent them in to the magazine, had our class not been mentioned in the magazine, I would not now be writing these boring words.

Susan Bartos, New Rochelle, N.Y.

Punned Foreign Phrases

YIPPE YI-YO CAHIERS—French Cowboy Film Journal.
MIRA, MIRROR ON THE WALL—Wicked Queen in *Snow Blanca* with a flair for the obvious.
FOR MANY ARE CALLED BUT FUHRER CHOSEN—Nazi Election.

Above, Foreign Co-respondents. Competitors were asked to define familiar phrase containing the punned version of a foreign word.

Report: Genuinely garish puns: more in French or Yiddish than Estonian—proving that parlez games are the quiche of death. Or quelque chose. Maintenant, les reprises: TAKE ME TO YOUR LIEDER. KVETCH 22. LONDON DERRIÈRE. STORY OF EAU. TEQUILA MOCKINGBIRD. GREER GARÇON. ALLES B. TOKLAS. CARRY A BIG SHTICK. ABSINTHE MAKES THE HEART GROW. TSURIS SHOOTIN'. THE QUALITY (or KOALA TEA) OF MERCI. A ROSE IS ARROZ. NEIN STORIES. HEIL BE SEEING YOU. THE OLD GREY MER. LIVRES OF GRASS. BIG HUILE. CHAUD BOAT. CIAO MEIN. SKOAL FOR SCANDAL. CHIC OF ARABY. É-COLE DAY IN HELL, and THINGS GO BETTER WITH COQ. Fin de reprises. Beaucoup de sexisme dedans. Fin de Seville liberties. Come back, shöen. Meanwhile, Grazie, Danke, Gracias, Hsieh, Merci, Pices, and Bashful.

FIRST CLASS OR TSURIS—Choice of seating arrangements on El Al Airlines.

Ed Schultz, N.Y.C.

SAMEDI MY PRINCE WILL COME—I also have dates for Thursday and Friday.

Nancy E. Ash, N.Y.C.

DOUZAINE DON'TS—The Twelve Commandments (revised paperback entitled *Livre to Heaven*).

Norman Brust, N.Y.C.

UPHARSIN'S WAITING FOR ME AND MY GAL—Beware of marrying a wallflower.

Fred Berg, Boston, Mass.

THEY'RE WRITING SONGS OF LOVE BUT NOT FOURMI—Cry of a maiden ant.

Sandra Rosenberg, Bayside, N.Y.

CACHET FALLING STAR—Cologne made expressly for Chevy Chase.

Anna Lambiase, Brooklyn

HUITIES—Breakfast des octogenarians.

Mark Wolfson, Spring Valley, N.Y.

THE BREAKFAST OF CHAMPIGNONS—Jacques Armstrong's cereal.

Miles Klein, East Brunswick, N.J.

FÊTE ACCOMPLI—The party's over.

Richard Smith, Brooklyn

BANK AMARCORD—Federico Fellini's credit union.

Bob Kocheck, Perth Amboy, N.J.

THE RED BADGE OF COURRÈGES—Blusher by noted designer.

Sandy Feuerstein, Long Beach, N.Y.

ARMOIRE SADAT—Member of Egyptian cabinet.

Zeke Zonker, Joliet, Ill.

MUCH ADIEU ABOUT NOTHING—Travelogue by the Invisible Man.

Donald M. Millinger, Rochester, N.Y.

CHAIM: A YANKEE DOODLE DANDY—Jewish soldier in the American Revolution.

Frank A. McNeirney, Brooklyn

VALSE EYELASHES—Makeup for the Merry Widow.

Mel Rosen, Stanfordville, N.Y.

A TALE OF TWO ZITIS—Dickens's pasta cookbook.

Hyman Levy, N.Y.C.

THE YENTA CONFERENCE—1945 meeting between Eleanor Roosevelt, Clementine Churchill, and Nadezhda Stalin.

Christy & Arnold Brown, N.Y.C.

MOT—L'histoire de Maureen Dean (traduit de l'anglais).

Jeanne Fried, Springfield, N.J.

BLANC CHECK—see "White Russian."

Anthony Gray, Closter, N.J.

MACRÊTE—The Loch Ness Monster.

Priscilla G. Osborne, Boston, Mass.

SOMBRERO-VER THE RAINBOW—Munchkin hat dance.

Jay Livingston, N.Y.C.

CHÉ STADIUM—Latin American ball park.

Steve Schwartz, South Salem, N.Y.

PÂTÉ AT BLACK ROCK—Gael Greene appraises the gourmet restaurants of Arizona.

Mary Fry, San José, Calif.

A FÊTE WORSE THAN DEATH—Cybill Shepherd Film Festival.

Tom Louis, Dobbs Ferry, N.Y.

NOCHES ANOTHER PRETTY FACE—Lady of the evening.

Beatrice Malon, Rego Park, N.Y.

ICI COME, EASY GO—Here today . . .

Beryl Downey, Newark, N.J.

THE LAST EN GRIS MAN—Militant in a Gray Flannel Suit.

William Fenner, D.V.M., N.Y.C.

CREATURE FROM THE BLACK LÉGUME—Del Monte's answer to Jolly Vert Giant.

S.B. Belen, Southfield, Mich.

MANQUÉ ON MY BACK—Not-quite-addicted drug user.

Doug Cassie, Old Saybrook, Conn.

WORKING WITHOUT A NYET—Amiable Moscow aerialist.

Ronald Linden, Princeton, N.J.

VENI, VIDI, VICHY—I came, I saw, I burped.

Joel Mansbach, Forest Hills, N.Y.

SODOM AND BEGORRAH—Racy Irish balladeers.

Jack Rose, N.Y.C.

BUERRE—Cholesterol Cookbook by Gore Vidal.

Rosa-Lee Listokin, Brooklyn

PRIX SOAK—Expensive car wash for racers.

Bruce Karp, N.Y.C.

HOW TO BE YOUR OWN BÊTE FRIEND—How-to book by Henry Jekyll, M.D.

Angelo Papa, Trenton, N.J.

CHALLAH FAME—New Brooklyn bakery.

C.J. Chatsworth, San José, Cal.

ONE PEUT-ÊTRE, TWO PEUT-ÊTRE, THREE PEUT-ÊTRE . . . Recipe from *The Uncertain Potato Cookbook.*

Margaux McMillan, Orinda, Cal.

PUTANA HAPPY FACE—Smile button worn by Roman prostitutes.

Stephen Pearlman, Los Angeles, Cal.

CALL ME A SCHLEMIEL—Opening sentence of *Moby Morris.*

Physic Bldg., SUNY, Albany, N.Y.

CHAI TOR—Mount Sinai.

Paula Van Aken, N.Y.C.

TUTU DIVINE—Margot Fonteyn.

Lucille Kadner, Los Angeles, Cal.

HERR—Germany's hit rock musical.

Myrna J. Glick, Wayne, N.J.

Book Retorts

1. Did you read that book on echoes?
2. Book on echoes? Book on echoes?

1. Did you read that book on crime in New York City?
2. Yeah, I stole it from the Canterbury Book Shop.

Above, book retorts. Competitors were asked for an all-too appropriate reply to "Did you read that book on . . .?"

Report: A huge entry, so right to the repeats: **1.** Did you read that book on modesty? **2.** Read it? I wrote it! **1.** Did you read that book on insomnia? **2.** Finished it at 5 A.M. **1.** Did you read that book—**2.** On ESP? **1.** Did you read that book on paranoia? **2.** Why do you ask? **1.** On sexual excess causing deafness? **2.** What? **1.** On memory improvement? **2.** I think so. **1.** On Barnes and Noble? **2.** Of course, of course. **1.** On levitation? **2.** Couldn't put it down. **1.** On milk? **2.** Skimmed it (or) Condensed version. **1.** On suicide? **2.** No, dying to. **1.** On the women's movement? **2.** My husband wouldn't let me. **1.** On speed reading? **2.** Ys. **1.** On the English language by Edwin Newman? **2.** No, but between you and I, hopefully I will. **1.** On basements? **2.** Best seller. **1.** On the CIA? **2.** Cover to cover. **1.** On the shelf? **2.** No, at the library. **1.** On the *Titanic?* **2.** Fortunately, no. **1.** *On the Waterfront?* **2.** No, at home. **1.** On palindromes? **2.** Did I? I did. **1.** On procrastination? **2.** Not yet. **1.** On Watergate? **2.** Not to the best of my recollection. **1.** Did you read that book on chopped liver? **2.** Did *I* read that book on chopped liver?

1. Did you read that book on the life of Henny Youngman?
2. Why, is one missing?

Terri Hallen, Stamford, Conn.

1. Did you read that book on snappy comebacks, you jerk?
2. Yes. . . . Make that no.

Debbie Bennett, Washington, D.C.

1. Did you read that book on Emperor CLAVDIVS?
2. Yes, wasn't it FABVLOVS?

Arch Napier, Tucson, Ariz.

1. Did you read that book on being a good listener?
2. Oh, look, it's snowing!

Larry Laiken, Bayside, N.Y.

1. Did you read that book on Art Fleming?
2. What is "Yes, Don Pardo, I did"?

Max Gilbert, Long Beach, N.Y.

1. Did you read that book on the sex life of the pygmy ants of Krakatoa?
2. Which one?

Margaux McMillan, Orinda, Calif.

1. Did you read that book on sexism in the office?
2. No, but I had my girl pick me up a copy on her lunch hour.

Anne Bernstein, Bronx;
Marilyn Crystal, Scarsdale, N.Y.

1. Did you read that book on Tyrone Power?
2. What's a Tyrone?

Evelyn Seltzer, New City, N.Y.

1. Did you read that book on the anatomy of waterfowl?
2. Does a duck have lips?

Chuck Stevick, Herminie, Pa.

1. Did you read that book on self-hypnosis?
2. Bow wow.

Mitch Gilbert, N.Y.C.

1. Did you read that book on manners?
2. Yes—so kind of you to ask.

Fanny K. Costello, Charleston, W. Va.

1. Did you read that book on American education?
2. No, man, I can't read.

Denise Bouchet, Chicago, Ill.

1. Did you read that book on how to get children to eat?
2. Yes, but it didn't explain how to cook them.

Paula Callan, N.Y.C.

1. Did you read that book on how the rich are different?
2. I'm waiting for the paperback to come out.

Sal Rosa, N.Y.C.

1. Did you read that book on improving work habits?
2. No, but I will after my nails dry—if it isn't five o'clock by then.

Simi Kirschner, Bronx

1. Did you read that book on the occult?
2. No, I didn't. And I especially didn't like that chapter on West Indies voodoo rites.

Richard Fried, N.Y.C.

1. Did you read that book on phobias?
2. No, I'm afraid not.

Carly Mary Cady, Los Angeles, Calif.

1. Did you read that book on squirrels?
2. No, I put it away somewhere and I can't find it.

Rose Corbett, Long Island City, N.Y.

1. Did you read that book on name-dropping?
2. No, I lent my copy to Jessica and Hume when they were sick and next thing I knew Mike lost it.

Stephen Gelb, Brooklyn

1. Did you read that book on murder for profit?
2. No, but my widow did.

Glenn T. Boyer, Middletown, N.Y.

1. Did you read that book on compulsive eating?
2. Yes, it was delicious.

Faith I. Luber, Newark, N.J.

1. Did you read that book on overpopulation?
2. No, the librarian said that it's on reserve until 1982.

Evelyn Seligman, Dollard des Ormeaux, Quebec

1. Did you read that book on exhibitionism?
2. Yes, I have it here under my raincoat.

Ellen Schreiber, Bronx

1. Did you read that book on piano playing made easy?
2. No—but hum a few bars and I'll fake it.

Anne Milton, San Francisco, Calif.

1. Did you read that book on tiresome writing styles?
2. I walk into Doubleday's. I pick up this book. The flap copy grabs me. I look at the first chapter. . . .

Ernie Norris, Hydes, Md.

1. Did you read that book on how to win friends more easily?
2. Yes.

Michael Marcus, N.Y.C.

1. Did you read that book on how to carry on more stimulating conversations?
2. No.

David R. Ammons, Andalusia, Pa.

1. Did you read that book on footwear through the ages?
2. Your mother wears army boots.

Rosemary Bascome, Shelter Island, N.Y.

1. Did you read that book on how to speak French fluently in two weeks?
2. *Si.*

B. Moria, Muttontown, N.Y.

1. Did you read that book on yogurt?
2. Yes. I borrowed it from Bagwar Tapagua.

P. Sipp, N.Y.C.

1. Did you read that book on how to say no?
2. Yes.

Richard Nathanson, Jericho, N.Y.

1. Did you read that book on world records?
2. Yes—in two hours, 32 minutes, twelve seconds—but I wasn't the first.

Barbara Babich, Orangeburg, N.Y.

1. Did you read that book on birth control?
2. Anthony, Sasha, Caroline, Sam, Maureen, Cindy, Max—be quiet. No.

Phyllis Ostrafsky, Brooklyn

1. Did you read that book on malapropisms?
2. I caroused it.

Don Wigal, N.Y.C.

1. Did you read that book on identity problems?
2. Who, me?

Elysa Hartstein, N.Y.C.

1. Did you read that book on the machine age?
2. No, but if you will leave the title, author, and approximate time of your call . . .

Bonnie Champion, N.Y.C.

1. Did you read that book on being your own best friend?
2. Yes, we liked it.

Lelia Vincent, Johnston, R.I.

1. Did you read that book on banking?
2. I started to, but I lost interest.

Eric C. Landman, Englewood, N.J.

1. Did you read that book on decision-making?
2. No. Should I?

Helene Levine, Rego Park, N.Y.

1. Did you read that book on willpower?
2. I couldn't put it down.

Sheila Kaplan, Brooklyn

Did you read that book on assertiveness?
1. If you say so.
2. No. Give me your copy.
3. Well, yes. And, please forgive me for asking, but do you think it's helped me? You don't have to answer if you don't want to.

1. Christine Ackerman, St. Louis, Mo.
2. Lou Grillo, West Hartford, Conn.
3. Mark Sherman, New Paltz, N.Y.

1. Did you read that book on winning friends and influencing people?
2. I read it in *Reader's Digest,* bugle lips.

John Hofer, Southboro, Mass.

TV Guide Listings

STOREFRONT DOCTOR—Dr. Morton lances a boil, prepares to go golfing, and refuses treatment to a sick woman because of spiraling insurance costs. Dr. Morton: John McMartin.
ILONA—Twice-divorced Ilona is a magazine editor and successful interior designer. In tonight's episode, Ilona discovers her date is homosexual. Ilona: Charlotte Moore. Bill: Charlotte Moore.
COMPUTER COP—A short circuit causes Astro to attack the police commissioner, clone himself, and become confused about a rabbit. Astro: Larry Kert.

Above, plots to be buried. Competitors were asked for one TV Guide listing for a familiar-but-flawed program.

Report: Fred Silverman could probably get a whole new season just from our duplicated entries. Among them: The Bionic Child, Cat, Nun, Butcher, Yenta, Transsexual, Bird, Actor, and Chef. Plus Bionic Acres and One Bionic Man's Family. Celebrity Checkers, Canasta, Quoits, and Poultry. *Poultry?* A few elderly jokes à la Frontier Accountant. The majority, original and wispy titles of which these may be a few: Me and the Pimp. Great Presidential Debates. Getting Off on Youth. Partners in Crime. Tooth Fairy. D.J.'s on Wheels. Backstage Actuary. The Sonny & Cher Altoona Open. Alaskan IRS Agent. Wide World of Dry Cleaning. Jim Goofus, Computer Programmer.

The French Surgeon. The Don Porter Show. And, The Candlemaker in the Woods. Don't ask.

INSECT THEATER—Common garden spiders are featured this week in an uncommon production of *Death of a Salesman.*

Jeff Monasch, Bklyn.

THE JACK PALANCE COMEDY HOUR—Joining Jack tonight is actor Robert De Niro. Jack and Robert play two zany doctors in a skit, and in the finale, salute the songs of Lerner and Loewe.

Mrs. Edith Rutman, Bklyn.

BIG SELLERS—*Exodus,* Chapter Eight. While Moses tries to reason with Pharaoh, Egypt is overrun by frogs, lice, and flies, and tempers flare. Moses: Hal Holbrook. Pharaoh: Jos. Wiseman.

Ellen Conford, Massapequa, N.Y.

JANE—Jane (Sandy Duncan) makes Mr. Rochester (Gale Gordon) furious when she accidentally sets fire to his mansion. Heathcliff the Doorman: Anthony Zerbe.

Carole S. Hoffman, Manitowoc, Wis.

LITTLE-KNOWN OPERAS—*Der Vinderschmeer.* Heinz flees to the forest hoping to break his loathsome habit. On Gaflooglenicht he meets the Kleinerkins, tiny peekers ruled by Lumpschen, Goddess of Knotholes. Heinz: Frucht Wahnsinning.

Albert G. Miller, N.Y.C.

THE NAPALM SHOW—Host Don Rickles welcomes a celebrity panel to view obscure talent. If, after 30 seconds, the contestant is deemed untalented by the panel, he is sprayed with a toxic defoliant. Tonight a man dry-cleans a goat. Steve Allen, Esther Rolle, Jodie Foster.

Mario A. J. Mondelli Jr., N.Y.C.

MURRAY—Murray's new co-workers in Los Angeles know lots of baldness jokes. But he gets homesick anyway and calls Mary. Mary's Voice on Phone: Jim Backus.

Bettina Conner, Washington, D.C.

WARLOCK AND FAMILIAR—Wendell discovers that Beelzebub has mites. Wendell: William Conrad.

Barbara F. Eisenberg, N.Y.C.

PAPERHANGER—Through a series of mixups, Billy finds himself assigned to wallpaper a haunted house. The fun begins when the walls start moving.

Richard P. Monley, Birmingham, Mich.

SHOPPING SPREE—Shopping tips and travel hints on a budget. Hosts: Sen. Strom Thurmond, S.C., and Sen. William L. Scott, Va.

Louise Chianese, Chicago, Ill.

BLUES GUYS KNOW GANDHI—Four fun-loving jazz musicians from New Orleans travel to India in search of enlightenment and play an impromptu gig with the daughter of an untouchable.

No Signature, N.Y.C.

CLOSET QUEEN—Victoria rearranges her wardrobe again and her clothes are not amused.

David J. Mackler, Rosedale, N.Y.

BARRY LYNDON—After a twilight stroll through the garden, Barry and Lady Lyndon enjoy a candlelight dinner.

John Welsh, Chicago, Ill.

AFTERMATH—Roberta and Larry Winter and son Forrest wait out the holocaust in their one-room fallout shelter. In tonight's episode, Forrest hides the fresh-water supply as a practical joke.

Martin Schenker, Washington, D.C.

I GOTTA BE ME—Sarah Coventry salesman faces possible disciplinary action for giving away friendship rings. Loman: Sammy Davis Jr.

Roger Talbot, Gardena, Calif.

THE HOLDOUTS—Some of the world's greatest athletes hang together to battle crime while waiting for their contracts to be renewed. Dr. J.: Julius Erving. Tiny: Nate Archibald.

Bruce Karp, N.Y.C.

THE SONNY & GREGG SHOW—Musical comedy.

Sal Rosa, N.Y.C.

DRAMA IN COURT—In response to defendant's 12 (b) (6) dismissal motion, plaintiff moves to amend his complaint. The judge raises the question of diversity of jurisdiction *sera sponte* and abstention is invoked.

M. L. Perlin, Trenton, N.J.

THE TIME VOYAGERS—Marion goes back to the year 1953 and purchases four Regency chairs for $45 apiece.

Amanda Raymond, N.Y.C.

SKY'S THE LIMIT! Norman Lear's latest about a wacky Mohawk family in Brooklyn. Tonight, Grandpa Sky (Chief Dan George) announces he wants to go back into the family's construction business. John: Michael Ansara.

Philip N. Hathaway, Bloomington, Ill.

OGG—Tonight, Caveman Ogg discovers his ear. Ogg: Morty Gunty. (90 min.)

Steven Gordon, N.Y.C.

MARLON BRANDO SHOW—Marlon and his assistant demonstrate the everyday, practical advantages of the solar wind vector, sundial, and body heat. Marlon: Marlon Brando. Assistant: Barbara Howar.

Ken Nicholas, Highland Park, Ill.

THE $20,000,000 PYRAMID. Exciting new game show pits a team of Egyptologists against a team of archaeologists to decipher new hieroglyphics.

Kevin Heisler, Charlotte, N.C.

HORSE CRAZY—Debut. A new comedy based on the hit Broadway play *Equus.*

Susan Salter, Southfield, Mich.

FAT LIKE ME—Myra Lint, svelte reporter for a major metropolitan newspaper, gets a new assignment: to disguise herself as fat and expose discrimination.

Marvin Melzer, Athens, Ga.

HOUSEHUSBAND—David drives the kids to school, plays tennis, washes the windows, and takes Geritol; his wife, Alice, decides to keep him.

Alexander Glatt, Bklyn.

TRANSPARENT!—Science fiction. Debut. Close-up opposite. (90 min.) (Pre-empts regular programming.)

D. Jean Mayer, Boswell, Pa.

UNEMPLOYED BILL—Bill gets up before noon and can't find any rolling paper, so he uses his college diploma.

Edward B. Leahy III, Putneyville, N.Y.

THE NEW JULIE SHOW—Julie Andrews recreates some of her best-loved characters. Tonight's guest star: Billy Mumy. Highlight: "Inclement Weather" medley.

Peter L. Vandenbrul, Poughkeepsie, N.Y.

REMBRANDT JONES—Eastern artist visits the West in the 1880s. Rembrandt rides out in search of a buffalo to draw.

Peter W. Warren, Billings, Mont.

THE ADOPTERS—Another setback for Sid and Marge. Gasoline costs are up and they can no longer drive to distant orphanages or black-market connections. Sid: Pat Boone. Marge: Donna Reed.

Dan Sherman, Albany, N.Y.

DEADWOOD—Each week a guest star plays the sheriff in this western saga. At the end of each segment, the sheriff is run out of town or meets an untimely end.

Simmie Bohey, Chicago, Ill.

THE FINE LINE—Great Granddaddy Fine, Grandpa Fine, Fred Fine, and seven-year-old Richie Fine (all widowers) live together and have all sorts of fun. This week: A fine romance.

Gary Geyer, N.Y.C.

MARIO AND ERNESTINA MELODY SHOW—Mario and Ernestina sing: "Do-Wacka-Do" and "Dang Me." Mr. Fix makes a shoeshine box. Tonight's guest: Laurence Olivier.

Toni Marco, Bklyn.

THE EAST-SIDERS—Brunch with Jean-Luc forces Rachel to confront her depression. Emily cancels her date with Tod.

Joe Enasconi, N.Y.C.

CHAD MICHAELS, WEST-SIDER—Young executive, bored with his Turtle Bay existence, finds he "gets off" on the West Side. Chad: Dean Pitchford. Girl in Bar: Alice Playten.

Glen Roven, N.Y.C.

POLICE DOG—Sgt. "Bowser" Anderson goes undercover to expose a shady obedience school. Plenty of car chases.

Len Prokine, Roslyn, N.Y.

FIGHTING RABBI—Rabbi Benjamin is attacked by thugs as he leaves the synagogue Friday night but turns the evening around when he discovers that his tormentors are Jewish.

Susan Kline, Minneapolis, Minn.

GO-GO BOY—Billy accepts an invitation to dance at the local women's club, then learns that his girl Gladys is a member.

Charles Librizzi, Atlantic City, N.J.

THE $25,000 SKY JUMP—Dressed as fowls of their choice, contestants compete for cash prizes while free-falling from a 747.

Frank Russo, Utica, N.Y.

PERKY AND ME—Seven-year-old boy and transistorized, invisible Chihuahua rescue stray hamster and help police solve baffling mass-murder case.

Linda J. Kern, Miami, Fla.

A WORD TO THE WISE—Dr. Featherwell explains the meaning and origin of the word "abhor."

Ken Coleman, Worcester, Mass.

FUNERAL LAWYER—Legal Aid lawyer and his secretary set out to prove his death was a case of murder, not suicide.

Dan Chayefsy, N.Y.C.

BARBARA WALTERS LIVE!—Tonight Amy Carter makes her singing debut ("Boogie Fever"). Other guests are Anson Williams ("Could It Be Magic?"), rock group Smooch, comedian Ronnie Schell, and the Flying Ferracutis. Barbara interviews Ilie Nastase and Premier Hua. The Rockettes. Bob Rosengarden Orchestra.

Charles Carson, Knoxville, Tenn.

WORLD CHAMPIONSHIP CHESS—Anatoly Karpov sits on an empty stage in the Philippines. Shelby Lyman, Commentator.

David M. Eisenberg, Silver Spring, Md.

THIEU'S COMPANY—Norman Lear's new series focuses on the shenanigans of former South Vietnamese cabinet members as they adjust to life in a Guam resettlement camp.

Edwin Schallert, Pacific Palisades, Calif.

THE DIVINE COMEDY HOUR—Hosted by Guru Maharaj Ji, the Perfect Master of Ceremonies.

Don Lessem, Cambridge, Mass.

CAPTAIN MARSUPIAL—Farmer Greenapple pets baby ducklings and sings a song about birthdays. Mrs. Bunny-Wunny shows how to wash hands and joins Mrs. Chickadee in a song about spring. Grandpa Timepiece teaches how to count from one to ten and reads the story "Baby Panda Plays the Drum." Daisy the Clown sings "I Like Chocolate in My Milk." The entire cast congratulates the Captain as he begins his 26th year on television. The Captain discusses suicide and its ramifications.

Douglas Braverman, East Meadow, N.Y.

GREEN ACRES 1975—Nguyen Cao Ky as a gentlemen farmer who settles in rural Kentucky. Tonight a neighbor's pig mauls a row of cauliflower, and Ky calls in air strikes.

Bill Goldschlag, N.Y.C.

HARVEY AWARDS—Television honors its invisible actors. Nominees include Carlton the Doorman and Don Pardo. Johnny Carson is guest host.

Lyell Rodieck, N.Y.C.

MONTY'S FLYING PYTHON CIRCUS—Carnival is sold after Monty and his friends are eaten alive by winged serpents. Next week in this time period: Herman's Flying Python Circus.

Alan Kroker, Oak Pk., Mich.

EYEWITNESS NEWS—Arabs and Israelis clash in Middle East. Students attack U.S. Embassy. Cost of living up .6 per cent in N.Y. area. Teachers threaten strike. Mayor Beame blames fiscal situation on GOP. Mets win, Yanks split. Roger Grimsby chides weatherman. (Repeat)

Thos. Van Steenbergh, Bergenfield, N.J.

CELEBRITY BULLFIGHTING—Leading Hollywood personalities try their hand in the arena of death. Host: Bill Dana.

Brian Joseph, Cambridge, Mass.

CELEBRITY QUOITS—Host Dr. Martin Abend welcomes Beverly Sills, Pelé, Bella Abzug, and Thomas Hoving. . . .

Norton Bramesco, N.Y.C.

NO HURRY!—A cat decides not to climb a tree. A pregnant woman has an uneventful ride in a World Trade Center elevator. Hurricane Hulga peters out at sea. Perry Como guest stars.

Fran Ross, N.Y.C.

UNDERWATER ADVENTURE—Jacques Cousteau and photographer unexpectedly encounter a giant white shark near Amity, Long Island. (Last in series)

Jacqueline Fogel, Jamaica, N.Y.

WHIPLASH!—Young lawyers chase laughs and ambulances in this new series. Tonight Morris and José defend a notorious tort-feasor.

Ms. Averill Kaufman, San Francisco, Calif.

ENRICO AND THE PAN—The adventures of a hospital orderly. (Premiere)

Seymour M. Weit, Bklyn.

ABERCROMBIE AND FETCH—The story of a boy and the dog that loved him.

Mike Rubin, Baton Rouge, La.

POLICE STURGEON—Friend of Flipper fights for law and order in this compelling undersea crime drama.

George Axelrod, N.Y.C.

MOVIE. THE BRIDE COMES TO SKIATOOK—In this tale of the Old West, the Marshal of Skiatook has gone off to marry. Upon returning, he is embarrassed to let the townspeople know she's a Communist.

Bill Emery, Oklahoma City, Okla.

BILL—Bill's watch stops and he discovers that there is no butter in the refrigerator. His mother is subjected to a cruel emotional outburst. Neighbor Julie summons the jeweler and together they calm Bill, who goes to the grocer and buys a pound of Danish butter for himself and a pint of strawberries for his mother.

Jane Saniford, Somerville, Ma.

I LOVE MEDEA—When Jason won't let her try out for the Club Argo, Medea talks Ethel into helping her in a zany scheme to kill little Jason.

Richard Helfer, N.Y.C.

BENIHANA—Each week two different strangers, seated next to each other at the counter tables of Benihana, tell their life stories. Skilled chefs provide a continuous background.

Joel Henkin, East Brunswick, N.J.

HOTEL COLLINGWOOD—Hijinks on the East Side of the Big Apple. 1,001 tales of suspense, drama, and mirth.

Dorothy Green, Yonkers, N.Y.

MASTERPIECE THEATRE—A series of dramatizations of forgotten classics. Tonight: part one of Alfred Bunn's *The Bohemian Girl.*

Ron Harvie, Quebec, Canada

LIVE FROM P.S. 197—From the famous auditorium on Kings Highway in Brooklyn, the school orchestra plays Handel's "Water Music Suite" and a medley of Burt Bacharach tunes.

Joel Crystal, Scarsdale, N.Y.

YOU BET YOUR ASS—A new game show where contestants play pin-the-tail-on-the-donkey for exciting prizes. Timothy Bottoms hosts.
Morleen Novitt, Jackson Heights, N.Y.

MISTER ROGERS' GHETTO—Today: a visit to a Cadillac Showroom.
Brian Plante, Staten Island, N.Y.

LAPPS SPEAK OUT!—This weekly PBS news and discussion show investigates the special problems of Laplanders.
Andrea Fagin, Brooklyn

MAYBE NEXT TIME—The sometimes funny, always entertaining story of Dr. Ehrlich's search for a cure for syphilis. A Tandem production.
Don Lessem, Cambridge, Mass.

NEW SOCIALIST MAN—Laboring to fulfill the five-year plan, Ivanovich conceives a fondness for his tractor.
Stephen Moss, Scarsdale, N.Y.

WASP JOURNAL—On tonight's show, Clarke chats with Mrs. Winston "Muffie" Bancroft about her book, *Gardening With Your Gardener.* Deena visits Bootsie Bostwick at her boutique, Bootsie Funky Nonni.
Nancy Joline, Huntington, N.Y.

WE DIG YOU THE MOST—A young widower and his nine children open a funeral parlor in midtown Cleveland.
Julian Bradford II, East Providence, R.I.

ORCA—Japanese animated cartoon about a reformed killer whale and his little friend, Buddy.
Judith Klein, East Brunswick, N.J.

THE WILLY LOMAN SHOW—Someone is selected from the studio audience; his life is then systematically shattered.
Warren Alexander, Brooklyn

HOLMES AND WATSON—Two detectives try to guess which of them is the robot. Roger Moore and Lee Majors star.
Elsie Angell, Greenville, R.I.

Whimsical Etymology

PUMPERNICKEL—1812 [Fr. *"Pomme pour Nicole"*]: Wholemeal rye bread. (Napoleon, retreating from Moscow astride his mare, Nicole, dined upon peasant food. He scorned the Russian black bread, suitable only as an "apple for my horse.")

Above, derivative humor. Competitors were asked to invent the whimsical etymology of an existing word.

Report: C.T. Onions would be proud of you. Most of you. I think. Maybe. Generally a feverish lot: some blatantly antisemantic. Pidgin Italian, Chinese or other did not seem, um, apropos. Speaking of which, ever notice how you never see any *baby* pidgins anywhere? Just asking.

NEEDLESS [OE Needles—more than one needle]: unnecessary. (In Old England it was discovered that using a double "s" in the plural of needle was pointless.)

Ms. Gene Winslow, Summit, N.J.

FISHMEAL [ME; OE Fisk + OE mael]: animal or vegetable matter ground and fed to fish. (Common use and spelling first seen in Amer. novelist H. Melville's first draft of *Moby Dick,* which began, "Call me Fishmeal.")

Carol Forrest, Hopewell, N.J.

MACARONI—U.S. 1940 [dialect version of "Mickey Rooney"]: wheat flour noodles, dried and prepared for eating by boiling. (Named by the Milanese chef Guido Baccala, a devotee of Andy Hardy films who also originated scungilli alla Lewis Stone.)

Heather Vaughn, Old Lyme, Conn.

HEMOGLOBIN—Span. 1520 [colloq. for "He's circumnavigating the world"]: a response attributed to Mrs. Ferdinand Magellan when asked, "Is your husband home?"

W. H. Richardson, Peace Dale, R.I.

HAIKU [ME "high I.Q."]: Japanese verse composed by persons who can count to seventeen.

Maria Conti, Warwick, R.I.

KRAKATOA—1883 [Malay: "Krak a toa"]: volcanic island near Java. (On opening night two temple dancers exchanged traditional pre-performance "good luck" wishes. Shortly thereafter they were crushed by flying boulders.)

Jack Rose, N.Y.C.

UGH—1776 [Amer. Ind. "Ugh!"]: expression originated with Algonquin Indian medicine men who foresaw plans for their country's Bicentennial.

Judy Juzaitis, Haddonfield, N.J.

FEBRUARY [Yiddish. Undesirable, cold, miserable]: second month. (FEH—who needs it?; BR—freezing; U.A.R.y—having characteristics of United Arab Republic.)

Stanley Joseloff, Cocoa Beach, Fla.

POLONAISE [Fr.]: cavalrymen in Napoleon's army played polo using a round loaf of dark bread as a ball; their horses emitted resounding "neighs" (nays) if, after the match, they were offered the bread instead of an apple. (see PUMPERNICKEL)

Thomas Van Steenbergh, Bergenfield, N.J.

EEL [Ital. "il"]: simplified American/English—That's a moray.

Mrs. Sylvia B. Jacobs, Old Lyme, Conn.

GNEISS: a foliated metamorphic rock. (Named by the Gnorwegian geologist, Gnicholas Gnelson, who declared, on its discovery in gnorthern Tibet, "That's gneiss, a gnew rock.")

Nancy Joline, Huntington, N.Y.

SALAMANDER—1897 [Corruption of Fr. *salle à manger*]: small, four-legged amphibian. (Name derived from the celebrated talking newt, François, exhibited at M. George-Framboise's Ménagerie de Paris. The creature, able to utter only the French for "dining room," died of mortification when given second billing to Henri, the yodeling quail.)

Jennifer Vaughn, Old Lyme, Conn.

MONSIGNOR [Ital. "My Lord"]: an honorary ecclesiastical title apparently named from the common reaction to new appointments: "My Lord! Why *him?*"

Msgr. A. V. McLees, St. Albans, N.Y.

LOLLYGAGGING: fooling around. (Coined in honor of Shirley Mae Parrish, who choked to death on a hard candy while her mother thought Shirley Mae was only "fooling around.")

Mr. M. S. Seacat, N.Y.C.

PRESIDENT [L. precedere, to go before + L. dentis, a tooth]: head of government. (From George Washington's reply when asked to be king, "First, let me go get my teeth.")

Anne Milton, San Francisco, Calif.

SCARSDALE: Westchester village. (Named by Roy Rogers on his first trip east; he was seated on a hill overlooking the Bronx River Parkway when his wife said, "Them's mighty funny horses." He replied, "It's cars, Dale.")

Pericles Crystal, Scarsdale, N.Y.

AUDITORIUM [L. audire, hear + taurus, bull]: a building for public gatherings. (It is often used by politicians or other orators for speech-making.)

William S. Klein, M.D., Silver Spring, Md.

PERCOLATOR—circa 1883 [It. "Porca latte"]: a kind of coffee pot. (Attributed to Giovanni Papuccino of Rome's Café Greco, who flatly refused to make American coffee because, he said, it tastes like "sow's milk.")

George Malko, N.Y.C.

HORS D'OEUVRE [Fr. "out of work"]: Lament uttered by chef to Louis XIV who dismissed the man for adding anchovy paste to the chopped-liver appetizers.

Steven D. Price, N.Y.C.

ACROBAT [Amer. colloq.]: small gold statuette awarded annually by the B. Lugosi Chamber of Horrors for outstanding achievement in vampirism.

M. Obarowski, Deerfield Beach, Fla.

TREE [from Latin tres, "three"]: because of the belief that plants were made on the third day of creation. (cf SEX)

K. B. Robinson, N.Y.C.

BOWDLERIZE—1818 [Gr. Br., after Rev. Thomas]: [redacted] upset with certain words in Gibbon's *The Rise and the* [redacted] *of the Roman* [redacted] and in Shakespeare's *Romeo and* [redacted], this British minister went about covering the eyes of readers with large stones so they could not read words such as [redacted], [redacted], and [redacted].

Don Wigal, N.Y.C.

Punned Quatrains

When Cleopatra's daddy died,
He left a fledgling sparrow,
They told her: "You rule Egypt's tide."
And she said, "MIA FARROW?"

I've been rereadin' books of mine—
One just ain't worth admirin'
Now Gore's enchantin'; Norman's fine
But oh, that WILLIAM STYRON.

Above, Me, a pharaoh? and William's tirin'. Competitors were asked for rhyming quatrains concluding with a punned famous name.

Report: Dine ashore. Tom is tryin'. A beam. You carry. Sell mah diamond. Chew and lie. If Scott fits Gerald. Sid, seize her. You, Gino, kneel. (E)clair booth loose. Al is fey. Who's kissing her now. Knicks on. Mark's pits. Dick & Tom's mothers. Ellen burst in. France is bakin'. Too loose, low track. Gertrude's tine. Marry and madden. Jack and her son. Surely black. Less brown. Fran's list. Louie's tea, aunt. Borrow his passkey. (Where Keats summers) Shelley winters. Sam's need. Her mon kill a brew. Darn knots. Roman pole and ski. Cart a burden. (Sleep on) Randolph's cot. William's afire. (Will) birch buy? (I didn't know) Anwar said dat. Frank and stein. Olive or twist. Her man woke and Sally ran. Marlin, brand O. Carry grant. Fadin' away. Hi, Lee's a lassie. Alix and her Pope. Stephen's on time. Beverly's ills. Her man Mel vill. Maria callous. Gym neighbors. James and Ali can, a manual can't. Pressed and forced her. A decanter. Yassuh, Ara fat. Louie passed her. Adam's myth. Eagle crow. O Mark, I am. Punch his pilot. And so Tibet.

Cats and cows and many mammals
Prefer an arid bed to bunk in.
Camels don't go in for swimmin',
But porpoise ISADORA DUNCAN.

Brad Fullagar, Bath, N.Y.

A Lennon verse makes Philip rave;
The queen is Ringo's fan;
The Prince of Wales is George's slave,
But I'll take PAUL CEZANNE.

Leslie Karst, Santa Cruz, Calif.

My clinic's full of specialists: Doc Wilson for the piles
(But his rates are somewhat higher than Blue Shield's);
For fractures you see Piker; for anxiety there's Miles—
If you're faint or seeing W.C. FIELDS

Harold Stone, N.Y.C.

You've *still* got it wrong! It was Norma flambée.
Lucia went mad in a spinney.
Aida was buried and the person who leapt
From a castle was TOSCANINI.

Barbara A. Huff, N.Y.C.

I can't wear small or medium—
(I'm built just like a moose.)
And yet I hate to ask for large.
I say, "ANITA LOOS."

Jack Labow, N.Y.C.

"This brew lacks something," frowned the witch.
"Perhaps a lizard's lung?
A bat's left ear? A rat's right eye?
I know! A MAO TSE-TUNG!"

Janet Lemkau, Plandome, N.Y.

When I took my friend Marge to the station,
She suggested we chat by the train.
I exclaimed, "There's no time for oration.
Either get aboard, MARJORIE MAIN."

Anne Hamill, N.Y.C.

We card players think we're immune to defeat.
A few setbacks at bridge do not daunt us.
A bad game of gin? Why, we'll bear it and grin—
But our losses at stud POCAHONTAS.

Richard Silvestri, Valley Stream, N.Y.

"Oh, spare me, Elizabeth! Pardon my lust!"
Essex cried as he knelt on the floor.
"While Your Majesty feels that my sentence is just,
I'd appreciate CLEMENT C. MOORE."

John A. Hertz, San Francisco, Calif.

To Paul VI, I said one day,
"That bride she'sa in fine fettle,"
Then I caught most of her bouquet,
And POPOCATEPETL.

Barbara O'Brien, Ridgewood, N.J.

There are rules in this gym;
Hang your towel on that rack
Fold your shorts in this locker
Take your JACQUES OFFENBACH.

Phil Levine, Bronx

Juan had the flu,
José slipped and fell,
Jorge had a belly ache
But LUIS BUÑUEL.

Angelo Papa, Trenton, N.J.

My dear, give me diamonds, not emeralds or rubies.
And those sweet little pearls by the rope'll
Not do, nor will sapphires or garnets or zircons,
And I simply CONSTANTINOPLE.

Lenore Millhollen, Phila., Pa.
J. Z. Harrison, Ridgewood, N.J.

Claude he hunted very bizzly,
Shot himself a great big grizzly;
But Claude, he liked his meat so rare
That, alas, poor CLAUDETTE COLBERT.

Judy and Keith Reemtsma, N.Y.C.

Sir Thomas watched, while ill in bed,
His men play on the telly.
"The strings are rather bad," he said;
"That is, all BOTTICELLI."

Ernst T. Theimer, Rumson, N.J.

Thoreau takes friend Ralph to Concert Hall
To hear Jenny Lind singing Sousa.
Thoreau cries "brava" at curtain's fall
Unyielding, EMERSON BOOZER.

Mrs. Joel F. Crystal, Scarsdale, N.Y.

Crosby showed up one hour late
And then refused to sing.
Which caused most everyone to say,
"How awfully RUDOLF BING!"

Bill Blow, Edison, N.J.

Young elite females with long fingernails
Can cause men intense agony.
So don't take any chances at coming-out dances:
Avoid any CLAUDE DEBUSSY.

Jay Livingston, N.Y.C.

Mushrooms were bought by the sheriff's boss,
A treat to which he was partial.
The sheriff tasted them first, of course,
His famous last words: "THURGOOD MARSHALL."

Lydia Wilen, N.Y.C.

"You look so surprised, Doc," the quiz-show czar said.
His doctor responded, "My God, man,
Your navel has moved to the top of your head!
I must say you're really BILL TODMAN."

Jack Rose, N.Y.C.

When Robinson was shipwrecked,
His bride repacked her trousseau.
"It's now been twenty years, by God
Guess that's THALASSA CRUSO."

Beatrice Bussey, Miami Beach, Fla.

Pa loaded rigs for Tel & Tel,
Ma worked for its supplier;
She claims she fell beneath his spell
Watching PAUL O'DWYER.

Arthur S. Ash, Mt. Vernon, N.Y.

The Parisian lass was an animal hater.
She stayed in New York at the Ritz.
"Ze city si belle," she recalled to her mater,
"Tout va bien, but ZASU PITTS."

Lee A. Davies, Douglaston, N.Y.

I cried with Anna Karenina
And was torn apart by Camille's fever,
But the tears flowed into buckets
At the plight of Uncle TOM SEAVER.

Jerry Lederman, Bklyn.

While fishing with Aunt Jane one morn
She put up quite a fuss.
Before we tossed her overboard
She threw HERODOTUS.

Fran Henderson, Piscataway, N.J.

Saladin fought his Christian foe
Armed only with a garrison.
History's tide was turned, we know,
When Crusader couldn't REX HARRISON.

Norton Bramesco, N.Y.C.

There's a charming café where I'm told the elite
Come to dine, as they call it, alfresco.
You can reach it by traveling west on Main Street
And then heading NORTON BRAMESCO.

Eve Jelof, Verona, N.J.

Who's Who in the Cast

PRYCE KNOWLTON (Paul Tel-Amadhavi, Second Reporter, a Townsperson) was last seen as the younger son, Styx, in David Mamet's *Foreclosure* and as Fetlock in the Actors' Theatre production of *Amato.* Mr. Knowlton played the uncle, Vanya, in Anton Chekhov's play of the same name, which he directed here in 1972.

EVANGELINE COMET (Maria Tel-Amadhavi) delighted audiences in Sayville this summer with her one-woman show, *Poetry to Music.* She appeared as Fanny in Molnar's *The Turbot* and is known to millions of TV viewers as Morgan Lamont, the matron-you-love-to-hate on the CBS daytime serial *City of Fear.* Ms. Comet is the daughter of the late Jane Feasible and makes her home with her husband, John Smith, and their cairn terriers in Rydell, New York.

HARRY FLAN (The Mummer) is a newcomer to the legitimate stage, but filmgoers will remember him in the title role of Luis Buñel's masterful *Enfant Terrible.*

Above, what's what with "Who's Who in the Cast." Competitors were asked for sample biographical notes. Thanks to Marshall Brickman.

Report: Most of you caught either a tone of provincialism, or at least nonprofessionalism, in productions far, far Off Broadway or the pretension of On. Here and there, jokes rather than parody, a common complaint, but what isn't? A breakout of thematic relentlessness: the woman producer benefacting male protégés; male directors fostering starlets; and specialty acts: transvestites, mutes, ghosts, letters of the alphabet, vegetables (you know, silly acting). Or dog stars (Sirius acting). Some drifted over 150 words. But what isn't? Sample titles: *Pride of the Yukon. Armadillos Are in Season. Fort Wayne! Apple Come Cider. Short Cut to Hell. Greece! Pour Me in the Cup Some Tea* (Yiddish theater). *Seabrook Must Not Be. The Mother Who Understood. Plane Jane and the Bear. Basiliske in the Foster Grants. A Fine Thing, Mr. Osborne. Ring on Appetizing. Johnny on the Pony 1-2-3. Don't Blame Kaiser Bill.* Arthur Kopit's *Methuselah's Revenge. Move Over, Mr. Milkwood. The Frontal Alphabet.* And the evitable *Postcards, Please!* But what isn't?

ALEX JOHNSON (The Gambler) is starring in his first adaptation for the stage. He has acted in various repertory companies while pursuing his vocation of poetry teacher at the elementary level. His experiences were published last year in a book, *Nine Again, Fine Again: How Young People Feel Words.*

FRESCA TODDLER (The Nun) appeared as a child in thirteen movies, including *House of Thrills* and *Lord of the Flies,* and on the stage in *The Five Little Peppers.* This is her first adult role, having just returned from six years in Paris, where she studied Platonic philosophy.

SONYA EMERSON (The Radio) has been the singing voice of Macdonald Carey and many others. She worked for the BBC Third Program for some time while her husband was stationed in England with the CIA.

Anne Jones, Riverdale, N.Y.

CHRISTOPHER SOMMERS (Hamlet) has appeared in summer-stock productions of *Very Good Eddie, Roberta, Spring Fever, Bernadine, Anything Goes,* and *The Boys From Syracuse.* It was his role as Antipholus in this last show which brought him to the attention of the producers and inspired them to cast Mr. Sommers in his first straight Shakespearean role. This marks his Broadway debut.

Jay McDonnell, N.Y.C.

MARK NORBIT (Harry) has worked as a singing waiter at Enrico's, the Six Fingers, and Leonard's of Valley Stream. He appeared in the spring 1977 Dristan commercial.

HARRIET NORBIT (Leslie) decorated her entire house by herself. She plays tennis twice a week but calls herself "just a hacker." Despite a hectic rehearsal schedule, she always has managed to prepare a hot meal for her family.

LES NORBIT (Marcus) recently retired from the cleaning business. He finds acting an exciting second career.

EUGENE NORBIT (Playwright) is a native of Long Island. He describes *Nepotists,* his first dramatic work, as "a searing exposé of the dishonesty and corruption that festers within the American family of our time."

J. Bickart, N.Y.C.

BRADFORD PARKER (Martin Dysart) is a long-time member of the Southboro Players, appearing most recently as Teyve in *Fiddler on the Roof* and before that as Herr Schultz in *Cabaret* and as Bellamy in *The Fantasticks.* Offstage, Brad is drama director at the St. Mark's School.

PHILLIP ARSINE (Alan Strang) followed up appearances on the Boston and Providence professional stages as Dr. Chasuble in *The Importance of Being Earnest* and as Li'l Abner in—you guessed it—*Li'l Abner,* with his this-season smash Southboro Players performance as Marat *(Marat/Sade).*

CHRISTIAN DUMONT (Young Horseman) unfortunately slipped a disk and is being replaced by his young son, Anthony, who was last seen in a Woodward School presentation as a noun.

John Hofer, Southboro, Mass.

MIMSY DRINKWATER (Bridget, Dr. Jekyll's Cook) is an apprentice this season at the Pleasant Valley Summer Playhouse. She is a student at the Bleery School in New York City, where she has auditioned for such roles as The Boy in Beckett's *Waiting for Godot,* and Letta, Biff Loman's date in *Death of a Salesman.* Mimsy's grandmother, Mrs. Mildred Cartwright Gordon Drinkwater, is a Pleasant Valley summer resident and a member of our distinguished board of directors. Mimsy reminds us she is a Leo.

Pat Haley, Keene, N.H.

ESTHER BLODGETT (Vicki Lester) was born in a trunk in the Princess Theater in Pocatello, Idaho. It was during a matinee on Friday and they used a makeup towel for her didy. When she first saw the light, it was pink and amber coming from the footlights on the stage. When her dad carried her out there to say "hello," they tell her that she stopped the show. So she grew up in a crazy world of dressing rooms and hotel rooms and waiting rooms and rooms behind the scenes, and she can't forget the endless rows of sleepless nights and eatless nights and nights without a nickel in her jeans. But it's all in the game and the way you play it and you've gotta play the game you know. When you're born in a trunk in the Princess Theater in Pocatello, Idaho.

Rosemary Bascome, Shelter Island, N.Y.

FARR RUMIER (Innkeeper) makes his stage debut in this production. He began his career as Moe Collier in the award-winning TV drama *Never Throw Me Away.*

LOLA LEMMING (Guest #1) will be recognized from her stunning portrayal as Babette in Morris Jurgen's *Closer You Come,* an All-Points Theatre Production. She is single, lives alone, and likes it.

CASEY USTED (Vagrant) makes a triumphant return to the New York stage after touring Europe with the Ice-Ickles Show as resident thespian. She is best remembered for her haunting portrayal of Minnie in Roger Ratner's *Dig Deeper the Ditches.*

R. E. Baron, Roslyn Heights, N.Y.

DUANE BOBICK (Swede), a former heavyweight boxing contender, is making his Broadway debut.

Cassie Tully, Monsey, N.Y.

HARVEY MUSKEGEON (Prince Calaf) is a member of the far-flung Muskegeon theater clan. Mr. Muskegeon has been seen as Charley in *Travels With Charley* and won critical acclaim as a miserable in the summer touring company of *Les Miserables.* Last year, he appeared on Broadway in the role of Czar Nicholas in *Anastasia.*

SONDRA KIPLING (Joseph Conrad, The Ghost). Miss Kipling has dazzled Broadway in successive seasons, first in 1976 with her triumph as Raskolnikov in *Crime and Punishment,* then in 1977 with her directorial debut, the smash hit *The Screwtape Letters.* She is married to the former John Warrens and says she doesn't know if she likes it as she has never tried it.

Eric W. Allison, Roslyn, N.Y.

ORLUCK (The Emperor), "Mars's greatest living actor," returns in his first appearance since his triumphant tour of Saturn. He starred in several media there, some of which are not yet known here. This marks the 865th production in which Orluck has appeared as The Emperor, in a career spanning over a millenium. As he aptly put it recently, "I have done everything. I am only sorry that I never accepted the offers from Hollywood before they destroyed themselves."

XRD-3 (The Empress). This popular android talk-show host was recently seen in the Feel-O-Vision production of *Oh! Calcutta!,* an ancient Earth-work revival in which it played all the parts.

Marvin Goodman, N.Y.C.

EVERETT STANDISH (Lord Phimby) is best known as the founder and first artistic director of La Commedia. Among those productions which have been graced by the Standish imprimatur are the first English-language production of *Ngama Bramdu Conake* ("the chief is God") by the avantgarde Nigerian playwright Blethé, and the Trenton premiere of the musical version of Steinbeck's *The Grapes of Wrath.*

R. Rubin, Minnetonka, Minn.

LAURA RADCLIFFE (Selina Wescott) has enjoyed a long and illustrious career in the cinema. Miss Radcliffe is assaying her first stage role in the Tappan Zee Playhouse production of Elliot Gruber's new comedy, *Time Will Out.* Her latest movie, filmed entirely in Japan, *Zork, Beast Among Beasts,* is expected to be released in the near future.

Sal Rosa, N.Y.C.

LUDWIG VAN BEETHOVEN (Composer). Mr. Beethoven is the composer of nine symphonies, five piano concertos, one opera *(Fidelio),* and other music. His career, which had been in eclipse in recent years, was boosted by two top-of-the-charts records, *A Song of Joy* and *Fifth,* as well as his Oscar-winning score for the film *A Clockwork Orange.* This is his first Broadway show.

Pericles Crystal, Scarsdale, N.Y.

CHRISTINE PEPPER (Rhonda). A former Harlette, this is her first first role in "legit." Literally born in a trunk, her earliest memories are of sitting on the lap of Murray the K backstage at the Brooklyn Paramount while her parents, the celebrated rock performers, the Cloydells, wowed audiences. She came in second for the lead in the recent Short Pier Theatre production of *Fantastick Greasy Hair.* Chrissy beautifully summed up her attitude to Walter Kerr: "The theater is where it's at, it's *dynamite!*"

David Yarnell, Los Angeles, Calif.

VIOLA SWATCH (Mrs. Humphrey Davis) was apprentice to a thimble collector when she was first discovered by the late Fritz Kreisler. For two years she worked as a busperson under Sophie Gimbel, or someone like her. After studies with Ulu, Stella, and Uta in Urdu, she was cast as understudy to Una Merkel in Long Wharf's *Journey Into Night.*

MARVIN BEDD (Himself) is the well-known radio voice of *The Fight Against Mopery.* He has been mistaken for the (TV) man who wakes up his wife to tell her that he isn't breathing. But he *is* the same Bedd who had a good checkup as a child fourteen years ago and is now back in the medium with his smiling daughters, Charlene, Mavis, and Benjamette.

OVA TANGUAY (Mrs. Arnold Rothstein) is known in Melba as the toast of Riga. Her mother was the first female to sing Desdemona. Ms. Tanguay was last seen off Broadway on Amsterdam Avenue. [Note: Freddy Silverman was to have played Lord Spelvin, but he's been bought by a competitor to be the lead in *Fardel's Bear.*]

Henry Morgan, Truro, Mass.

BOBBY JACK PARDEE (Antonius Flavius). From opening night, when his 33-minute soliloquy drew a standing ovation from both audience and fellow cast members, Bobby Jack has continued to shine as Broadway's brightest star. An All-American at LSU and a Rhodes Scholar, this brilliant Bobby Jack-of-all-trades has proved conclusively, "I can do anything I put my mind to." He spends his leisure time sky-diving, reading, and is currently learning Sanskrit. Renowned as a master chef, Bobby Jack prepares the food devoured during the second-act orgy scene.

Judith Klein, East Brunswick, N.J.

. . . he played the eponymous hero in Jonson's *Eponymous* and on TV created the role of the The Man Behind and to the Left of Senator Montoya in the Watergate hearings . . .

K. B. Robinson, N.Y.C.

LES MEEHAN (McMurphy) has appeared with a variety of companies, including Charles Ludlam's Theatre of the Ridiculous, the Theatre of the Semi-Precious, the Theatre of Cruelty, Paul Sills's Storybook Theatre, and the Theatre of the Absurd-to-Say-the-Least, among others. He has been directed by such radical theater thinkers and tinkers as Serban, O'Horgan, Wilson, and Foreman. Mr. Meehan is presently an outpatient at the New York State Mental Institute and is making his Broadway debut.

Nikki Rosa, N.Y.C.

GERALD FINCHAMBER (Jason Sparrowjade) appears onstage for the first time since his defeat for re-election to Congress, playing the role created by Albert Littleton and supposedly modeled after Gerald. Gerald claims that there doesn't seem to be much difference between acting and politicking.

Mike Firth, Dallas Tex.

JACK JOY was *the* piano player in *the* club in Buffalo while in his teens. He bachelored in music at Philadelphia College and mastered at CCNY. Thereafter he was pianoistically on tap in the Hamptons; Montego Bay, Jamaica; and in Nantucket. He has pitted for several opera companies. He is a favorite accompanist for auditions, but will not play *The Impossible Dream* unless the fate of North America depends upon it.

Helen Zimmerman, Freehold, N.J.

KATHARINE BELLOWS (The Mute Girl) has played similar roles in the productions of *Darling, I Can't Hear You* and *Mime Time.* Originally from California, she studied with Norma San Quentin at the Marin County Hysterical Theater Unit before making her San Francisco debut as Lupé in *Wolves, Sheep, Goats, and Lupé.* Other credits include the well-received whistlestop tour of *Othello* and the all-star Tungsten Workers of America Industrial Show. Her most recent appearance as Lily/Billie in the revival of *The Prism Shattered* led to her being cast as The Mute Girl. Miss Bellows lives in New York, collects mice, and will leave no immediate survivors.

Larry Laiken, Bayside, N.Y.

HERBERT SEYMOUR, M.D. (Doctor Lomax) makes his debut in this production, but his name is familiar to *Playbill* readers, since he has served as house physician for many of Broadway's most distinguished houses. . . .

Lenahan de Rouin, Glen Ridge, N.J.

Famous Guide to New York

A Guide to Living in New York by JOSEPH HELL*R

In the city where I live everyone is afraid of someone. (Or some thing.) The tenant (even a person who owns his own house) is afraid of the landlord. The landlord (including homeowners ha ha) is afraid of the tax assessor. And so forth. I am afraid of walking in the park (the same seems true of my dog ha ha) and I would not advise a stranger to walk there after dark. I try to tell this to my daughter. This makes her unhappy. Or she claims it does. (I do not know why and she cannot tell me or will not tell me. It doesn't matter.) I am afraid of her.

Above, an excerpt from "Famous Tips to Tourists." Competitors were asked for hints on city survival in the style of a well-known person.

Report: A plethoric gallimaufry of tourist tips. Some gratuitous. Which is to say that duplications came not so much *within* this competition as *between* it and previous "in the style of" contests. Nonaggression pacts might well be signed for most-easily-mimicked styles—those of Gertrude Stein, Ogden Nash, e. e. cummings, the Bible, Shakespeare come to mind readily. Mark you, these parodies were not badly done, just overdone. Less predictable were tips from the following: Jerry (What's the Story?) Rosenberg. John V. Lindsay. F. Scott Fitzgerald. Gene Shalit. C. Dickens. T. Sorensen. J. D. Salinger. F. Dostoevsky. E. A. Poe. W. Cronkite. C. Jorgensen. R. D.

Laing. H. D. Thoreau, Anita Loos. Wm. Spooner. Lorenz Hart. Rev. Billy Graham. Ethel Merman. Dick and Jane. J. P. Donleavy. P. G. Wodehouse. T. S. Eliot. A. Buchwald. Groucho. Proust. John Locke. Don Marquis. Lewis Carroll. Helen G. Brown. Leo Rosten. V. Nabokov. J. Keats. W. F. Buckley Jr. Dorothy Parker. H. Melville. Casey Stengel. W. Churchill. E. Lear. H. P. Lovecraft. Aileen Mehle. Asimov. Joyce. Hunter Thompson. Philip Roth. Ionesco. Drs. Martin Abend and Alex Comfort. And others too luminous to mention. Oh yes, and K. Vonnegut. Listen. So it goes.

Quelques "Tips" Pour Survivre A Nouveau York, PAR M. BERLITZ

1. N'engagez pas en combat avec les pickpoches à l'airporte.
2. En l'hôtel, barricadez la porte, et stickez une chaise sous le doorknob.
3. Avoidez le subway, spécialement le Pelham Un Deux Trois.
4. En Times Square, ne dicker pas avec les jeunes filles.
5. Eschewez toujours le Side Quest.
6. Forswearez aussi le Side Est, excepté le Pays Dry Dock (ou tout est at).
7. Wastez no temps chercher pour un station-comfort. Bitez le bullet et hasten back à votre hôtel.
8. Parlez le jargon américain. Par example:
   a. So's your old man. (Votre père est aussi un stinkaire.)
   b. Ishkabibble. (Je should worrié.)
   c. Hot diggety dog. (Chaud diggety chien.)
   d. You're the cat's pajamas. (Vous êtes le chemise de poussé.)
   e. Oy-vey! (Sacrebleu!)

Albert G. Miller, N.Y.C.

Hints à la MILDRED NEWMAN AND BERNARD BERKOWITZ

Q. I've heard there are muggers in New York. What if I'm approached?

A. You have many qualities that make you worth knowing. Smile and introduce yourself proudly.

Q. But this guy's a crook with a knife!

A. As long as you have a sense of your own worth, what others might or might not think about you won't matter.

Q. But you misunderstand! It's not rejection I'm afraid of . . .

A. As your own best friend, you have an obligation to yourself not to squander too much of your own valuable time and attention on others. Run!

Angelo Papa, Trenton, N.J.

A Portrait of New York, by GERTRUDE STEIN

Inland by the sea sinks the city. See the sinking city by the sea. Cities cannot sink except to rise again. By our Hudson shores we see the city rise it rises stone by stone and stone of wood. And salt can we can we see our city rise. Salt of the sea and salt of the earth it is a joy to see and be. By our shores buy our stores sex and oars Saks indoors. Saks or backs and home of Mayor Beame. New York is old new joy. Do not fail to rise. Subways kill not buses. Buses are busses. Subways sink they do not rise. Go by bus buses cannot kill they are busses busses thrill. New York is thrill. Subways hate subways hurt. Buses make survive. Ride the buses stay alive. And do not sink.

James Fechheimer, Glen Head, N.Y.

ROBERT FROST

Whose hoods these are I think I know,
He's hiding in the Village, though;
It should be safe to take a Knapp,
And maybe I can beat the rap.
He drives his cab from morn to night
In the city he calls forsaken;
And woe to you should you complain
About the road not taken.
The man next door may deal in stolen goods;
It matters not that he scorns common labors.
Your proud possessions are forever safe,
Remember that good fences make good neighbors.

Richard J. Hafey, Morningdale, Mass.

MOTHER GOOSE

Jack be nimble, Jack be quick
Jack jump over the sidewalk ick.

Linda Quirini, Greenville, R.I.

ELIZABETH B. BROWNING

How do I live here?
Let me count the ways.

I live here by my wits,
And any bread my hands can reach
When feeling outta sight.

Teresa J. Sandiford, Huntington, N.Y.

GROUCHO MARX

Last night I shot an elephant in my pajamas. How he got into my *apartment* I'll never know. He must've walked across from Central Park. And speaking of walking across Central Park, it's time to play "You Bet Your Life."

Thos. Van Steenbergh, Bergenfield, N.J.

GREGOR SAMSA (KAFKA)

Check the newspapers for the Board of Health's list of convivial restaurants.

Sandra Wapner, N.Y.C.

Memoir of a Journey, by SIR ARTHUR CONAN DOYLE

As our carriage rattled through the streets, my companion, peering through a window very nearly black with grime, observed an array of thieves, dope peddlers, and cutthroats, many of whom had been released unpunished from courtrooms that very morning. Ending his impenetrable silence at last, he remarked, "We can assume, my dear fellow, that Professor Moriarty has taken up residence in New York."

Jerome Coopersmith, Rockville, Ctr., N.Y.

RODNEY DANGERFIELD

. . . When I was a kid, if you wanted a pen you'd go into a bank and take it. Now, if you take a bank, they'll give you the pen . . .

Frances Larson, Guilderland, N.Y.

CLIVE BARNES

New York is a cold, heartless place where your mind, body, and pocketbook are in constant danger of assault. I don't know much about saving your body, but you could do much toward saving your mind and pocketbook by staying away from *Penguin,* the new musical which opened at the Billy Rose last night . . .

Joel F. Crystal, Scarsdale, N.Y.

Fear of Driving, by ERICA JONG

To survive in New York (first) don't own a car. God knows I'm scared of driving in this city. Never mind that I'm breezing through traffic, that I know how to use (the big three) my brake, clutch, and accelerator, I'm convinced that if I grow overconfident, really *relax,* an accident occurs instantly. I can see myself (it's raining, of course) lying in the street, my vehicle crumpled like tin foil and buses tiptoeing around me.

Behind the wheel of a car (usually rendered *hors de combat* by Braille-system parkers) I depreciate rapidly. My ganglia go into reverse, my kidneys strip gears, my fingers (and toes) refuse to defrost, and for one screaming moment, it's touch and go with my emesis reflex. And that's before I even turn on the ignition. Believe me, it's better to take taxis.

Norton Bramesco, N.Y.C.

"Around That Corner," by IRNA PHILIPPS ("Queen of Soaps")

New York is a funny town . . . big and boisterous, yet small and intimate. It's the kind of town where you can turn the corner and run into anyone. Why, just the other day, I turned the corner and ran into my daughter's best friend . . . (FADE TO FLASHBACK)

ME: Alyssa, my daughter told me you dropped out of school and came to New York to seek fame and fortune.
ALYSSA: Fame and fortune my foot! (bursting into sobs amid the throngs of Manhattan). I'm pregnant! The father is your husband's boss.
ME (to myself): The father of her baby is the man I thought had been faithful to me since his wife became terminally ill.
(FADE TO PRESENT)

Yes, New York can break your heart. Just watch out turning those corners!

Lydia Wilen, N.Y.C.

EDWIN NEWMAN

Visitors to the city should be warned about the widespread abuse of language which prevails. There is a spectrum of misuse which ranges from the common obscenity, vulgarity, and wretched syntax of the streets to the subtler, but no less pernicious, abuses of the world of advertising (where *gifts* are inevitably *free* and *like* has permanently replaced *as*). But being a journalist I find the playful newspaper headline particularly odious. Such things as OUT TO LUNGE, THE LONG AND THE SHORT OF IT, and NO NOOSE IS GOOD NOOSE are the bummers that bother me.

George Fairbanks, Nutley, N.J.

NEW YORK TRANSIT AUTHORITY

Aviso. La via . . . es peligrosa. Quédese adentro. *No* salga afuera.

Cynthia Dantzic, Bklyn.

New York, by JAMES A. MICHENER

In the beginning, when the earth was being formed, an event of some significance occurred in the area which would one day be known as New York City. The structure of the earth was made up of several layers of molten lava and igneous rock, topped off by a hard crust. Sometime around 2 billion years ago, the molten lava broke through this crust, resulting in a multitude of large holes. Man first arrived in New York City about 10,000 years ago. Within 100 years and seven months he had invented a new crust with which to cover the roads and fill in the large holes. This city is about due for a second repaving, and until then, visiting motorists are warned to avoid 54th Street, the West Side Highway between 79th and 125th, Sixth Avenue between . . ."

Anne Miller, Teaneck, N.J.

Hunting the Wild Apartment, by HARRIET VAN HORNE

No bloodthirsty abode-killer I. But nostalgia for dear, dead days beyond recall, not to say self-preservation, requires getting the apartment, ferocious rarity though it be in these parlous times. There is no mistaking the nasty, brutish sounds omitted by this dastardly beast. Frighteningly unique are the death rattles in its pipes, as to us frail, quivering mortals are the pounding boom booms from above, the cackling and howling from its sides, the clankings from below. Once tracked, in our hunger for the tender grace of a day that is dead, to its odoriferous lair, it must be attacked mightily with scraper and paintbrush, hammer and screwdriver, broom and mop. Tamed and on a *lease,* 'tis a poor thing but verily our home.

Jack Paul, Bklyn.

About the Author

MARY ANN MADDEN is a contributing editor at *New York* Magazine, where these competitions first appeared, causing concern and infection. A former merchant wayfarer, Ms. Madden is an avid collector of foreign matter. Currently she is pursuing her hobbies of snail darting and embrochure in a lavishly appointed Manhattan apartment owned by her cat, Grace.